Ethics in British Children's Literature

Bloomsbury Perspectives on Children's Literature

Bloomsbury Perspectives on Children's Literature seeks to expand the range and quality of research in children's literature through publishing innovative monographs by leading and rising scholars in the field. With an emphasis on cross and inter-disciplinary studies, this series takes literary approaches as a starting point, drawing on the particular capacity for children's literature to open out into other disciplines.

Series Editor: Dr Lisa Sainsbury, Director of the National Centre for Research in Children's Literature, Roehampton University, UK.

Editorial Board: Professor M. O. Grenby (Newcastle University, UK), Dr Marah Gubar (University of Pittsburgh, USA), Dr Vanessa Joosen (Tilburg University, The Netherlands).

Titles in the Series:

Ethics in British Children's Literature: Unexamined Life Lisa Sainsbury
The Styles of Children's Literature: A Century of Change Peter Hunt

Ethics in British Children's Literature

Unexamined Life

Lisa Sainsbury

Bloomsbury Academic
An imprint of Bloomsbury Publishing Plc

B L O O M S B U R Y
LONDON • NEW DELHI • NEW YORK • SYDNEY

Bloomsbury Academic
An imprint of Bloomsbury Publishing Plc

50 Bedford Square	1385 Broadway
London	New York
WC1B 3DP	NY 10018
UK	USA

www.bloomsbury.com

BLOOMSBURY and the Diana logo are trademarks of Bloomsbury Publishing Plc

First published 2013
Paperback edition first published 2015

© Lisa Sainsbury, 2013

Lisa Sainsbury has asserted her right under the Copyright, Designs and Patents Act, 1988, to be identified as Author of this work.

British Library Cataloguing-in-Publication Data
A catalogue record for this book is available from the British Library.

ISBN: HB: 978-1-4411-3983-2
PB: 978-1-4742-2282-2
ePDF: 978-1-4411-2495-1
ePUB: 978-1-4411-9077-2

Library of Congress Cataloging-in-Publication Data
Sainsbury, Lisa (Lecturer in children's literature)
Ethics in British children's literature: unexamined life/Lisa Sainsbury.
pages cm
Includes bibliographical references and index.
ISBN 978-1-4411-3983-2 (hardcover) – ISBN 978-1-4411-2495-1
(pdf) – ISBN 978-1-4411-9077-2 (epub) 1. Children's literature, English–History

For Emilia

Contents

Figures   ix

Acknowledgements   x

Introduction: Unexamined Life in The Inferno   1
     Ethical exchange   1
     Ethics in British Children's Literature: Coming to terms   5

1   The Sin of Indifference (Part I): Beyond Naughty   11
     Indifferent territory   11
     Reading naughtiness   19
     The badness in between   27
     The ever-present danger of indifference   38

2   The Sin of Indifference (Part II): Discovering Evil   41
     A thousand diabolical expressions   41
     Rebuttable presumptions   48
     The death of childhood   50
     Touching evil   58
     The poetry of evil   70

3   Moral Ammunition: Growing Out of Dissatisfaction through
     Ethical Life   73
     Fighting for right   73
     Genre and the radicalization of family   83

4   Midnight Philosophy and Environmental Ethics   99
     A land ethic in the making   99
     Biotic communities   112
     Epiphany in green   122
     Paper-makery   129

5   The Making of Monsters: Duty, Gender, and the Rightness of Wrong   135
     Law breaking   135
     Alone about The Chase   138

Redeeming care   145
Flourishing futures   152
New consequences   160

6   The Greatness of Apple Seeds: Ethical Relationships in
        Miniature Literature   169

Conclusion: Through the Library . . . Towards a Life Examined   191

Notes   195
References   207
Index   215

Figures

1.1 Who would not be GOOD to look so lovely   16
1.2 Who would be NAUGHTY to look so ugly   17
1.3 Visual recrimination   29
1.4 Compensation and forgiveness   30
1.5 Badness bites   32
1.6 Pushed into badness   35
4.1 Docile bodies interned   109
4.2 Slow contemplation   110
4.3 Sprouting paper-makery   132
6.1 The embrace of moral agency   188
6.2 Losing responsibility?   190

Acknowledgements

This book could not have been completed without support of various kinds, and I remain indebted to many people who have contributed to the book in different ways. At institutional level, I am grateful to Roehampton University for granting me a period of leave to complete the book, and in particular to the staff of the Department of English and Creative Writing and the National Centre for Research in Children's Literature whose patient understanding throughout the writing process is much appreciated. The Children's Literature Collection at Roehampton proved an invaluable resource and our specialist librarians, Julie Mills and Julie Harrison, deserve thanks for their help with this project. A number of people have also been generous and helpful in granting permission to use material in the book, including: John Agard, Marigold Atkey, Trish Beswick, Paola Bottalla, Raymond Briggs, Hayley Davidson, Alexis Deacon, Sian Hardy, Oliver Jeffers, Sarah McMahon, Janetta Otter-Barry, Nicky Potter, Nick Sharratt, Florence Shepherd, Samantha Shea, Caroline Sheldon, Christopher Sutherns, and Jacqueline Wilson.

Many individuals have offered advice and assistance. Sincere thanks are due to those who shared in the evolution of this book: Laura Atkins, Steve Banting, Jane Carroll, Susan Hancock, Jenny Hartley, Peter Hunt, Jenny Kendrick, Jane Kinglsey-Smith, Mark Knight, Gillian Lathey, Clare McManus, Laura Peters, Pat Pinsent, Kimberley Reynolds, Sarah Solly, Liz Thiel, Kay Waddilove, Alison Waller, and Jenny Watt. Special thanks go to Emilia Lamkin and Neal Richardson for their constant encouragement and support.

Finally, I would like to thank David Avital, Anna Fleming, Rosie Pattinson, and all staff involved at Bloomsbury.

Poetry cited from *The Young Inferno* (2008) by John Agard throughout is reproduced with the kind permission of John Agard, Frances Lincoln Children's Books and Caroline Sheldon Literary Agency.

In Chapter 1 an extract from 'On the Perils of Indifference' by Elie Wiesel is reproduced. Originally given as a speech, 12 April, 1999. Copyright © 1999 by

Elie Wiesel. Reprinted by permission of Georges Borchardt, Inc., on behalf of Elie Wiesel.

Parts of Chapter 4 first appeared in P. Bottalla and M. Santini, eds (2009) *What Are Little Boys and Girls Made of?* Padua: Unipress, as 'A Boy's Duty', pp. 67–85. Used by permission of Unipress, via Cesare Battisti, 231–35121 Paodova, Italy.

Introduction

Unexamined Life in The Inferno

In the middle of my childhood wonder
I woke to find myself in a forest
that was – how shall I put it – wild and sombre.

Agard, 2008, Canto 1: 1–3

Ethical exchange

The journey from life unexamined to a life examined begins in moments of
moral awakening such as those described by Dante Alighieri in the fourteenth
century and John Agard in the twenty first; awakenings that illuminate a path
into ethical being and moral courage. Agard's 'seeker'[1] in *The Young Inferno*
(2008) wakes not 'Midway along the journey of our life' (Dante: C. 1: 1[2]), but
'In the middle of my childhood wonder' (C. 1: 1) at a much earlier moment
of emergence into ethical life than Dante the Pilgrim. Agard's every-child is
disorientated, with 'nowhere to turn but tracks and tracks of gloom', until he
meets Aesop, his guide through the nine circles of hell. Agard expressly selects
Aesop (instead of Dante's Virgil) 'whose fables Dante might have read in Latin
translation and whose African ancestry is often forgotten',[3] though it also seems
significant that *Aesop's Fables* are widely associated in the twenty-first century
with moral education and childhood culture. It is implied that the seeker will
be guided into ethical being through recourse to historically rich literary and
cultural traditions, as represented by Aesop, having woken into a new stage
of moral consciousness. This type of awakening is marked also by Hegel, who
observes, 'Education is the art of making people[4] ethical. It considers them as
natural beings and shows them the way to a second birth, the way to change

their original nature into a second, spiritual, nature, and makes this spiritual level *habitual* to them' (2008/1821, p. 159). For Agard and Hegel, the journey to moral agency can be considered a second birth through which the child wakes into a new phase of awareness that transforms the individual into a being of a different (moral) order and it is a second birth that presses close upon the first, so that it occurs during childhood or adolescence.

When Agard's young seeker exits hell into the companionship of a bookish Beatrice, his 'pulse leapt to the sound of her name' (C.13: 15) and the narrative closure supports Agard's introductory observation that 'behind this adventure into Hell lies a search for love.'[5] However, there is an understated irony in Agard's allusion to love, for he refers not simply to the 'erotic love' derided by Kierkegaard for its preference of one person 'above all others' (1998/1847, p. 19), but to a virtuous love that recognizes the challenges posed by evil as an obstacle to goodness. Furthermore, the seeker's discovery of love is grounded in literature and in an ethical passage to the sort of moral agency described by Iris Murdoch in *The Sovereignty of Good* (1970),[6] which finds its expression in a virtue that embraces love as it extends towards goodness:

> Instances of the facts, as I shall boldly call them, which interest me and which seem to have been forgotten or 'theorized away' are the fact that an unexamined life can be virtuous and the fact that love is a central concept in morals. Contemporary philosophers frequently connect consciousness with virtue, and although they constantly talk of freedom they rarely talk of love. But there must be some relation between these latter concepts, and it must be possible to do justice to both Socrates and the virtuous peasant. (Murdoch, 2001/1970, p. 2)

Significantly contributing to an inclusive philosophical drive in the twentieth century (Bertrand Russell is also representative of a shifting momentum in philosophical thought in the modern era), when Iris Murdoch observes that 'an unexamined life can be virtuous' she challenges Socratic wisdom[7] expressed in Plato's *The Last Days of Socrates* (c.390–80), 'for a human being a life without examination is actually not worth living' (2010, *Apology*, 38a), and also puts virtue in the reach of children. Murdoch's insistence that virtuous love can emanate from a being unconscious of virtue thus touches her 'virtuous peasant' (p. 2) and the child – for the newly awakened seeker has not examined life in Socratic terms. This is not equivalent to saying that young children are (yet) capable of leading a complete moral life, because Murdoch observes that 'Moral change and moral achievement are slow' (p. 38) and that it involves an ongoing process that on one level requires knowledge and a degree of maturity:

> . . . at the level of serious common sense and of an ordinary non-philosophical reflection about the nature of morals it is perfectly obvious that goodness *is* connected with knowledge: not with impersonal quasi-scientific knowledge of the ordinary world, whatever that may be, but with a refined and honest perception of what is really the case, a patient and just discernment and exploration of what confronts one, which is the result not simply of opening one's eyes but of a certainly perfectly familiar kind of moral discipline. (p. 37)

This type of patience, discernment, and moral discipline might be beyond most children (and most adults actually), but Murdoch's perception of human love and goodness allows for an inner and preconscious reaching to others that must begin somewhere; for Murdoch goodness comes gradually into focus as knowledge is refined. A lack of measured experience does not refuse goodness though, rather the child grows towards knowledge and virtue through a process of observation that leads away from 'selfish care'[8] (p. 82). Consequently, it seems that Murdoch's conception of virtue pulls in two directions, recognizing the value of an unreflective love that can exist in the present being of an individual (peasant[9] or child), and also appreciating the developmental aspects of growth into a more deeply knowing love – and in this tension can be seen her affirmation of an unexamined life. This satisfies Peter Hollindale's cogent argument in *Signs of Childness in Children's Books* (1997) that a full comprehension of childhood values its *presentness* (and unexamined status in Murdoch's terms) in addition to the more dominant cultural perception that childhood is preparatory and developmental.

Hollindale posits that books are instrumental in 'helping a reader to build and diversify her sense of childhood possibility' (p. 20), and he describes the process by which books allow 'the conjunction of exterior with interior action' (p. 20). The significance of such an exchange can be seen in Murdoch's advocacy of a goodness that is unseen, also accepting that it can be inferred from visible actions. Like Aristotle,[10] Murdoch recognizes good as 'the object of life', although action is not central to Murdoch's philosophy, and it is her recognition of the importance of *inner* workings – of the character and emotions, for example – that makes her thinking so useful as a way into considering the drive to moral life in children's literature. Hollindale also claims for children's literature a 'distinguishing property' (p. 47) of childness that is both present and evolving, chiming with Murdoch's understanding of moral possibility. Childness wrests from a landscape of 'linguistic poverty' (p. 45) a positive and dynamic way of articulating childhood that offers an alternative to the negative connotation of 'childish' and 'juvenile':

> I propose 'childness', therefore, as a critical term with wider relevance. For the child, childness is composed of the developing sense of self in interaction with the images of childhood encountered in the world . . . For the adult, childness is composed of the grown-up's memories of childhood, of meaningful continuity between child and adult self . . . For the child, childness includes the knowledge and acceptance that one *is* a child; for the adult knowledge and acceptance that one isn't . . . This compound of cultural and personal attitudes is articulated in a text of children's literature, and the *event* of children's literature lies in the chemistry of a child's encounter with it. (p. 49)

Hollindale's chemical encounter is figured in *The Young Inferno*, which also offers a vision of childhood that is simultaneously present and becoming, passive and reactive, as confirmed by the closing lines: 'I danced in the chemistry of her eyes/ and I could have chilled out there for ever. /She made that library a paradise./ Yes, that May Day meeting began my own spring' (C. 13: 25–8). Agard's seeker is content to stay ('chilled out') within the confines of the knowledge-giving library, yet this Eden of ethical becoming marks a period of growth and renewal at the same time. In the chemical reaction between the seeker (child) and his Beatrice (book), Agard conveys the *event* described by Hollindale and implies a young reader ready to engage with the demands of moral life as envisaged by Murdoch. Indeed, Murdoch argues that 'The development of consciousness in human beings is inseparably connected with the use of metaphor' (p. 75), such as that played out in *The Young Inferno*. Metaphors are 'fundamental forms of our awareness of our condition' (2001/1970, p. 75) and they reach their apotheosis in 'good art'[11] that 'shows us how difficult it is to be objective by showing us how differently the world looks to an objective vision' (p. 84). Murdoch attributes great depth and significance to metaphor and this does not preclude the idea that metaphors can be most meaningful when stripped down and simple. Figuratively speaking then, at their most basic, metaphors might be considered childly (Hollindale's adjectival companion to childness), shaping our moral landscape from the moment re-presentation can be grasped and this understanding grows alongside moral discipline until good art can be appreciated by a highly developed consciousness (and this is the point at which Murdoch 'returns'[12] to Socrates). Goodness, intrinsic and underlying, is there to be seen by those who look (within the pages of a book), since in Murdoch's view, 'Goodness is connected with the attempt to see the unself, to see and to respond to the real world in the light of virtuous consciousness' (p. 91), and in Beatrice the seeker finds 'the shadow who guides my inner spark' (C.13: 24).

Ethics in British Children's Literature: Coming to terms

In the interplay traced between *The Young Inferno, Signs of Childness*, and *The Sovereignty of Good* can be found the roots and central concerns of *Ethics in British Children's Literature*, a series of disquisitions that consider and demonstrate at close range various (and by no means all) ways in which contemporary British children's literature engages in ethical discourse at the level of philosophical enquiry. Since the end of the Second World War, books for young people have increasingly endeavoured to involve children and adolescents in an exchange of ethical thinking, implying readers who are ready to think in the present, and willing to engage in a process of philosophical envisioning. The post-1945 demarcation for *Ethics in British Children's Literature* is partly a practical circumstance of material management, but primarily it is embedded in my conviction that there is a flowering of ethical discourse in children's literature during this period. I concur with Hollindale's view that 'children's literature in the postwar years, growing steadily in artistic confidence, has engaged more openly with the "flickering drama of the mind and soul"'[13] (1997, p. 40). The chronological boundaries of my discussion are flexible though, for no book is produced in a sociocultural vacuum and an awareness of the historical traditions out of which my focus texts grow underpins my discussion of individual books and spheres of ethical enquiry. I could not envisage a discussion of evil in children's literature without recourse to Stevenson's *Treasure Island* (1883), for example, and discussion of masculine duty in B.B.'s *Brendon Chase* (1944) is incomplete without reference to Jefferies's *Bevis* (1882), thus my bounds yield to the demands of a particular topic or discursive thread.

The geographical focus of *Ethics in British Children's Literature* is grounded in my sense that discussions of philosophy in relation to British children's literature tend to begin with Locke and end with Rousseau; it seems important to move along the conversation. British children's literature is not commonly associated with philosophy (moral or otherwise); in part because Britain has not produced a philosophical blockbuster along the lines of Saint-Exupery's *The Little Prince*

(1943), Jostein Gaarder's *Sophie's World* (1991), or *Where Were You, Robert?*
by Hans Magnus Enzensberger (1998) and because philosophy was and is not
commonly taught in schools in modern Britain (while it has long featured on
school curricula in many other European countries such as France and Norway).
However, my experience of teaching and researching British children's literature
confirms that there are numerous British books that explore ethical issues, and
which utilize manifold strategies (such as thought experiments or Socratic
dialogue) to engage young readers in philosophical thinking. Contemporary
British children's literature makes a significant contribution to the field of
ethical discourse with a range of diverse writers – such as Nina Bawden, Aidan
Chambers, Vivien Alcock, Peter Dickinson, Jan Mark, Ann Schlee, Melvin
Burgess, Malorie Blackman, Geraldine McCaughrean, Raymond Briggs, Gillian
Cross, Jan Needle, Terry Pratchett, Philip Reeve, or Jenny Valentine – returning
to areas of ethical concern repeatedly throughout their writing careers. Moreover,
during this period, a number of books for children have been published that
deal with philosophy as a central theme: for instance, the creative enquiries of
Dorothy L. Sayers's *Even the Parrot* (1944) and Ian Gilbert's *Little Owl's Book of
Thinking* (2004); or novels such as Jill Paton Walsh's *Unleaving* (1976), Gillian
Cross's *A Map of Nowhere* (1988), or Terry Pratchett's *Nation*[14] (2008).

Since *Ethics in British Children's Literature* is centrally concerned with books
for children that are morally aware at the very least, some explanation is required
as to distinctions I make between moralizing (on the cognitively restrictive
end of the moral scale) and ethical discourse (which encourages philosophical
enquiry) in children's literature. I accept that while moralizing often seeks to tell
children what to think, it can also contribute to a process whereby children are
shown *how* to think. During the eighteenth century, one of the most popular
exponents of this balancing act was Maria Edgeworth, for as Mitzi Myers argues
in 'Socializing Rosamond' (1989), Edgeworth skilfully combines form and
ideology in 'philosophic tales' that teach girls to think (pp. 54–5): 'The structure
and theme are one, the narrative consequences emerging naturally from the
Edgeworthian educational posture' (p. 55). I agree with Myers that Edgeworth's
tales are grounded in moral philosophy, but the impetus in Edgeworth's stories
is towards socialization, rather than philosophical enquiry for its own sake (and
this is the aspect of children's literature that most interests me in this book).
Authors denigrated for the moral stricture of their writing – from Ana Laeteia
Barbauld in the eighteenth century to Enid Blyton in the twentieth century –
often produce work that is more ethically complex in their approach than critics
allow, as demonstrated by my discussion of Mary Martha Sherwood's *Brotherly*

Love (1851) and Blyton's *Naughty Amelia Jane* (1946) in Chapter 1. Matthew Grenby offers an overview of the critical debates framing moral and instructive writing in *Children's Literature* (2008), observing that a 'dwindling of faith in the potential and necessity of didactic literature no doubt helped to hasten the decline of the moral tale in the early twentieth century' (p. 82). Grenby reflects on the connection between didacticism and the moral tale, arguing that literature for children continues to be instructive in the twentieth century, but rather than explicitly pointing lessons, modern moral tales such as Berlie Doherty's *Dear Nobody* (1991) 'have shied away from offering any simple, confident solution to the problems they represent' (p. 76). I would add that this open-ended approach to thinking through problems offers a platform for philosophical thinking, while the 'specific lessons taught by . . . moral tales', such as obedience and prudence (Grenby, 2008, p. 70) prior to the twentieth century tend to eschew philosophy in favour of a more directed moralizing of the sort derided by Nietzsche as '*herd-animal morality*' (2003/1886, p. 125).

Common to ethical discourse and moralizing is a didactic impulse that can be as liberating as enslaving, and in *Ethics in British Children's Literature* I demonstrate the positive didactic drive in a selection of books for children that opens the way for moral agency. Many philosophers concern themselves with the education of children – from Plato and Aristotle, through to Locke, Rousseau, and Singer – but none is more engaged with the ethical education of children in modern Britain than Bertrand Russell. In *On Education* (1926), Russell rejects the Arnoldian tradition for being exclusive and aristocratic (2010/1926, p. 26), the Augustinian insistence on original sin, and 'Rousseau's belief in natural virtue' (p. 82), arguing that moral education should be available to all children and opining that 'The raw material of instinct is ethically neutral, and can be shaped either to good or evil by the influence of the environment' (p. 82). Russell envisions a philosophical approach to teaching and learning whereby 'the education of character must begin at birth' (p. 21) and which champions intelligence as a virtue of moral character: 'The desire to instill what are regarded as correct beliefs has made educationalists too often indifferent to the training of intelligence' (p. 39). Russell invests in an 'open-mindedness' and 'curiosity' through which 'we should all learn to be able to think for ourselves about matters that are particularly well known to us, and we ought to have acquired the courage to proclaim unpopular opinions when we believe them to be important' (p. 44). Russell offers a range of strategies to develop this sort of intellectual courage, and in relation to this book his valuing of dreams and imagination seems especially pertinent as he observes: 'To kill fancy in childhood is to make a slave to what exists, a creature tethered to earth and therefore unable to create heaven' (p. 77). Related to this is Russell's advocation of a love of books and reading, with the reservation that 'The books that are his[15] own property should, as far as possible, be good books, such as Lewis Carroll and *Tanglewood Tales*, not mere trash' (p. 96). Russell does not expand on the value of these particular books, but I want to link his affirmation of literature as a path to philosophical enquiry to Agard's bibliographic epiphany in *The Young Inferno*. When Agard's seeker exits the ninth circle, he is surprised as to the other road along which Aesop directs him: 'Back in the Upper World of familiar faces/ I didn't expect to see a vision – /not in the library, of all places' (C. 13: 1–3). Through his seeker's astonished response, Agard challenges any preconceived notion that the library might be antithetical to the vision required of moral teaching or philosophizing. His hooded hero might not think to find moral guidance in a library, but Agard's investment in literature is unsurprising given that he has long engaged with political and moral issues in his poetry for young people.

If I might stretch a metaphor, *Ethics in British Children's Literature* explores a limited selection of texts pulled from the shelves of Agard's library in a process mindful of Schopenhauer's 'well-arranged' library:

> As the biggest library if it is in disorder is not as useful as a small but well-arranged one, so you may accumulate a vast amount of knowledge but it will be of far less value to you than a much smaller amount if you have not thought it over for yourself; because only through ordering what you know by comparing every truth with every other truth can you take complete possession of your knowledge and get it into your power. You can think about only what you know, so you ought to learn something; on the other hand, you can know only what you have thought about. (2004/1851, p. 89)

Reflecting the inclusive conditions of Russell's philosophical education, I have chosen books from a range of genres – encompassing thrillers, satire, historical fiction, and naturalistic writing – and literary forms – including picture books, poetry, novels, and short stories – some popular and some little known outside of critical circles, which span the contemporary period of writing for children since 1945 and which in different ways educate the reader, in Russell's terms, encouraging courageous thinking. Close reading of a small number of focus texts in each chapter allows for sustained and in-depth demonstration of *how* books encourage philosophical enquiry and seek to engage the reader in an exchange of ethical discourse. I ponder not only the ways in which philosophical theories might be applied to children's books – though this is an important aspect of this book, for application and discussion of specific philosophical theories shows how thinking around a problem or idea might develop – but the ways in which children's literature might be considered philosophical as well. Russell observes that training in moral character should be 'nearly complete' by the age of six ([p. 58] his treatise is idealistically specific at times), suggesting that this early education serves as groundwork for entry into a deeper and more considered mode of moral life envisaged variously by Hegel, Murdoch, Russell himself, and by a large number of writers for children from the mid-twentieth century who recognize the virtue of life unexamined in the present and the potential for life to be examined in the future.

The first two chapters of *Ethics in British Children's Literature* explore the concepts of good and evil; concepts that are fundamental to ethics and which have a particular relationship to children's literature and notions of childhood. I mostly omit discussion of fairy-tale and high fantasy – genres which are frequently associated with the representation of good and evil in children's literature and which have been frequently discussed in this context.[16] Much high fantasy (though of course there are exceptions) figures evil as an external force, often demonic or supernatural that works on humanity and, since I choose to focus on the human conditions of good and evil as explored variously by Murdoch, Midgley, and Svendsen, an emphasis on realism – with excursions into romance, satire, dystopia, and domestic fantasy – makes for an illuminating discussion of the ways in which 'evil makes itself known, first and foremost, in human interaction' (Svendsen, 2010/2001, p. 14). Chapter 1 focuses on naughtiness as an ambivalent concept that encompasses both good and evil, moving on to consider badness and its relationship to good and evil. Chapter 2 concentrates specifically on evil, paying particular attention to its relationship with constructions of childhood in society, media culture and books for children. Chapters 3, 4, and 5 centre on areas of ethical enquiry that have a particular relevance to children's literature and childhood: family and community; environmental ethics; and sexual politics in the gendering of duty. Discussion of these rich and thorny ethical fields is necessarily limited and in each chapter I open windows onto restricted areas of ethical-literary concern. Boundaries are drawn, for instance, through recourse to a particular philosophical approach (as in Chapter 3 wherein the Hegelian vision of ethical life provides an overarching focus for discussion of family and society) or via a generic focus (such as the emphasis on anthropomorphic literature in Chapter 4). Chapter 6 explores miniature literature as an area of writing for children that magnifies a range of ethical issues and offers a means of pulling together thoughts unfurled in earlier chapters.

This book establishes contemporary children's literature as a field rich in ethical discourse and that variously challenges Russell's conviction that 'ready credulity in the face of repeated assertions is one of the curses of the modern world' (p. 183). Russell argues that schools must do what they can to guard against this, but this book shows that contemporary British writers for young people offer an array of philosophical tools necessary for fighting and vanquishing such credulity.

The Sin of Indifference (Part I):
Beyond Naughty

There was every accent you could imagine –
howls of pain uttered in every language.
I asked my teacher, 'Why all this wailing?'

'These are the people who sat on the fence.
They cared neither for good nor for evil.
Theirs was the sin of indifference.'

Agard, 2008, C.3: 13–18

What is indifference? Etymologically, the word means 'no difference.' A strange
and unnatural state in which the lines blur between light and darkness, dusk and
dawn, crime and punishment, cruelty and compassion, good and evil.

Elie Wiesel, 1999[1]

Indifferent territory

Indifference is the first sin encountered by the hooded hero of Agard's *The Young Inferno* on his descent into the nine circles of hell and eventual exit into ethical wisdom and moral agency, for as Aesop explains to his young seeker, indifference cares not for good or evil. Without such care, the seeker's path surely remains embroiled in the 'tracks and tracks of gloom' (C.1: 12) of his wilderness nightmare, for ethical life requires an understanding of good and evil; moral education is redundant if indifference negates care, blinding the seeker to the good which should guide him and the evil to be eschewed. In *The Nicomachean Ethics* (c.335–23 BC),[2]

Aristotle marks out good as the object of life, remarking that 'Every art and every investigation, and similarly every action and pursuit, is considered to aim at some good' (2004, p. 3), and Lars Svendsen observes that 'evil can be understood as everything that hinders the realization of a good life' (2010/2001, p. 25) – good and evil shape each other, but there are shadows in between that prevent knowledge of either. Speaking as one who has endured the wretchedness of evil, Elie Wiesel identifies these shadows as the mark of indifference; in his view the ultimate sin and the ultimate punishment. Indifference is seductive and avoids troubling about the pain and despair of others; indifference renders the lives of others meaningless and leads to inhumanity; 'indifference is not a beginning, it is an end'. When he speaks of indifference in 1999, Elie Wiesel is at once 'the young Jewish boy from the Carpathian Mountains' who experienced 'the eternal infamy' of Auschwitz and Buchenwald, and 'the old man I have become'. On his final release from Buchenwald, 'there was no joy in his heart. He thought there never would be again' – though this modal phrasing suggests that Wiesel has again discovered joy. Certainly not joy in the failures of a millennium that 'cast a dark shadow over humanity', rather in moments of human response and intervention that allow the young boy and the old man to walk together 'towards the new millennium, carried by profound fear and extraordinary hope'.

Wiesel looks back on a twentieth century marked by good, evil, and indifference, and in a speech touched by personal experience of each, he reaches for a philosophy that might approach indifference. As he looks forward to a new millennium, Wiesel passes on a philosophical be(quest) to the young people imagined in Agard's seeker: 'Is there a philosophy of indifference conceivable?' he asks and this question is left open for consideration by the young seeker once the inferno has been traversed. To answer Wiesel's question ringing from the depths of Buchenwald, the seeker must observe the broad moral terrain of human sin presented to him in Agard's inferno – ranging from drink-driving to military dictatorship – relevant to the sociohistoric circumstances of young people of the twenty-first century; he must observe and he must then respond and intervene once he has returned to the Upper World. Wiesel is keen to alleviate and prevent the suffering of children: 'What about the children? . . . When adults wage war, children perish', yet his questions are not directed only at adults. When Wiesel asks, 'What about the children?' he addresses the suffering and abused, and also the questioning child who once he was – the 13-year old boy he brings to life in *Night* (1958) who is 'deeply observant' (2008/1958, p. 3) and full of difficult questions about his faith and life – and those questioning children of the future. The young people implied in *The Young Inferno* are those who are willing to take

Aesop's hand and look about them to discover good and evil in opposition to the end that is indifference.

Attending now to Agard's seeker, I want to consider whether such a young person, having woken recently from 'childhood wonder'[3] could have any understanding of good and evil. Let us imagine him a (would-be) reader, an every-child of Britain past and present, immersed in centuries of childhood culture; in its toys and books and games and rhymes. Might such a child know anything of good and evil and might such a child be susceptible to the sin of indifference? In order to ponder these questions, I shall take a brief philological detour, revealing that young people are immersed in the semantic foothills of good and evil from infancy. As the rhythms of popular culture intone: 'When she was good/ She was very, very good,/ But when she was bad, she was horrid' (Longfellow, c.1850),[4] and since at least the fifteenth century in art and literature, children and childhood have been conceptualized in part through language that appears morally charged, sliding on a scale of good to evil. Dichotomous reductions render children good or bad, virtuous or wicked, obedient or naughty, stacking them neatly on schoolroom and nursery shelves in jars labelled accordingly – although shelves are susceptible to gravity if not securely hung and jars are prone to chip or fracture as Lewis Carroll suggests figuratively in *Alice's Adventures in Wonderland* (1865) when Alice tumbles down the well lined with 'cupboards and book-shelves' and an empty jar 'labeled "ORANGE MARMALADE"' (2009/1865, p. 10). Alice might be experiencing a disorientating fall, nonetheless she proves herself a considerate child on the path to moral agency, albeit her good intentions are ironized by their ludicrous situation: 'she did not like to drop the jar, for fear of killing somebody underneath, so managed to put it into one of the cupboards as she fell past it' (p. 10). Alice's care for others exhibits the potential for moral growth, although the empty jar hints that the systematic and ordered shelving of nursery and schoolroom could impede ethical *agency*.

The Oxford Book of Children's Verse (Opie and Opie, 1973) confirms usage of evaluative epithets from the fifteenth to nineteenth century (Table 1.1), and poets approach childhood matters diversely through evangelistic exhortation, or satirical subversion, yet common to each of the extracts I have selected is the employment of epithets suggestive of moral appraisal. Children were and continue to be categorized variously as wicked, good(ly), bad, sweet, or naughty, and such branding gave rise to extensive debate in the twentieth century, since typically it is driven more by sociopolitical forces and ideological precepts than by ethical considerations. Furthermore, this

Table 1.1 Epithets applied to children in verse published between 1478 and 1862 (from *The Oxford Book of Children's Verse*, edited by Iona and Peter Opie, 1973).

A Goodly Child
It is to a goodly child well fitting
To use disports of mirth and pleasance
Anon, c.1478, p. 6

A Schoolmaster's Admonition
Good children, refuse not these lessons to learn
Anon, c. 1625, p. 21

To My Youngest Kinsman, R.L.
With wicked children do not play
Abraham Chear, 1672, p. 34

The Description of a Good Boy
The boy that is good,
Does learn his book well
Henry Dixon, 1728, p. 54

There was a Naughty Boy
There was a naughty boy,
A naughty boy was he
John Keats, 1818, p. 148

The Story of Fidgety Philip
See the naughty, restless child
Heinrich Hoffmann, 1844/1848, p. 208

A Farewell
Be good, sweet maid, and let who will be clever
Charles Kingsley, 1856, p. 227

John, Tom, and James
John was a bad boy, and beat a poor cat
Charles Henry Ross, 1862, p. 231

---

process of epithetical judgement objectifies children/childhood, rather than perceiving the child as a moral subject on the path of moral development. Contemporary educational discourse considers extensively the repercussions of labelling children, focusing on areas such as deviance and disability; as Barbara Riddick observes, 'Among some educationalists there is a strong belief that "labelling" children is harmful. The basic argument is that labelling can lead to stigmatisation, and give the child and adults involved negative expectations' (2000, p. 654).[5] I shall consider stigma further later; for now the evident proliferation of such debates serves to emphasize the historic, escalating, and widespread tendency to label children and that some of this labelling – as reference to children's poetry confirms – enters the semantic domain of good and evil. Consequently, Agard's young pilgrim is susceptible to indifference in the face and good and evil; so familiar is he with epithets worn thin through ubiquitous and constant usage, that he is unlikely to consider what they might suggest or mean. This is not to say that the individual child will not respond to epithets applied to her/him, rather that overuse might obscure meaning and render anodyne the most complex and important of concepts.

Literary markers suggest that childhood has long been swathed in language associated with morality, but whether the praising of good boys and the censure of bad girls invests in ethical enquiry or even confers moral status is questionable. When my neighbour tells me in passing that her son has been a good boy today, she is not confirming his moral character; she means that he ate his carrots and endured his morning nap without complaint. In this instance, the appellation 'good boy' assesses socially acceptable behaviour and is the language of social *mores*, as opposed to morality.[6] Conversely, the anonymous writer of 'A Schoolmaster's Admonition' (Table 1.1) is concerned with 'The pathway to virtue',[7] claiming that the lessons in mores and morals conveyed through this poem will lead to glory, virtue, and grace. The tone is forcefully didactic though, 'I likewise command thee this lesson to keep' (p. 22), and the road to virtue prescriptive, 'Play not, nor laugh not, thy master to fret', hence the implied reader is encouraged to accept the conditions of virtue outlined as fact, and there is no space for thinking about virtue conceptually. Each of these brief examples, although concerned with different moral categories, invests in moralizing rather than philosophizing and reveals some of the ways in which childhood is hemmed in by the language of good and evil. However, the terms used to conceptualize children are not restricted to 'goodly', 'bad', 'virtuous', and 'wicked' for there are loose threads in the linguistic armoury of childhood with which Agard's pilgrim might begin to unpick the stitching of moralizing and take up the needle of ethical enquiry.

One such loose thread can be identified in the concept of naughtiness, for naughtiness is conceptually ambivalent and (at least) one of its etymological branches is correlate with childhood.[8] Of the various morally indicative labels conferred on children, 'naughty' has come to have especially close associations with childhood, an alliance that gained momentum during the eighteenth century. This alliance is captured in a pair of images painted by Thomas Duché

Figure 1.1 Who would not be GOOD to look so lovely. To all sweet tempered industrious & obedient Children. This plate is dedicated by their obedient Servant, Tho.s Lovegood (inscription on plate).

Source: Published in London, 25 March, 1790. Print attributed to Henry Birche, after Thomas Spence Duché, published by Benjamin Beale Evans. Acquired by the British Museum in 2010. © The Trustees of the British Museum.

Figure 1.2 Who would be NAUGHTY to look so ugly. To all pouting lazy illtemper'd lying & disobedient Children. This plate is dedicated by their obedient Servant, Tho.s Lovegood (inscription on plate).

Source: Published in London, 25 March, 1790. Print attributed to Henry Birche, after Thomas Spence Duché, published by Benjamin Beale Evans. Acquired by the British Museum in 2010. © The Trustees of the British Museum.

and engraved by Henry Birche in 1790 (Figures 1.1 and 1.2), offering an irreverent insight into the ambivalent aspect of childhood naughtiness. Eric Ziolkowski observes in *Evil Children in Religion, Art and Literature* (2001) that dualistic and stereotypical distinctions in post-enlightenment art and literature often depict boys as naughty and girls as good,[9] and naughtiness is attributed only to boys in *The Oxford Book of Children's Verse*, yet here is a naughty girl who challenges the traditional refrain, 'Sugar and spice/ And all that's nice,/ That's what little girls are made of'.[10] Duché's depiction of frowning girlhood could be seen to test prevailing conceptions of femininity, however the inscriptions beneath the images – dedicated to *all* good and naughty *children* – indicate an interest in childhood vagaries that embrace boys and girls; accordingly the virtues and vices outlined are gender-neutral. Assuming that the same sitter has been used for both images,[11] this child embodies goodness *and* naughtiness, suggesting – together with the interrogative use of modal auxiliaries in the title, 'Who would?' – that there is a matter of choice in goodness and naughtiness; that these are not enduring, essential qualities of childhood or identity. Indeed, the titular emphasis on appearance indicates that these are external qualities, reflected in physical demeanour, behaviour, and temper.[12] The possibility of change and choice challenges the impulse to label and categorize, so although these images seem to invest in labelling, actually they undermine this process. The tone of levity is also striking, for the signatory play of 'Tho.s Lovegood' undercuts an investment in goodness over naughtiness and the humorous juxtaposition of images evidently parodies the moralizing tone of some prominent late eighteenth-century children's literature. Any didacticism detected in the 'Naughty' image is surely thwarted by the comparative approach, and this points to a general ambivalence towards the concept of naughtiness. Naughtiness implies behaviour in need of correction, but equally this behaviour is often tolerated, enjoyed and even admired – consider that Tom Kitten 'was very naughty, and he scratched' in a classic work of children's literature 'Dedicated to All Pickles'.[13]

C. T. Onions's (1966, p. 604) etymology traces *naughty* to the Old English word *naught, nothing*, which passes into adjectival use by the fourteenth century as '*naughty*'. Generally meaning *poor* or *needy*, this relation to poverty or lack also takes on a more specific, judgemental quality, relating to that which is *bad* or *of inferior quality*. This ambivalent shift is interesting since *naughty* comes to mean *morally bad* and it is reasonable to speculate that the related notion of lack came specifically to refer to the lack, or absence of good; as Mary Midgley observes in *Wickedness* (1984), 'Evil, in fact, is essentially the absence of good, and cannot be understood on its own' (2001/1984, p. 14). Equally enticing is Saint Augustine's shuddering at the 'darkness of that infant mind' and his impression that the infant boy 'with his mind unawakened . . . possesses nothing,'[14] for in this observation childhood is brought into the etymological amalgam of lack and wickedness. The fourteenth-century usage remains evident through to the sixteenth century as manifest in *Foxe's Book of Martyrs* (Foxe, 1563)[15] when the fisherman Rawlins White addresses a 'false' preacher at the stake: 'Ah thou naughty hypocrite, doest thou presume to prove thy false doctrine by scripture?' (2009/1563, p. 122). Onions notes that by the sixteenth century, naughtiness has taken on a playful quality and children familiar with *Foxe's Book of Martyrs* (which remained popular throughout the nineteenth century) would eventually come across conflicting and milder definitions of naughtiness that implicated them directly. Since the seventeenth century, *naughty* has come to denote waywardness or an inclination to disobedience and is associated increasingly with childhood misdemeanour as suggested by the Birche engravings. In summary then, the etymological evolution of *naughty* mingles notions of lack, wickedness, and childhood misbehaviour: *naughty* is empty and inconsequential; *naughty* is deviant and dangerous; *naughty* is childlike and changeable; *naughty* is the lack of goodness, and yet in its journey away from extreme wickedness, it embraces the possibility of good. It appears that *naughty* is full of ethical possibility for Agard's seeker misdirected by epithetical excess and it could offer a way of avoiding the inferno's fence of indifference.

Reading naughtiness

To recognize untruth as a condition of life: that, to be sure, means to resist customary value-sentiments in a dangerous fashion; and a philosophy which ventures to do so places itself, by that act alone, beyond good and evil.

Nietzsche, 2003/1886, p. 36

Naughtiness is proposed as a starting point for the philosophical expression and exploration of good and evil in children's literature for the properties of resistance inherent in its ambiguous nature. When focused on naughtiness, we have not yet arrived at good and evil, although in Nietzsche's vision, philosophy must seek to move beyond good and evil – and any investment in moral absolutes – if it is really to engage with the conditions of morality. Naughtiness is never less than, nor only a childly version of good and evil – it moves between and beyond this prepositional perspective and thus finds a way to negotiate or evade the moralizing strictures of its conception. Naughtiness tangles with good and evil without finally settling for one or the other, recognizing them in absence and drawing attention to its relationship with them. Agard's seeker can then reach beyond good and evil, back – and so forward – to naughtiness if he wishes to avoid Aesop's first circle of hell.

Naughtiness in British children's literature since 1945 is contradictory and full of tensions that both evade and elicit philosophical debate – and no wonder given a literary journey that has sought variously: to condemn naughtiness (Sherwood's *The History of the Fairchild Family*, 1818–47); to ridicule naughtiness (Stevenson's 'Good and Bad Children', 1885); to heroize the naughty child (Potter's *The Tale of Peter Rabbit*, 1902[16]); to subvert moralizing stricture from inside the conditions of naughtiness (Belloc's *Cautionary Tales for Children*, 1907); and to validate and admire the ingenuity of naughtiness (Crompton's *Just William*, 1922–70). It can be demonstrated that naughtiness is the language of conservative moralizing, even so naughtiness refuses to be bound by the reductive opinions of the moral-bound bourgeois. Consequently, it is worth taking a close look at how it functions in children's books central to the development of naughtiness in British children's literature. *Naughty Amelia Jane* (1946) by Enid Blyton and *My Naughty Little Sister* by Dorothy Edwards (1952) are popular children's texts produced just after the end of the Second World War that have remained in print ever since. These books offer naughtiness as a source of amusement to their young implied readership and instances of naughtiness are central to story structure, while differing in their approach to and conception of naughtiness.

Benjamin Spock's *Baby and Childcare* (1946) brought practical childcare into the middle-class British home and is indicative of a cultural preoccupation that yielded the *My Naughty Little Sister* series and programming such as the BBC radio's *Listen with Mother* during the 1950s. Dorothy Edwards's series is centred in the domestic sphere of family life and approaches naughtiness with an emotional understanding imbued (if unintentionally) with the childcare advice of Spockian expertise, the sympathetic pedagogy of Rousseau or Froebel, the psychoanalytic concern of Freud, or the cognitive psychology of Piaget. Recently psychologized, the young child is endowed with traits, such as naughtiness, that are recognized as predictable, inevitable, manageable, and temporary (as long as they *are* managed) aspects of childhood. The epithetical phrase 'my naughty little sister' is ubiquitous, and it does not serve to isolate or stigmatize the child, rather it confirms that naughtiness is typical for children of her age. The phrase retains a possessive, adjectival, and comparative emphasis – revealing as much about the narrator as her younger sister – but it does not carry the titular and nominal force of the foregrounded adjective in *Naughty Amelia Jane*, therefore the syntactical structure of Edwards's phrase suggests a temporary naughtiness that does not reflect character. The narrative tone is of knowing tolerance and the stories engage in observational humour, depicting the antics of a robust child as she soaks her clothes while illicitly fishing, or unwittingly cuts up a bridesmaid's dress in a fit of creative enthusiasm. Indeed, the conditions of naughtiness in *My Naughty Little Sister* – stubbornness, mild disobedience, fidgeting, grumbling, and answering back – seem to indicate situational response typical of a 3- or 4-year-old, although little sister's precise age is not provided: 'A long time ago when I was a little girl, I had a sister who was littler than me' (2002/1952, p. 1).

Naughtiness is presented as symptomatic of a developmental stage to be grown out of; it is not an intimation of moral status. Naughtiness is infantilized, patronized, and distanced from the implied reader, 'There, wasn't that bad of her? I'm glad you're not like that' (p. 14). This 'badness' is qualified by little sister's age and is a comment on external behaviour, as opposed to her moral identity; it is not equivalent to saying that she is, or is going to be, a bad person. The narration is retrospective and informed by adult experience that can explain and psychologize naughtiness, 'Shall I tell you why my naughty little sister hadn't wanted to eat her breakfast? *She was too excited.* And when my naughty little sister was excited, she was very cross and disobedient' (pp. 10–11), though in its phrasing and diction it recalls the superior attitude of an older sibling (and implied reader) who is safely past the 'naughty stage'. Naughtiness is thereby contained in early childhood and supervised by adult mediation; controlled in this way, naughtiness presents no danger to social structure, nor does it reveal moral character. Implicit in the exchange between protagonist (naughty child) and narrator (older/adult sibling) is the notion that maturity eschews naughtiness, leaving it behind along with milk teeth and fairy dolls. Naughtiness is endearing, amusing, and the stuff of nostalgia in *My Naughty Little Sister*, lending little to the fabric of moral life.

Naturally, the book's engagement with naughtiness suggests that an improper response to it might have implications for the future of the moral agent. Little sister is reprimanded for naughty behaviour, '"You are a bad child. You've disturbed all the little baby seeds"' (p. 30), and in line with Rousseauian tradition the consequences of her misdeeds serve to discipline and educate. Naughtiness is thus arbitrated through a familial structure that accepts naughtiness as 'normal' and responds to it with firm compassion. Conversely, no such acceptance is discernible in Enid Blyton's *Naughty Amelia Jane* in which naughtiness has an ostracizing effect. In each of the 11 short stories about Blyton's naughty doll, Amelia is singled out from the other toys in the nursery: 'There was one very naughty toy, who often made the others really angry' (2001/1946, p. 2); 'The toys surrounded the naughty doll' (p. 15). Naughty Amelia Jane is cast as a stranger who challenges modes of social interaction sanctioned by her social group:

> She hadn't come from a shop, like the others, but had been made at home. Shop-toys nearly always have good manners, and know how to behave themselves – but Amelia Jane, not being a shop-toy, had no manners at all, and didn't care what she said or did! (p. 2)

In Erving Goffman's terms, this initial otherness is rendered permanent through stigmatization that is forged by the ideological expectations of the nursery. Amelia Jane is stigmatized on account of her homemade (lower/working-class) origins and her consequent ignorance of (middle-class) social mores. Determined through social discourse, naughtiness is attributed to class, and ensuing educational deficiencies are manifest through 'naughty' behaviour that threatens social order. So, instead of being classified as typical childhood behaviour, naughtiness is rendered deviant. Each story involves episodes of naughtiness followed by punishment and recrimination, establishing a narrative pattern with a didactic thrust towards goodness. Reading on this surface level, naughtiness is easily recognized, challenged, and suppressed, however a closer look at the dominance of naughtiness in these stories reveals that the drive to goodness is ostensible and that Amelia Jane's stigmatization is deceptive. Goffman points out that stigma can lead to negative discrimination, alienation, and a reduction in life chances for the individual[17] (1968/1963, p. 15), though his emphasis is on social identity, and I want to consider how stigmatization impacts on the literary status of naughtiness in Blyton's stories.

That naughtiness is the leading player in these tales is signalled by the 'Naughty' epithet utilized throughout. The stories revolve around Amelia Jane purely because she is naughty; as the blurb on the back cover declares: 'She's big! She's bad! She's the terror of the toy-cupboard!' Amelia's naughtiness has accorded her iconic status in a culture that has kept her in print for over 60 years. Stigma isolates and magnifies naughtiness, so that it becomes the focus of attention in every story and its epithetical status makes it an umbrella term for a range of concepts and behaviours. Naughty behaviour ranges from the mild to the extreme, including impolite retorts, '"Pooh! said Amelia Jane rudely. I shan't!"' (p. 5), and cruel behaviour, 'She went up behind the pink rabbit and snipped his tail off!' (p. 8); naughtiness is articulated in terms of lack: ' "You have never done a good or brave thing all the time you have been with us" ' (pp. 16–17); and 'naughty' Amelia is variously described as 'a perfect nuisance' (p. 5) and a 'wicked, wicked doll' (p. 8). The expression and construction of naughtiness here echoes its etymological journey and shapes it as a concept that is morally complex and diverse, extending from lack of manners to physical abuse, from mischief to wickedness.

In common with Birche's 1790 prints, *Naughty Amelia Jane* might well attempt to banish naughtiness from the nursery by making it unattractive, for Amelia Jane is described as 'a big, long-legged doll with an ugly face, a bright red frock, and yellow hair' (p. 2), but if ousting and rejecting naughtiness was the intention it seems that like Milton, Blyton is unknowingly of the devil's party. Far from being rejected, as Amelia's stigmatization might suggest, naughtiness is inflated and embraced. Naughtiness is evidently pleasurable for Amelia Jane who 'loved doing naughty things' (p. 10) and is a source of constant hilarity: Amelia Jane's default reaction to her own naughty actions is laughter; the toys frequently laugh as they exact punishments on Amelia Jane; and the narrator's tone is of amused admonishment, 'Oh, Amelia Jane, you are just a humbug!' (p. 99). Naughtiness is both entertaining and desirable and is key to the recurrent pattern of these stories; it is not actually the promise of goodness that drives them, instead the return to naughtiness expressed in the closure of each story. Eight of the stories end with an explicit observation that Amelia's struggle towards goodness is transient: 'And you will be pleased to hear that she certainly *was* good for a little while, but I'm afraid it didn't last for very long!' (p. 21). Direct address is often employed to entice the reader towards the impending return to naughtiness in the next story: 'But alas! When they went back home again, Amelia Jane forgot all her good ways. Read on and you will see!' (pp. 52–3). Naughtiness only concedes the briefest of victories to goodness before it rises once more.

Can goodness be perceived in terms of victory at all though? As is true of naughtiness, degrees of goodness are in evidence in Blyton's stories: Amelia's recognition of and response to kindness in others is a type of passive good, while her capacity for selfless bravery is active (e.g. when she climbs the chimney to rescue a kitten she has endangered). However, naughtiness and goodness are not of the same order, for just as wickedness comes under the epithetical embrace of 'Naughty', so too does goodness. Although Amelia exhibits good behaviour, *Naughty* Amelia Jane she remains, and so the pendulum swings from wicked to good in a vacillating arc of naughtiness articulated in the book's closing lines:

'Oh, I'm so glad you've forgiven me, Toys! I won't be naughty again.'

Well, the toys didn't believe *that*, of course – they knew Amelia Jane too well! . . .

'She's like the little girl in the nursery rhyme,' said the bear to the clown. '*You* know – when she's good she's *very, very* good – but when she's bad she's horrid!' (p. 186)

The intertextual reference points to naughtiness as a cultural tradition of which Naughty Amelia Jane is a part, highlighting the ethical performance of Blyton's popular stories for young children. Blyton's tales are not philosophical, yet they illustrate and play with the moral extremes located in naughty ambivalence; using naughtiness as a repository for these complex concepts, they place goodness and wickedness within the remit of the nursery and by association childhood. Russell observes that good habits and ambitions require stimulation in early childhood and it seems that literature such as this might be considered a feature of the early moral training Russell calls for (2010/1926, p. 58).

My Naughty Little Sister and *Naughty Amelia Jane* employ a convention of series literature, freezing childhood at a particular stage so that stories can be repeated in a familiar cycle. While they deal differently with naughtiness in the present space of the childhoods they construct, each book anticipates an unspecified future of *potential* ethical maturity. Through naughtiness, goodness shimmers on the horizon and in this way such books offer clues to Agard's youth in search of the moral life, although this is not true of all texts that feature protagonists identified by epithetical traits that could be deemed naughty. 'Dennis the Menace' (1951–present), a long-running comic strip from *The Beano*, and Francesca Simon's *Horrid Henry* series (1994–present) invest in caricature and exaggeration to exploit the humorous potential of menace and horridness, but the conceptual constraints of such texts result in a one-dimensional focus on the characteristics in question. These stories adhere relentlessly to the horrid and the menacing because there is no forward impetus in which a future of moral/immoral development is anticipated and in this sense such stories lack moral momentum. I do not mean that they are morally irresponsible, rather that they do not anticipate moral agency; they simply are menacing and horrid now. Interestingly, although a range of concepts, behaviours, and attitudes are identified as 'horrid' in *Horrid Henry*, 'Henry threw food, Henry snatched, Henry pushed and shoved and pinched' (1995/1994, p. 7), Henry is never described as naughty.[18] It could be that the term is too mild to be considered relevant or overly infantile in the vein of *My Naughty Little Sister*, notwithstanding the ambivalence of naughtiness (understood in its widest sense) would be problematic in a text that hangs on unequivocal horridness.

Children's literature deals in the main with childly aspects of naughtiness, so it is inevitable that the nature and usage of naughtiness change in line with shifts in perceptions of childhood. In the ardent Evangelism of Sherwood's *The History of the Fairchild Family*, naughtiness is a behavioural manifestation of the 'sin in men's hearts'; indeed, Emily Fairchild's 'sad temptation' (1824/1818, p. 115) in 'The All Seeing God' is described as 'her own naughtiness' (p. 121) and linked directly to the fact that 'fear of God was not in the heart of Emily' (p. 116). Comparison with another of Sherwood's stories *Brotherly Love* (1851)[19] reveals that the ambivalent core of naughtiness can transcend ideological distinctions though. Here naughtiness is presented as an inevitable behavioural condition of early childhood and young Reuben is similar to Dorothy Edwards's little sister in this. Reuben's 13-year-old brother Marten is expected to care for him on the basis that Reuben is too young to keep himself out of harm, being 'not yet half that age' (undated/1851, p. 5). Reuben is the only character to whom naughtiness is attributed in this tale, the narrator describes him as 'looking, I am sorry to say, very naughty and selfish'(p. 39), but his naughtiness is treated quite differently from Marten's conceit in believing himself good and beyond temptation. Reuben is only mildly reproved by the narrative tone 'I am sorry to say' and his behaviour is explained as an emotional response to frustration, 'he was really wishing Marten to give up his own desires to attend to and humour his' (p. 39). In this instance, Sherwood presents naughtiness as an emotional, rather than cognitive response; as David Carr observes, 'if it makes sense to speak of at least some affective states – those of animals and infants – as genuine emotions, then feelings need not *always* be cognitive and would not in that case be inevitably liable to rational assessment' (2009, p. 35). Reuben's naughtiness is not subject to moral judgement because it is not presented as the product of a rational being; Reuben is not a culprit, rather 'the poor little victim of his brother's self conceit' (p. 52). Furthermore, when placed in mortal danger of drowning by Marten's negligence (and not his naughty behaviour), Reuben is protected by his heavenly Father whose 'eyes are ever on infants, the loveliest beings of his creation' (p. 84). Naughtiness is not *sinful* in this instance, instead a condition of childhood used to expose the presence of sin in others. Reuben's human condition means that he too has sin in his heart, even so his naughtiness here is not presented as an aspect of this sin. The naughty infant garners love and protection, while simultaneously demonstrating the necessity of Divine guidance for, 'unless he is guided in all his actions by his heavenly

Father, he is sure to go wrong, let his age or condition be what it may' (p. 93). So, in Sherwood's writing, naughtiness is both evidence of human sin and of childhood disposition that eludes moral scrutiny; this discrepancy poses questions that disrupt tidy morality.

Nineteenth-century evangelist writing takes a different stance on naughtiness from children's literature in modern Britain, still the ambivalent nature of naughtiness endures and looks towards both good and evil in the process. Naughtiness has the propensity to be immoral in Nietzsche's terms, as he asks: 'Is a moralist not the opposite of a Puritan? That is to say, as a thinker who regards morality as something questionable, as worthy of question-marks, in short as a problem? Is moralizing not – immoral?' (2003/1886, p. 158). Much of Sherwood's writing exemplifies the morality Nietzsche rejects here, but his question mark can be located in the very gap opened by naughtiness. Immorality designated thus is the destination of Agard's seeker as he ascends from the circles of hell to find the Upper World rendered question markable. Indeed, his first utterance is framed as a question to Beatrice, 'lost to the world in a book' (2008, C.13:4):

> I could have said, 'That book, is it scary?'
> or something like, 'Have you got the time?'
> Instead, I mumbled, 'Are you the good fairy?' (C.13: 7–9)

That the seeker associates the book Beatrice reads with fear points to the danger recognized by Nietzsche in 'resist[ing] customary value-sentiments' and *The Young Inferno* adds to this the notion that literature is best placed to discover, question, and resist the 'correct beliefs' (p. 39) scorned by Russell in order that 'Our purposes should be our own, not the result of external authority' (Russell, 2010/1926, p. 35). The allusion to time here is ambiguous, suggesting the seeker's own sense of having lost (mortal) time while in the underworld, and also that the task ahead will challenge the limited time available to mortal experience. The precise nature of the guide/seeker's task is not articulated, although the assignation of *good* to Beatrice suggests that he must seek the moral territory that will save him from eternal torment in hell's circles. Of course, the 'good fairy' is also an iconic motif of literary tradition and so his guide is figuratively comprised of literature and books; she is 'poetry in motion' (C.13: 12). Accordingly, it seems that the long usage of naughty ambivalence in literature should be advantageous for Agard's seeker, surfacing from hell into a living library versed in the evolving conditions of good and evil and ready to serve the young pilgrim in the rejection of indifference.

The badness in between

The Young Inferno traces an adolescent awakening to sin and places his infernal tour between the states of childhood wonder (pre-inferno) and [young] adult moral agency (post-inferno). Agard explains in the introduction that he wanted to stay true to 'the symbolic significance of numbers' in Dante's epic poem, and so Agard hopes that the 13 cantos of *The Young Inferno* 'sounds about right for a teenage reader', [20] suggesting that the growth into moral agency begins around the age of 13 for most people. From Agard's point of view then, the state of childhood wonder is morally unconscious and the awakening to sin articulated in the poetry of his *Inferno* does not imply a preteen readership. As my exploration of naughtiness in children's literature demonstrates, however, moral concepts and semantics are introduced to childhood culture and literature intended for and enjoyed by younger readers.[21] Literary naughtiness serves as a sort of moral training ground that does not commit to good or evil, nonetheless a number of books for younger readers take a more ethically aware and challenging stance than *My Naughty Little Sister* or *Naughty Amelia Jane*. In Gillian Avery's academic romp *The Warden's Niece* (1957), for example, the parodic treatment of the usage and status of badness in education works covertly to provoke contemplation of its ethical status, while Diana Wynne Jones's comic fantasy *Wilkins' Tooth* (1973) explores the powerful and rippling consequences of doing 'a bad act disguised as a good one' (2002/1973, p. 91), confronting directly a range of moral categories, such as kindness, fairness, good, bad, and even evil. If good and evil sit at either end of an ethical scale, then books for younger audiences tend to approach the concept of evil with caution, nudging towards it through a consideration of badness, which is frequently presented by writers and philosophers as an ancillary ethical concept to evil. So, although badness is often treated as ethically moderate in relation to evil, it is no less significant, especially since encounters with badness are relatively commonplace (and even young children are likely to be familiar with badness), while, as Terry Eagleton points out, 'evil is not the kind of thing we bump into every day' (2010, p. 128). It seems worthwhile then to consider the treatment of badness – and its dichotomous relationship to goodness – in two popular books for younger readers that make use of their formal properties to open up ethical concepts for consideration.

The Elephant and the Bad Baby (1969) by Elfrida Vipont and Raymond Briggs is a picture book for young children that leaves questions suspended in a manner that equips the young thinker for a journey into the deeper realms of human experience. Nicolette Jones observes, 'A certain moral anarchy in the text makes

Vipont an interesting counterpart to Briggs, in whose own books, where there is conflict between protagonists, it is never clear-cut who is wrong and who is right' (Briggs and Jones, 2003, p. 22). Ostensibly it is a book about badness, though close attention reveals a loving goodness that transcends the badness it appears to invest in. A vista of expressionless sky overhanging an empty sward on the edge of an unidentified town gives a visual hint of the silences that mark this playful book. The conditions of badness when an elephant and a bad baby meet in the middle of nowhere are never established, nor are they explained. We have already seen that labelling is a common strategy for containment and control in children's literature, yet the nominal phrase 'Bad Baby' is never justified here (as it is in *My Naughty Little Sister* and *Naughty Amelia Jane*), and consequently it is not clear where this appellation originates; it is not apparent who has identified the baby as bad or to what the badness refers. Is the baby's badness essential and inescapable – or is his badness merely the circumstantial play of alliteration? Is the baby 'chosen' by the elephant because his badness is somehow evident and in need of reward (a riotous ride through town from a like-minded partner) or recrimination (verbal chastisement from an adult who has disguised the romp as a lesson in good manners)? These questions are not answered and the title's hanging judgement is challenged by a text that does not directly expound on its labelling.

The baby's badness might be taken as a form of naughtiness, of course, and the inherent ambiguity of naughtiness is relevant to a text full of unresolved gaps. It could be argued that, although not explicitly stated, the baby's badness is located in his lack of manners, as suggested by the elephant's admonishing accusation: ' "You haven't ONCE said please" ' (1971/1969, p. 23).[22] There is bathos in this accusation for it takes no account of the string of thefts that precede it; thefts instigated by the elephant and acquiesced to by the Bad Baby. There is no sign that either the elephant or the Bad Baby acknowledge wrongdoing, and the verbal narration does not comment when 'the Elephant stretched out his trunk and took an ice-cream for himself and an ice-cream for the Bad Baby' (p. 9). However, while the verbal narration is silent on the stolen ice creams, pies, and buns, Briggs's accumulative line drawings confirm that the thefts have been noticed; thus the verbal and visual aspects of the picture-book work in counterpoint (Figure 1.3). Anger is conveyed through the facial and body expression of the shopkeepers who pursue the miscreants on every page turn and the chase appears to be a morally loaded accusation – 'stop thief!' – although this accusation is not made verbally. When the chase is abruptly terminated by the Elephant, outrage is directed solely at the Bad Baby, as the Elephant and

Figure 1.3 Visual recrimination (p. 15, 1971/1969).

Source: *The Elephant and the Bad Baby* by Elfrida Vipont, illustrated by Raymond Briggs (Hamish Hamilton, 1969). Text copyright © Elfrida Vipont Foulds, 1969. Illustrations copyright © Raymond Briggs, 1969.

vendors point at the Bad Baby with a reproving exclamation, '"Just fancy that! He never *once* said please!"' (p. 26). Theft is undercut by the focus on manners and moral concerns are overridden by a preoccupation with social mores. Vipont and Briggs's irony might intend to point out the moral hypocrisy of adult-child power relations, or to suggest that too much emphasis is given to manners and etiquette in bourgeois society when there are more important social issues at stake – but their target is not of primary concern. The philosophical potential of this book is located in the ironic (counterpoint) gap opened between morality and mores, and it is the gap itself that is pertinent here.

It is in this gap that the baby's badness is both identified and obscured. If he is bad because he lacks manners, what of his criminality? The Bad Baby is not verbally admonished for thieving and his accomplice is not blamed. The Elephant initiates theft and runs riotously, 'rumpeta, rumpeta, rumpeta, all down the road'; perhaps he is beyond moral recrimination because he is not human. Considered metaphorically, the point may be that while bad manners might seem childly, amusing and harmless, unchecked they will lead to crime on a much larger, elephantine scale. Just as we might begin to reflect on the nature, consequence, and extent of badness it seems to fade into the background and into the childly vulnerability that manifests itself when faced with collective, authoritative fury. The Bad Baby is diminished visually in this moment – hunched on the ground with his back to the viewer – and the incongruity of 'bad' and 'baby' is emphasized in Briggs's emotive image. The Bad Baby does not apologize for his wrongdoing, though he does ask politely (lesson learned) for the ultimate source of comfort: ' "PLEASE! I want to go home to my Mummy!" ' (p. 26); he seems exhausted by his efforts to live up to his name and turns instead to the good.

In the return home to mother's kitchen and bed, the baby does not face the punishment that might be expected after a day (or a life) of badness. Instead the Bad Baby is comforted with 'pancakes for everybody' (p. 31) and a maternal care that asks no questions when confronted with son, elephant, and crowd of recently disgruntled shopkeepers. Goodness is not expressly determined here, but the expanse of the elephant's hug, the laden tea table, and mother's smile set up a challenge to badness; this unidentified warmth *feels* and *looks* good as reflected in the baby's grin (Figure 1.4). Iris Murdoch observes, 'Goodness appears to be both rare and hard to picture. It is perhaps most convincingly met with in simple people – inarticulate, unselfish mothers of large families – but these cases are also the least illuminating' (2001/1970, pp. 51–2). Certainly *The Elephant and the Bad Baby* is not illuminating and its closure reaches for that rare goodness that is likely to evade most of us. It is a goodness that forgives and a goodness that is patient with the everyday badness that most people fall into; an everyday badness that makes the Bad Baby typical. The Bad Baby cannot be entirely wicked, for wickedness has no room for the goodness invested in that kitchen; like most people he will lapse into the badness that renders him human. Sundown cannot vanquish badness and he remains bad in the closing line of the book: 'And the Bad Baby went to bed' (p. 32), yet the embrace of his

Figure 1.4 Compensation and forgiveness (pp. 30–1, 1971).

Source: The Elephant and the Bad Baby by Elfrida Vipont, illustrated by Raymond Briggs (Hamish Hamilton, 1969). Text copyright © Elfrida Vipont Foulds, 1969. Illustrations copyright © Raymond Briggs, 1969.

mother's kitchen suggests that good is at least possible. Good is not something that the baby becomes – repentance and recrimination are not relevant for a sinner unconscious of sin – more precisely, the bad is bathed in and surrounded by good; this, it seems, is an excellent place for moral life to begin.

Regardless of how the closure is interpreted – for Murdoch's notion of loving goodness is only one way of reading it – *The Elephant and the Bad Baby* poses a series of questions about the nature of badness and its relationship to moral character, punishment, reward, and goodness. These questions are posed through a number of silences: the epithetical reference to badness is not explicated; the picture-book form exploits the gap between mores and morals in its use of visual/verbal counterpoint and irony; and the closing process of reward ignores the badness that precedes it. A range of peritextual, textual, and literary devices playfully contribute to the philosophical potential of an ostensibly simple picture book for young children. Good and bad are, quite literally, put on the table in *The Elephant and the Bad Baby,* alongside mother's sugar and lemon; they are on the menu should the reader choose to engage. In Jacqueline Wilson's illustrated novel *Bad Girls* (1996), the level of engagement with badness is more direct, and this aspect of the book might seem to limit its philosophical potential (as it does in Blyton's *Six Bad Boys*[23] [1951], for instance). Wilson's books are well known for their willingness to tackle 'unflinching subject matter',[24] though only to describe her novels as 'issue books' would be to underestimate the attention given to *ideas* alongside issues in books such as *Bad Girls.* Certainly *Bad Girls* deals with the issue of bullying, but the subject is one of several vehicles for a broader consideration of good and bad. Furthermore, the combination of Nick Sharratt's line drawings and Wilson's verbal text serves to unsettle the concept of badness and to reach beyond the direct treatment of issues; once again, the form of children's books offers a way in to ethical considerations.

This 'unsettling' process begins with the titular labelling familiar to the sociocultural conditions of childhood and a cover illustration that might seem to identify the 'bad girls' as Mandy the protagonist and Tanya, an older girl who befriends Mandy. However, this identification is troubled by the opening of the first chapter, which visually and verbally offers different referents for consideration: 'They were going to get me./I saw them the moment I turned the corner. They were halfway down, waiting near the bus stop. Melanie, Sarah and Kim. Kim, the worst of all' (2006/1996, p. 2). From the outset of the first chapter, it appears that the girls tormenting Mandy, the protagonist, are the nominal 'bad girls', and this is supported by a range of descriptors used to qualify their badness (their leader Kim in particular): 'so scary' (p. 4); '. . . wicked, wicked, wicked'

(p. 14); '. . . really nasty big girl' (p. 27); 'a nasty piece of work' (p. 29). Badness here is defined in terms of a callousness that diminishes the life experience of other people, and conceptually it is the most extreme interpretation of badness in *Bad Girls*, coming close to Schopenhauer's vision of *Schadenfreude*, which he argues is closely related to cruelty as the antithesis of pity; for Schopenhauer '*Schadenfreude* is diabolical and its derision is the laughter of Hell' (2004/1851, p. 140). In *Bad Girls*, this badness is evoked figuratively both visually and verbally: when Kim teases Mandy about her older mother: 'It felt as if she were biting me . . . Cruel little nips, again and again' (p. 7). The pain caused by Kim's cruelty can be seen and consequently badness is made visible (Figure 1.5).

Badness refuses to stay in focus in *Bad Girls* though and different categories of badness are soon introduced. Reflection on these categories is prompted early on through a question posed by Mandy's protective mother: ' "Aren't we bad girls?" said Mum' (p. 38). Mandy's mother is referring to the fact that they have decided to take an unnecessary day off after Mandy's road accident (precipitated by Kim and her cronies), and the allusion to the book's title is telling. Mandy's mother only playfully concedes to badness here nonetheless – as we will see – parental responsibility for guiding the child to moral agency is an important ideological strand of *Bad Girls*. Moreover, this wordplay implies that Mandy's status as victim of cruelty does not preclude her from being or becoming bad and so Mandy's entry into dubious moral territory with Tanya – it transpires that Tanya regularly shoplifts – is foreshadowed. The brash, kind, and troubled Tanya is the friend Mandy has long dreamed of, still she introduces Mandy to criminality and another category of badness. Mandy decides eventually to overlook Tanya's thievery and accordingly the shadow of badness casts over Mandy too: 'I decided I didn't care what Tanya did. I had to have her as my friend no matter what' (p. 122). This brief overview demonstrates some of the ways in which the cruelty established at the

Figure 1.5 Badness bites (p. 7, 2006).

Source: Image taken from *Bad Girls* by Jacqueline Wilson and illustrated by Nick Sharratt, published by Random House. Used by permission of Nick Sharratt and David Higham Associates Ltd.

opening of *Bad Girls* is overlaid with different types of badness that transform the title into an ethically framed interrogative.

This interrogative framing is underscored by literary techniques that directly address the reader and encourage consideration of the ethical dilemmas established by the unfolding plot. For example, Mandy is shown explicitly to ponder the moral conditions of Tanya's first theft, a hairband that she gifts to Mandy:

> And if she *had* stolen it, then what?
>
> I knew it was wrong to steal things. Especially from people like Mr and Mrs Patel, who didn't make very much money out of their corner shop. Although it was only a hairband. A little, velvet, scrunchie hairband that only cost a pound or two. It wasn't as if it was really valuable.
>
> Tanya hadn't stolen it for herself. She'd stolen it for me, because I was her friend. And she didn't have any spare cash of her own. She didn't get proper pocket money every Saturday like me. She had hardly anything at all. So it wasn't really too awful for her to take it, was it? (p. 84)

The questions opening and closing this sequence resemble the technique of Socratic address, seeking to draw the reader into Mandy's 'conflicting thoughts buzzing round in [her] head' (p. 84), and to demonstrate that moral choice is challenging and isolating. Moral choice is presented as an inner conflict that must finally be made alone by the moral agent. This moment seems neatly to illustrate Murdoch's observation that 'a peculiar feature of moral choice . . . is the strange emptiness which often occurs at the moment of choosing' (2001/1970, p. 34). Murdoch's emptiness articulates a *moment of potential* and a *setting the self apart from* that is always daunting; especially for a child cocooned in parental love. Initially Mandy finds the moral task overwhelming and almost as diminishing as the bullying she has experienced, which would do little to sell the concept of moral agency to young readers if Mandy did not survive and grow in moral strength through the process. This moment of isolating decision making is balanced by a plot device – the arrival of a teacher with new teaching methods – that elicits a controlled discussion of the moral and social issues raised by bullying. 'Circle Time' allows Wilson to pose and answer a range of different questions related to bullying, significantly demonstrating that collective response to and responsibility for ethical issues is possible, just as Russell implies when he argues that schools ought to take responsibility for the building of moral character.

In the pursuit of badness, *Bad Girls* seeks to understand the causes of different grades of badness such as cruelty, criminality, and cowardice. Much socially aware children's literature that explores the ethical conditions of badness attributes it at least partly to social background: Enid Blyton's *Six Bad Boys* pinpoints working mothers as the root cause of adolescent delinquency; Melvin Burgess's *Junk* (1996) presents Tar's heroin addiction and eventual violent behaviour as the consequence of mental and physical abuse by alcoholic parents; and Anne Cassidy's *Looking For JJ* (2004) locates negligent maternal care as the catalyst for juvenile murder. As a writer sensitive to the social conditions of childhood, Wilson also seeks to offer socially sympathetic grounds for the unruly behaviour of her protagonists; in *The Story of Tracy Beaker* (1991), for instance, Tracy's destructive truculence is explained by her mother's abandonment of her, and this sociological approach to moral issues is also evident in *Bad Girls*. Mandy's weakness in the face of bullies and moral temptation is set in the context of overprotective parenting, and Tanya's thieving is explained as a reaction to her mother's suicide and a life spent in care. This picture of social responsibility for badness would seem to absolve the individual and is evasive in the terms set out by Midgley:

> There is at present a strong tendency for decent people, especially in the social sciences, to hold that it has no internal causes in human nature – that it is just the result of outside pressures which could be removed. Now obviously there are powerful outside causes. There are physical pains, diseases, economic shortages and dangers – everything that counts as 'natural evil'. There are also cultural factors – bad example, bad teaching, bad organization. (2001/1984, p. 2)

While Midgley accepts that social factors must be considered, 'The idea that we must always choose between social and individual causes for human behaviour, and cannot use both, is confused and arbitrary' (p. 2). Midgley is interested in establishing the human causes of moral evil and to understand why 'People often do treat each other abominably' and 'constantly cause avoidable suffering' (p. 2). Although *Bad Girls* is not quite interested in moral *evil*, it does invest in the idea that people cause each other suffering, and also demonstrates, as Midgley insists, that 'Nothing has one sole cause' (p. 3). Taking a slightly different, but related line on this, Eagleton argues that 'action which has a cause [can] be freely undertaken' (2010, p. 3) and that 'reason and freedom are closely bound together. For those who do not grasp this point, trying to account for wicked acts is always a devious attempt to let perpetrators off the hook' (p. 7). So although *Bad Girls* is mindful of social factors governing human behaviour, various strategies are employed to show that it is possible for individuals to take responsibility for their actions and that social class and upbringing do not solely determine behaviour. Indeed *Bad Girls* interrogates its social conscience from within, opening gaps to be debated in the position it might appear to take.

Positioned as an outsider in *Bad Girls*, Tanya is supported by the book's liberal sociopolitical position; it exposes the sort of prejudice that perceives Tanya to be 'a bad influence . . .' on account of her background (p. 88) as an unjustifiable cause of human suffering. Thus far, *Bad Girls* invests in the social scientific approach outlined by Midgley, yet otherness also functions as an interrogative tool and therefore her authority is necessarily reinforced by the implied author and the ideological subtext. For example, Tanya probes Mandy's first-person narration from a position of *sympathetic otherness,* destabilizing – though not entirely rejecting – Mandy's depiction of maternal overprotection and infantilization. Mandy's views are reenforced by Sharratt's illustrative commentary (Figure 1.6), verbal and visual texts combining to suggest that Mandy's susceptibility to victimization and desire for Tanya's friendship (whatever the consequences) are rooted in her mother's treatment of her. Maternal restrictions are perceived as negative and undermining, until Tanya weakens the narrative perspective, commenting for example that ' "Your mum nags because she's absolutely dotty about you, anyone can see that" ' (p. 113); Tanya's challenge reveals that there are different ways of seeing and that understanding other points of view is

Figure 1.6 Pushed into badness (p. 6, 2006).

Source: Image taken from *Bad Girls* by Jacqueline Wilson and illustrated by Nick Sharratt, published by Random House. Used by permission of Nick Sharratt and David Higham Associates Ltd.

morally constructive. Once Mandy properly is able to see her mother as a source of loving care, Mandy is better able to respond to her mother's views and to stand up for her own opinions; she actively looks to herself, rather than passively blaming others for her misfortune. This proposes the idea that goodness and badness are within the remit of the individual; that good and bad are affected by circumstance, but not reducible to it. Though there are a number of ways of approaching this, the balance between individual and social responsibility is reminiscent of Schopenhauer's notion of will:

> That one man is wicked and another good does not depend on motives and external influences such as teaching and preaching; and in this sense the thing is absolutely inexplicable. But whether a wicked man shows his wickedness in petty injustices, cowardly tricks, and low villainy, practised by him in the narrow sphere of his surroundings, or as a conqueror oppresses nations, throws a world into misery and distress, and sheds the blood of millions, this is the outward form of his phenomenon or appearance, that which is inessential to it, and it depends on the circumstances in which fate has placed him, on the surroundings, on external influences, on motives. But his decision on these motives can never be explained from them; it proceeds from the will, whose phenomenon this man is. (1969/1851, pp. 138–9)

Schopenhauer refuses the idea that good and bad can be explained through circumstance alone, insisting that any decisions made by the moral agent instead 'proceed from the will'. Interpreting Schopenhauer in optimistic terms (if this is possible), Mandy's struggle with moral choice can be read as a fight between will and circumstance; she wills to be good and, although the circumstances of her upbringing temporarily cause her to ignore the moral jeopardy of friendship with Tanya, the strength of her will to goodness wins through. On the other hand, Kim's persistent cruelty points to a will to badness; no explanation is given for Kim's bullying behaviour and though the 'Circle Time' episode speculates about possible motivations, readers are left to contemplate the idea that some people 'intentionally [do] acts that are wrong' (2001/1984, p. vii) – one of Midgley's definitions of wickedness – and thus *Bad Girls* introduces the notion that bad people exist, regardless of circumstance. *Bad Girls* manoeuvres between positions, giving space for young readers really to think about the nature of badness.

Although *Bad Girls* establishes different ethical categories of badness and is more expressive about its conditions, in common with *The Elephant and the Bad Baby*, it closes with an affirmation of goodness. Each of these books for younger readers offers a comforting closure, investing in a protectionist paradigm that could be seen as evasive, or even dishonest about the challenges of moral agency and the prevalence of evil as an aspect of human experience. However, Kierkegaard observes in *Works of Love* (1847) that it is never easy to be good, or to love truly (goodness for Kierkegaard is bound up with a selfless, suffering, and tested love that is rooted in God's love); hence he deliberates not on love, but on *works of love*. Indeed, novel and picture book each contain aspects of this constantly tried love/goodness; Mandy suffers for love and the baby's mother feeds the whole community love to compensate for filial badness. The affirmation of good that closes *Bad Girls* and *The Elephant and the Bad Baby* does not render goodness more powerful than bad – badness is given more space in both books – instead it directs the implied reader towards moral life. This moral life involves a regard for other people expressed through a friendship and love that properly sees the other's point of view; maternal love sees beyond the baby's badness and Mandy's love/friendship is seen through moral understanding. Moreover, badness is not vanquished in either book; Kim is not reformed and the baby is still bad, ergo badness underlies the turn to good. That love is the key to moral life is clear though and these books symbolically offer this positive potential for goodness to their young readers, as does *The Young Inferno* when the seeker becomes 'lost in the orbit of Beatrice' (C.13: 19).

Out of context, the seeker's enamoured response to Beatrice might seem trite after a tour through the regions of hell, but it is significant that this otherworldly creature is forged in literature (rather than religion), and the fact that he meets her at 'precisely nine o'clock' (C.13: 14) marks the beginning of a new life phase in harmony with Dante's numerical symmetry. Agard's seeker and implied reader require this reassurance, since it is unclear how to approach love in an increasingly secular society where love is no longer shored by Kierkegaard's faith, or the conception of God's love in *The Divine Comedy*. A solution to this comes from Iris Murdoch, for whom the notion of good transcends God and this understanding of loving goodness seems especially relevant to a period of British children's literature that is no longer dominated by theology. Murdoch offers a vision of moral life that does not abandon God, recognizing that true attention to any other human or to God ultimately requires goodness. Murdoch rejects the validation of 'intelligence' and 'force of will' in the existential visions of Heidegger and Sartre, along with the contrasting and 'vanishing images of Christian theology which represented goodness as almost impossibly difficult, and sin as almost insuperable and certainly as a universal condition' (p. 49). Murdoch and Agard are united by an optimism that anticipates and affirms a secular loving goodness; an optimism tempered by Melvin Burgess's *The Baby and Fly Pie* (1993), a dystopian reminder that indifference remains a present and future threat to goodness. No longer are we in the territory of literature for the youngest readers, for here badness grows up and turns towards evil.

The ever-present danger of indifference

The Baby and Fly Pie is a young adult book that wrenches its implied reader out of a childness that might reassure with a measured and hopeful rendition of badness into a landscape of disturbing images that designates childhood grotesque and innocence impossible or stupid. For much of the novel, a kidnapped baby is quietened by masking tape strapped across her mouth and when finally removed, 'a big black hole opened in the middle of her face. And she screamed – and she screamed and screamed and screamed. It was so loud it seemed to split the air' (1995/1993, p. 68). The infant's cry is an aperture into which good and bad fall indiscriminately. Burgess's novel is set in a unspecified future London, teeming with avarice and rubbish picked over by the 'rubbish kids' who populate the municipal underbelly of capitalism. Burgess's novel is elliptical and intensely symbolic, overlaying in its depiction of ruthless street urchins a Dickensian idealism that renders them pitiable with a more uncompromising political edge located in a contemporary evil that chokes Manila, Mumbai, Rio de Janeiro, Jakarta, and every city in which poverty is forced to live on the waste of affluence.[25] *The Baby and Fly Pie* is a deeply philosophical book that calls for moral values and an ethical framework to human being missing from the London that Burgess conceives.

In *The Baby and Fly Pie*, the ambition of every rubbish kid is to 'make good', an ambition bereft of morality, and underscored by an individual desire to escape suffering. As the book's narrator Fly Pie explains, 'We call it making good. It's plans and dreams and you can't always tell the difference. Everyone's going to make good but not many do' (p. 18). The opportunity for Fly Pie and his friend Sham to make good comes in the form of Sylvie, a baby who has been taken from her wealthy parents and held to ransom by a local gang. Fatally injured, one of the gang members dies in the boys' cardboard hideout, leaving them with the baby and dreams of a future built on 17 million pounds. However, the boys' notion of making good is challenged and overturned by Fly Pie's sister Jane, who believes that they can make good of a different nature; a good forged in honesty, trust, and faith in fellow humanity:

> She said we had to behave like proper people. People didn't judge you by what you did, she said – they judged you by what you were inside. We just had to be *like* that enough and the good would come without us even trying. (p. 60)

Jane convinces the boys that if they treat the baby with loving care and if they shun the life of stealing and prostitution imposed on them by Mother Shelly and the world of the Tip, this will be recognized by Sylvie's parents and the authorities. However, this is a society indifferent to the experience of rubbish kids – 'People pretend that they take you to nice villages and towns where you have a proper life but we know better that that. The kids see everything' (p. 3) – and it becomes clear as the novel unfolds that nobody will ever look to see good in them. Jane clings to her faith in goodness until the end, forgiving Sham's betrayal of her, just as she clings to Sylvie in the faith that humanity is good and loving.

It is through these very different versions of making good that Burgess tests and provokes his implied reader. Each is articulated and challenged repeatedly by a range of characters and thus a dualistic formulation of good encourages contemplation of *how* and *what* it means. The open ending of *The Baby and Fly Pie* as Jane is left to an (un)certain death on a country road, her hands and lap weighted with stones, leaves readers to ponder the possibility and nature of good in an apparently faithless and Godless world. Burgess's darkly fantasized London lacks moral and theological structure, notwithstanding his depiction of Jane echoes the sufferings of Christ and the moral vision of countless philosophers. Indeed Jane's is the sort of goodness epitomized by Christ in Kierkegaard's vision of love:

> Just imagine ... Christ in that moment when he was brought before the Council; imagine the raging crowd [...] Imagine how many insults, how much derision, and how many mocking taunts were shouted [...]. But he discovered nothing; lovingly he hid the multitude of sins – by discovering nothing. (1998/1847, pp. 287–8)

Jane discovers nothing and lovingly she hides the multitude of sins in her acceptance of death; she is not Christ and yet the echoes of Christian mythology in Burgess's representation of Jane are necessary to the ethical wasteland he conjures. Jane discovers nothing, still perchance Burgess's reader will learn that goodness can transcend indifference. *The Baby and Fly Pie* might seem a hopeless vision of humanity, but in Burgess's comparative articulation of good lies space for thought, possibility, and moral agency. Moreover, pessimism is not a vice to hope's virtue, as Hollindale points out, sometimes 'it is important to go against the human grain and respect pessimism' (2011, p. 99). Pessimism with moral purpose is a potent antidote to indifference.

In common with some of the books for young people explored in Chapter 2, *The Baby and Fly Pie* conceives evil as human and mundane, refusing the ultimate evil of indifference in its depiction of a courageous and faithful young girl. Accordingly, Burgess's novel takes an older and wiser seeker back to the fence of indifference, seats him upon the fence, and then dismantles it from beneath him. Burgess's novel underscores Wiesel's point that 'indifference can be tempting – more than that, seductive' (Wiesel, 1999) through Jane's exceptional response to situations that those around her fail to confront. Wiesel explains that indifference has the capacity to deny humanity and to leave our neighbour's pain and despair meaningless and thus 'indifference reduces the other to an abstraction'. If novels for young people are able to demonstrate the moral imperative in exposing the suffering of others, then they are engaging young readers in one of the most crucial areas of ethical concern.

The Sin of Indifference (Part II):
Discovering Evil

. . . it is certainly easy to see that the one who loves, who discovers nothing, makes a very poor showing in the eyes of the world. To make discoveries even with regard to evil, with regard to sin and the multitude of sins, to be the shrewd, sly, foxy, perhaps more or less corrupt observer who can really make discoveries – this is highly regarded in the world. Even a youth upon first stepping out into life is very eager to divulge how he knows and has discovered evil (because he is reluctant to have the world call him a simpleton).

Kierkegaard, 1998/1847, pp. 283–4

A thousand diabolical expressions

Kierkegaard's uncourageous youth succumbs to the allure of evil because the rewards of love appear unattractive in comparison, conversely Agard's seeker has been awakened to the world's evil in order to embrace love in a denial of Wiesel's indifference. In Kierkegaard's view the knowledge of evil holds no interest for the loving soul; love eschews evil and 'In this the one who loves is like the child' (p. 286), and his position might seem to contradict or deny Agard's. Kierkegaard is articulating a love that refuses engagement with evil though, rather than a love that is ignorant of (or indifferent to) evil, and in this Agard's seeker moves into the embrace of Kierkegaard's love. In Kierkegaard's terms then, the seeker's journey must involve a return to that state of childhood wonder;[1] a journey back towards a knowing that is simultaneously unknowing.[2] However, since Kierkegaard speaks of Christian love, its relevance to the notions of love (good) and sin (evil) is questionable in *The Young Inferno*, which are only loosely framed through Christianity. Agard's hell works as a figurative space to demonstrate the contemporary evils of *this* world, rather than focusing on the notion of punishment in the next, still there is something that *The Young Inferno* and *Works of Love* have in common. Both evidently recognize the worldly allure of evil and attempt to strip away the glamour that leads Eagleton to observe that sinners in the cast of *Brighton Rock's* Pinkie 'are more spiritually glamorous than the boringly well-behaved' (2010, p. 56) and later to declare 'the idea that evil is glamorous is one of the great moral mistakes of the modern age' (p. 120). For Kierkegaard and Agard, deglamorizing evil involves demonstrating that evil has no access to love, albeit different categories of love and that evil must be eschewed by loving goodness (Murdoch points out that the concepts of love and good are closely related). Agard's seeker confronts false love and glamour directly in the second circle of hell and illustrates his point through widely recognizable cultural references:

> Turning to my teacher, Frankenstein said,
> 'Why bring a boy here? You should know better.
> What does he know of love? Besides, he ain't dead.'
>
> 'It is good that the lad should see for himself
> how love still shoots its burning arrows
> into souls that lived their lives all for the flesh . . .'
>
> My teacher winked at me kindly as he spoke.
> 'These days the young have old heads on their shoulders.
> They've seen it all in magazines and soaps.' (C.4: 19–27)

In these lines, 'they've seen it all' can be discerned Kierkegaard's concern for the youth eager to divulge his knowledge of evil, but rather than encouraging a return to a childhood that invests innocently in the *wonder*ful, *The Young Inferno* provokes a questioning wonder at the extent and range of evil through its descent into hell and its invitation to get moral wisdom through reading. *The Young Inferno* draws on a wide-ranging cultural history encompassing *Aesop's Fables*, Dante's *Divine Comedy*, plus the diasporaic rhythms of youth culture that have enriched Agard's poetry since the 1960s, and its willingness directly to confront youth with evil can be located in a particular tradition that reaches back to Robert Louis Stevenson's *Treasure Island* (1883), a novel that challenged the conventions of children's literature from within.

Long John Silver's malign absence has shadowed and enlivened children's literature for over a century; an evil of the genus Aquinas outlines when he suggests that 'the first evil is when the thing generated does not attain its specific form, as when something less than a man is generated' (1998, p. 569). Stevenson's Sea Cook encapsulates this 'something less '; a *something* that manifests itself in ghostly lack beyond the 'moral actions' that Aquinas identifies. Indeed, *Treasure Island* evinces evil partly through the Sea Cook's acts of mutiny and murder, which satisfy the terms of evil established by a range of philosophers: Silver's actions are '*apt to produce or increase any pain, or diminish any pleasure in us; or else to procure us any evil, or deprive us of any good*' (Locke, 2004/1690, p. 216); Silver desires power over other individuals, 'for the service of his own will, and tries to destroy their existence when they stand in the way of the efforts of his will' (Schopenhauer, 1969, p. 362); and simply, Silver 'intentionally [does] acts that are wrong' (Midgley, 2001/1984, p. vii). However, the essence of Silver's enduring and pervasive evil is located in the moments of absence that open and close *Treasure Island*. Evil is frequently associated with destruction, negation, and non-existence, thus 'the good or evil of action, as of other things, is due to the fullness of being or the defect of being' (Aquinas, 1998, p. 568), and 'Evil, in fact, is essentially the absence of good' (Midgley, 2001/1984, p. 14). Consequently, it is Silver's absence that is perhaps more unsettling than his duplicity and violence:

> How that personage haunted my dreams, I need scarcely tell you. On stormy nights, when the wind shook the four corners of the house, and the surf roared along the cove and up the cliffs, I would see him in a thousand forms, and with a thousand diabolical expressions. (2011/1883, p. 11)

Silver is not named here and Jim has not met him at this point, nonetheless his absence is powerfully affective; it acts on Jim and produces the sort of fearful response to 'uncertain' evil described by Hume: 'We find that an evil, barely conceiv'd as *possible*, does sometimes produce fear; especially if the evil be very great' (1978/1739–40, p. 444). Hume explores the affective power of uncertain evil, maintaining that the passion of fear ensues from it (as hope arises from uncertain good). Jim's dread comes from the enormity of an evil that is almost inconceivable and that lacks physical presence, and its significance for Hume lies in the fact that evil is produced by these passions, so evil is as likely to emanate from Jim's fear, as it is from Silver's actual presence. This movement between certainty and uncertainty is key to the play of evil in *Treasure Island*, which considers evil to be both a psychological product of the imagination (uncertain evil) and as an essential character trait (certain evil); therefore Stevenson's moral challenge to the implied reader lies in the shift from imagined to actual, absent to present.

Treasure Island is fascinated by a complex and varied wickedness expressed in 'a thousand forms', yet this haunting extends beyond the non-specific and incomprehensible to the realm of active human experience in which duty and moral considerations are complicated by the awareness and experience of evil. Evil is not located in the child in *Treasure Island*, even so Jim Hawkins is touched and changed by the evil he encounters. Wickedness is presented as an inescapable aspect of human experience and a feature of human character to which any moral agent is susceptible. When Silver arrives to make terms at the stockade, irresistibly Jim is drawn to the 'monster' whom he knows to be responsible for 'a human life cruelly cut short' (p. 79):

> I will confess that I was far too much taken up with what was going on to be of
> the slightest use as a sentry; indeed, I had already deserted my eastern loophole,
> and crept up behind the captain . . . (p. 105)

Jim directly confesses to a dereliction of duty that leaves the stockade improperly defended, but the language used to qualify his confession is ethically equivocal and admits to something beyond being a poor sentry. Jim's 'loophole' is a common feature of medieval castellation – and appropriate to Stevenson's defensive stockade – though its more recent association with technical evasion[3] reverberates through the sentence, betraying a desire to shirk sentry duty. Furthermore, Jim's 'creep[ing] up behind the captain' is expressed in language connoting devious intent, thereby intimating that Jim's behaviour is more underhand than he is willing to admit, or able to recognize. This semantic deviance echoes the shifts in allegiance that occur throughout *Treasure Island*, and here Jim's instinctive desire to observe and come closer to Silver overrides moral obligations to Captain Smollett's party. Jim's allegiance shifts partly because good and bad are not presented dualistically in *Treasure Island*, hence it is difficult to identify 'the good'. It also shifts because Stevenson demonstrates the allure of evil (foreshadowed in Jim's fearful imaginings, which in Hume's terms could lead Jim to do evil); an allure that poses questions about Jim's own moral agency and potential for immorality. In the ethical scaffolding of *Treasure Island* is located the immoral question marking that Nietzsche calls for in *Beyond Good and Evil*; the challenge to a puritanical vision of morality that undoes ethical interrogation with its certainty.

Treasure Island charts the tenebrous waters of good and evil,[4] bringing together poles that are frequently isolated in constructions of childhood and in associated literary genres, such as fairy tales or moral and instructive tales. Stevenson credits his young implied reader with the ability to grapple with moral complexities and romance becomes a vehicle to explore shades of human motivation and behaviour, rather than promulgating Christianity and Empire as in precursors such as *The Coral Island* (1858). As Peter Hunt reflects, 'it may be that it is the developing reader who is brought up short by (and intellectually nurtured by) the dark and unsettling side of the book which questions accepted attitudes to good and evil'.[5] Instead of telling readers how and why to think about moral issues, *Treasure Island* renders morality uncertain in the voice of its impressionable narrator; moral authority is not centred in the narrator and readers are left to think through the implications of, for example, Jim's sympathy for Silver in the closing lines of the book:

> The formidable seafaring man with one leg has at last gone clean out of my life; but I daresay he met his old negress, and perhaps still lives in comfort with her and Captain Flint. It is to be hoped so, I suppose, for his chances of comfort in another world are very small. (pp. 182–3)

'Formidable' is a suitably slippery term, embracing both the sinister and the masterly, suggesting that Silver is to be feared and simultaneously admired. Jim's reference to 'another world' nods vaguely towards religious notions of damnation, though *Treasure Island* does not employ the Christian ethical framework typical of children's literature in the nineteenth century. In sidestepping the Christian trappings of chivalrous adventure, Stevenson avoids engaging with dominant, theological conceptions of childhood, which in their certitude render difficult any philosophical speculation about good and evil.[6] These conceptions predate Stevenson by centuries, as confirmed by Eric Ziolkowski in his historical, cultural, and theological exploration of evil children, *Evil Children in Religion, Literature, and Art* (2001), and consequently Stevenson's circumvention can be seen as radical in its unsettling of long-established ideas.

Ziolkowski focuses on the development of a motif in 'literature, hagiography, art from antiquity to our own time, and . . . in contemporary film' that has its origin in 'the mockery of Elisha by a mob of boys on his way to Bethel' (p. xi), and his findings are framed by two conflicting 'theological assessments of the human being' that feed into constructions and depictions of childhood:

> On the one hand, the image of the killer child would seem to crystallize the doctrine of original sin, whose mythological foundation is established in Genesis 2–3. On the other hand, the image of the violated or murdered child can almost inevitably – and most understandably! – evoke the thought of Jesus' ascription of a heavenly innocence to children, coupled with his dire warning to any adult who might corrupt them. (p. xi)

Such dualistic visions of human being have exerted a tenacious influence on theories and representations of childhood, through Aquinas, Rousseau, Sherwood, Wordsworth, (past Stevenson), Burnett, or Barrie. In the twentieth century, these images are overlaid with the psychoanalytic theories of Freud and Jung, so that theological and psychoanalytic permutations of sin and innocence fuse into a contradictory and often disquieting amalgam. In the late twentieth century, these images were grafted onto the British consciousness by media coverage that depicted innocence and sin literally hand in hand after the murder of a toddler by two 10-year-old boys in 1993. As Eagleton discusses the James Bulger case by way in to his discussion of evil, he contends that it should not be surprising to discover that children can kill, 'Children, after all, are only semi-socialised creatures who can be expected to behave pretty savagely from time to time' (2010, p. 1), and Eagleton puzzles over the ensuing 'outcry of public horror' (p. 1). Surely the horror comes, at least partly, from such a rare instance of childhood extremes converging; when child murders child we are confronted in a terrible, definite, and final manner with the contradictions central to prevailing notions of childhood. While Eagleton displays intellectual arrogance in his dismissal of public grief, he is right to question the terminology and philosophical grounds that condition the case – Eagleton discusses the instinctive and defensive attribution of evil to the killers by a police officer at some length – for it has significance that extends beyond that terrible afternoon in Liverpool. Quite apart from the appalling details of this case involving children as perpetrators and victim, public horror might also be located in its disquieting conceptual conditions – and Chris Jenks also affirms the importance of teasing out the 'nature and import of that unease' over the murder (2005/1996, p. 119). Childhood sin originates in a theological concept that remains central to configurations of childhood, yet is anachronistic in a multi-faith and increasingly secular society. Accordingly childhood brought under the microscope of the judicial system and tabloid press is bound to be profoundly and widely unsettling. When Eagleton's police officer claims to have recognized evil in the young killers, he is directed by a cultural and social history that reaches back to Ziolkowski's Bethel boys, but which has lost touch with its religious foundations.

In *Childhood* (1996), his sociological exploration of the conditions and composition of childhood, Chris Jenks concurs with Ziolkowski that 'Throughout the historical and cross-cultural literature on childhood what seems to emerge is two dominant ways of talking and thinking about children' (2005/1996, p. 62). Jenks employs the mythological images of the Dionysian (evil) child and the Apollonian (innocent) child to identify these 'codes', thus allowing for two traditions that 'are too old and pervasive to be explained in terms of . . . cultural regimes' (p. 62). Ziolkowski's theological focus leads him to make visible the sinful image of childhood and to suggest that the concept of evil children is more widespread than commonly accepted. He implies a sociological myopia in Western, contemporary society that clings to the image of childhood innocence. Jenks is more explicit and suggests that 'the conceptual space of childhood' prior to 1993 was largely perceived 'as innocence enshrined' and that for this reason 'the murder was not just disturbing, but was, quite literally, inconceivable' (p. 119). Prior to moving into the philosophical territory of Nietzsche and Foucault to consider ways in which the conceptions of childhood might be reconsidered and brought closer to children's various and actual experiences of society and being human, Jenks contends that 'it was not just two children who were on trial for the murder of a third but childhood itself' (p. 127). If childhood as society understands it died in 1993, what has taken its place? Jenks does not fully answer this question, though he observes that listening to children could be a way forward, recognizing that children are rarely allowed to express their own experiences and that their voices are rarely trusted when they do speak. However, a move towards hearing the child is gathering momentum, as exemplified in *The Story of Childhood* (2006) by Libby Brooks, in which she talks to nine different children about their experiences of growing up in modern Britain. Brooks contends that

> . . . the arena of childhood will situate some of the most exciting ideological battles of this century, and that progressive thinkers must begin their interrogation of that territory now. In a secular, pluralist society, where adults and children wear the same clothes and read the same books, how do we reach a consensus on the kinds of morals, ambitions and characters we want to share with our children? (p. 4)

Whether consensus is possible or desirable is debatable; nevertheless an interrogation of childhood territory is essential if it is to be trusted as a site of moral development. Brooks is right to point to the rupture in the ideological underpinning of childhood sprung from secularism and pluralism; indeed Stevenson recognized this over a century ago – different historical conditions, similar ideological rupture – and his legacy continues to be mapped. During the early twentieth century, in *A High Wind in Jamaica* (1929) by Richard Hughes, echoes of Silver's murderous piracy are internalized by semi-socialized children who veer between naked tenderness and invulnerability. As Emily Bas-Thornton wonders about the limitations of a piratical career, she comes to recognize that 'Gone, alas, was any shred of confidence that she was God. That particular, supreme career was closed to her. But the conviction that she was the wickedest person who had ever been born, this would not die for much longer' (2002/1929, p. 116). *A High Wind in Jamaica* offers a more sustained consideration of childness (and one evidently influenced by Freudian theory) than *Treasure Island,* an emphasis that flows through Golding's *Lord of the Flies* (1954) and on into books for children such as *The Trial of Anna Cotman* (1989) by Vivien Alcock, or *Pictures in the Dark* (1996) by Gillian Cross, but in common with Stevenson's masterpiece these books open philosophical discourse in their interrogation of good and evil. While Stevenson's influence is not overt in any of the texts discussed in this chapter, in their open and challenging examination of good and evil they reach back to *Treasure Island*; as Hunt declares, 'In the history of children's literature it is a landmark, a turning point'.[7] I propose that it is to this tradition of literature – a literature that invites children to think about the very categories that define them – that we might look for ways of negotiating the conditions of childhood.

Rebuttable presumptions

Anne Fine's *The Tulip Touch* (1996) and *Angela and Diabola* (1997) by Lynne Reid Banks are radically different in style and approach – the former, a hyperbolic black comedy and the latter, a menacing psychodrama – nonetheless each confronts directly Ziolkowski's and Jenks's competing childhoods and in so doing they reengage with the discourse of good and evil through children's literature. They offer timely philosophical interventions into debates verging on hysteria in the British press;[8] both books were published in the aftermath of the 1993 murder into a sociocultural and political landscape that had, in Chis Jenks's terms, virtually killed off childhood and was openly expressing its anxiety about children through media reporting and government legislation. A particularly contentious area of childhood legislation moving into the 1998 Crime and Disorder Act was the rebuttable presumption of *doli incapax* (incapable of crime) applied to children from 10 to 13 years of age. Dating from the 1933 Children and Young Persons Act, the irrebuttable presumption of *doli incapax* 'conclusively presumes that a child less than ten-years-old cannot legally be held responsible for their actions, and so cannot be convicted for committing a criminal offence' (Youth Justice Board),[9] but the

> rebuttable presumption of *doli incapax* applies to children in criminal proceedings of ten to thirteen years of age: children in this age range are presumed not to know the difference between right and wrong and, therefore, to be incapable of committing a crime because they lack the necessary criminal intent. This is an additional requirement to proving mens rea. The presumption can be rebutted if the prosecution can show, beyond reasonable doubt, that the child concerned had 'mischievous discretion'; that is, that they were aware that their actions were 'seriously wrong' (as opposed to merely naughty or mischievous). (Walsh, 1998)

The 1998 Crime and Disorder Act eventually abolished the rebuttable presumption for tens to thirteens, arguing that it was archaic (Consultation Paper, 'Tackling Youth Crime', 1997) and that there could be 'No More Excuses' (title of White Paper, 1997) for youth crime. In her challenge to New Labour's reassessment of the youth justice system, Charlotte Walsh offers a brief history of challenges to the rebuttable presumption, observing that the debate gained momentum in1994. Mr Justice Laws insisted in a 1994 court ruling that 'this presumption at the present time is a serious disservice to our law' and that 'I would hold that the presumption relied on by the defendant is no longer part of the law of England'[10] – his ruling was overturned by the House of Lords, eventually to become law in 1998. Walsh does not make the connection, but it seems unlikely that Mr Justice Laws – presiding over a case of motorcycle theft in Liverpool – was not influenced by the events of 1993 and the ensuing media commentary on youth crime. I deal with this issue at some length, not to debate the age of criminal responsibility[11] in the United Kingdom, rather to demonstrate that the 1993 watershed put child morality on the public agenda. It framed questions about the developmental conditions of moral agency, asked whether young people are capable of serious crime as opposed to mischief, and whether their actions might be considered evil.

A close look at the deviations in translating *doli incapax* from the Latin points to ambiguities surrounding childhood and child crime. *Doli incapax* is currently translated by Her Majesty's Youth Justice Board as 'incapable of crime',[12] but a 1997 Home Office consultation paper, 'Tackling Youth Crime',[13] translates *doli incapax* as 'incapable of evil', while referring to it elsewhere in the report as not knowing right from wrong. Semantically and philosophically, these translations cover different (though related) ground – to be capable of crime is quite different from being capable of evil. For instance, Eagleton distinguishes between immoral behaviour (crime falling into this category) reflected in actions and 'bound up with material institutions' (2010, p. 151), and evil, which 'is a condition of being as well as a quality of behaviour' (p. 152). In contrast, Svendsen's reading of the moral optimism in the thinking of Kant and Hegel renders crime *and* evil social forces that contribute progressively to an ethical society – and from this perspective crime and evil begin to conflate (2010/2001, pp. 62–5). Returning to the interpretation of *doli incapax* then, it seems reasonable to suggest that the terminological slippage reflects tensions surrounding childhood crime and ideology during this period, evading the contradictions inherent in conceptions of childhood that allow for both innocence and evil. Evidently, judicial review seems incapable of confronting coherently these ideological, philosophical, and ethical dilemmas and so it seems important that books published for children, such as *Angela and Diabola* and *The Tulip Touch*, are willing to unpick the semantic and ideological conditions of childhood. These books imply that the prevailing images and ideals of childhood deny children moral agency because they originate in adult preconceptions about childhood and, in exposing the conceptual imagery of childhood, they invite their implied readers to think about the conditions of good and evil in terms of human being and the social experiences of childhood. Significantly, they tap into issues that open up the related moral terrain for consideration by young people.

The death of childhood

Angela and Diabola can be considered a thought experiment that cross-examines childhood conceptualized through dominant images of good and evil. Banks employs a combination of satire and black humour to inquire whether it is possible for individual children purely to be good or evil and in asking this she interrogates institutions that shape childhood, such as family, church, and school. Banks imagines what it might be like if the extremes of childhood ideology were given human form, born into a family, and sent to primary school. This idea is preposterous of course, still it is born of the absurd (and potentially damaging) demands made on real children when dominant ideology expects compliance to notions of innocence (Angela) and original sin (Diabola) – and Banks's dark satire lines up these conceptions for philosophical target practice. Formulated through Baudrillard's visual semantics, *Angela and Diabola*

> conjure[s] up the perversity of the relation between the image and its referent, the supposed real; the virtual and irreversible confusion of the sphere of images and the sphere of a reality whose nature we are less and less able to grasp. (1987,[14] p. 13)

Baudrillard refers to the 'diabolical seduction of images' (p. 13), suggesting that reality can only be grasped if a way is found to see beyond the image. This seems especially important in relation to a childhood that has been 'killed off' by fear that there is nothing beyond the images it has invested in for so long. Taking the images of childhood to their extremes, *Angela and Diabola* undoes their seductive potential and in the process offers young readers a figurative exchange that (re)thinks childhood.

Angela and Diabola relates the early childhood and schooling of anti-thetical twins; their oppositional nature is apparent from the moment of delivery when Angela announces her arrival with 'a sort of polite little cough' (1997, p. 8), followed by a punching, kicking, and yelling Diabola who bites the midwife 'severely on the thumb' (p. 13). From the outset, Angela and Diabola are caricatures frequently placed in farcical or extreme situations; they personify ideas about good, evil, and childhood rather than denote fully psychologized humans/children in realistic circumstances. Caricature lends itself to satire, also distancing the implied reader from the object and allowing for detached consideration of the concepts and ideas outlined. For example, Diabola's actions seem to play out a version of evil that is extreme in the manner of cartoons: 'When she was one and a bit, the cat objected to having its tail pulled. It turned on Diabola, most unwisely, and bit her. She put both her chubby little hands round its neck and in three seconds it was dead' (p. 32). This rejects the Romantic affinity between child and nature, pointing simultaneously to the amoral artifice of this brand of evil. Svendsen elaborates on the nature of evil (that appears to be at work here) and admits to his own fascination with the concept:

> This fascination was a result, most especially, of our tendency to regard evil as an *aesthetic* object, where evil appears as something *other* and therefore functions as an alternative to the banality of everyday life. We're steadily exposed to more and more extreme representations of evil in films and such, but this form of evil doesn't belong to a *moral* category. (Svendsen, 2010/2001, p. 9)

Diabola's evil is not an ethical concern in Svendsen's opinion and, by association, nor is Angela's goodness, rather these creatures are living incarnations of aesthetic ideals and powerless to act with moral agency as a result. Through inviting readers to consider whether these aesthetic objects can ever be subjects, *Angela and Diabola* points out the conceptual obstacles to becoming a seeker in Agard's terms and simultaneously undermines them.

As *The Young Inferno* implies in its historical inventory of evil acts, ideas, and individuals, evil has to be recognized and understood in its full destructive and negative capacity if its threat to goodness and the moral life is to be appreciated; it is difficult to be good if we have only an inchoate notion of what constitutes evil. The very idea of needing to understand evil in order to understand goodness (and vice versa) invests in dualism, and this comparative approach to difficult concepts is likely to be accessible to young readers familiar with fairy tales such as the Grimms's 'Ashputtel', wherein Ashputtel is 'good and kind to all about her' in contrast to her stepsisters who are 'foul at heart' (1977/1815, p. 34). *Angela and Diabola* questions the restrictive application of these concepts to childhood, its exaggerated approach to dualism serving as a way in to philosophical thinking. In his ' "rehabilitation" of the concept of evil' (p .9), Svendsen observes that evil is difficult to talk about in a society no longer shaped by Christian doctrine and that ' "evil" can refer to such a diverse number of phenomena that the concept seems beyond our comprehension' (2010/2001, p. 18). Banks's dualism offers a way of *approaching* evil, though the extremes she invests in reach beyond dualism, towards Baudrillard's notion of the ecstatic; Angela's goodness is more good than Ashputtel's, and Diabola's evil is more evil than the stepsisters'. Moreover image contains value and as Baudrillard proposes, 'We will not oppose the beautiful to the ugly, but will look for the uglier than ugly: the monstrous' (2008/1983, p. 25). In order to find a path to a childhood of moral agency, *Angela and Diabola* expresses the ecstatic that 'is an immoral form, while the aesthetic form always implies the moral distinction between the beautiful and the ugly' (p. 26). Baudrillard's distinction between the ecstatic and aesthetic apparently challenges Svendsen's observation that aesthetic evil 'doesn't belong to a moral category', but Svendsen refers to an aesthetic that overrepresents through repetition and saturation, so that the aesthetic image becomes detached from any sort of moral framework. Svendsen and Baudrillard each articulates a system of representation that reaches beyond morality, an excessive thrust to extremes that *Angela and Diabola* expresses in its depiction of good and evil children.

Angela embodies perfection and is described variously as 'a beautiful child' (p. 9), 'the darling little creature' (p. 9), 'a very, very special baby' (p. 9), 'a dear – sweet – beautiful – perfect little girl' (p. 11), and as having an 'extraordinarily loving and caring nature' (p. 38). Angela's status as a child is not initially doubted by those around her and the epithets applied to her are commonly associated with newborn infants and children; she fits with the Rousseauian and Romantic notions identified as prevalent by Jenks. There is no place in this cult of childhood[15] for Diabola though, for she challenges contemporary expectations of innocent infancy from the outset, forcing her mother to ask after Diabola's birth, ' "Gracious me! What is it?" ' (p. 13). As a newborn, Diabola's violent and vengeful behaviour, '. . . the baby twisted its face and tried to bite . . . It managed to get in a good kick in the nurse's stomach' (p. 13), substantiates the Augustinian notion of original sin. As Saint Augustine observes in precise detail, original sin manifests itself in infantile aggression: 'I have myself seen jealousy in a baby and know what it means. He was not old enough to talk, but whenever he saw his foster-brother at the breast, he would grow pale with envy' (1961, p. 28). Augustine's confessional reworking of his own childhood shaped the narrative form and stance of some of the most influential Puritan and Evangelist writers for children, such as James Janeway and Mrs Sherwood, who profess that children must be made aware of their sinful state at the earliest opportunity; religious convictions that are virtually redundant in late twentieth-century British society and culture. Consequently, the dualism that now characterizes childhood evil in opposition to innocence is void of the values from which it evolved, a situation parodied through Banks's inadequate vicar who 'simply couldn't believe in evil, which vicars are definitely supposed to do' (p. 22). The church is depicted as incapable of advising or supporting a society, which has (re)discovered that children can do evil and is anxious about the related threat to innocence. Appellations applied to Diabola – she is portrayed variously as a 'little monster' (p. 47) and 'a wild thing' (p. 114) – are frequently linked to the naughtiness of early childhood,[16] but so extreme is her nature that it confounds even the epithetical excess of childhood semantics:

The problem was Diabola's nature. This was not merely *un*loving and *un*caring, but the complete opposite of Angela's.

Diabola's nature could best be described as hateful, spiteful, destructive, vindictive, repulsive, and many other '-fuls' and '-ives'. Plus some '-somes' and '-ings' as well, such as loath*some* and disgust*ing*.

> But just *how* -ful, -ive, -some and -ing she was, her parents had yet to learn.
> (p. 38)

As demonstrated by this dualistic wordplay, reference to one twin draws on an understanding of the other, suggesting that innocence and evil are related concepts. This again raises Midgley's point, 'Evil, in fact, is essentially the absence of good, and cannot be understood on its own' (2001/1984, p. 14); the italicized prefixes in '*un*loving and *un*caring' suggest that Diabola's nature is related and opposed to Angela's, and lacking (absence) in comparison also. This philosophical lack might seem contradicted by the excessive adjectival catalogue used to describe Diabola's nature (rendering her 'larger than life', more rather than less), but words themselves are absented in this passage and Diabola is *un*described by suffixes dislocated from the verbs and nouns that would usually function descriptively. The semantic play encourages thoughtful consideration of the potentially damaging conceptual imaging of childhood, also parodying the labelling common to childhood culture. It draws attention to the 'routines of social intercourse in established settings' (Goffman, 1968/1963, p. 12), which are used thoughtlessly and rendered invisible (though no less harmful to the individual) through overuse.

Indeed, Diabola's uglier than ugliness shifts into the immoral space of Baudrillard's ecstatic; moving out of moral and even human being. When Angela is asked how Diabola behaves in class, Angela responds to their confounded parents that ' "she doesn't behave" ' (p. 100), and Angela cannot elaborate on what she means by this; actual childhood experiences such as attending school do not match the conceptions of childhood that she and Diabola represent. This exchange directs another parodic dig at unreflective childhood parlance, also emphasizing the empty character of Diabola's monstrosity, 'watching Diabola, they began to understand. Diabola didn't behave badly. She didn't behave well. She didn't *behave* at all. In some curious way, she just *was*' (p. 101). Diabola cannot be assessed through social mores, or ethical codes of good and bad, for she exists outside of the value systems that shape childhood. This does not mean that Diabola has no impact on those around her, because her evil is a destructive and negative force that emanates from her. For example, her unresponsiveness to parental care pushes her father to abandon her on the way to school, and when he attempts to explain his actions, Diabola denies him both parenthood and being: ' "I left you," he said, "because I am sick and tired of talking to you and being nice to you and having you treat me as if I were nothing." . . . She said, "You are nothing" ' (p. 106). If Diabola is absolute evil then she opposes existence and, as such, she lacks possibility; Diabola is impossible.

It follows that if Diabola represents an impossible vision of childhood, so too does Angela. This logic is more difficult to detect in the early stages of *Angela and Diabola*, because the middle-class society[17] into which the twins are born recognizes Angela as the desirable countenance of childhood imagery. Angela has 'soft hair . . . smoothed down tenderly on her forehead.' (p. 24) and is 'beautiful and angelic, like a painting by Botticelli' (p. 131), while Diabola is a 'most hideous little baby' (p. 12) with 'hair stuck out in puce corkscrews around her face. She looked like someone in a comic-book who's had a terrible fright' (p. 24). Angela is valued over Diabola in part because she conforms visually to notions of innocence, soothing adult anxieties related to its loss. As Brooks observes, 'At the very base of fears for and of our children is the ideal of childhood innocence, and the terror of what might stem from its corruption. It is images of children that have always made this ideal flesh' (2006, p. 53). Flesh, even in infancy, can never be ideal though and Brooks's idiomatic phrasing reveals a contradiction that *Angela and Diabola* also emphasizes and that encourages readers to consider whether Angela's goodness is as unthinkable and unacceptable as Diabola's evil. Bank's intertextual referencing points to the artificiality of associated images, suggesting that each concept is as impossible as the other in real terms. Accordingly, Angela's father observes, ' "Nobody should be perfect. I want her to be normal and ordinary and have faults like other people" ' (p. 61). Instinctively recognizing that his daughters are spawned from anachronistic theological ideology, Angela's father seeks the vicar's help to exorcize Diabola's evil and Angela's perfection, but the vicar refuses to touch Angela, ' "There is nothing in Scripture about getting rid of goodness," he said firmly' (p. 61). Banks thereby reflects the tenacious, ideological grip of childhood innocence, while simultaneously demonstrating its impossibility.

Designated '*Sinister*' (p. 16) by the midwife, the unsettling birth scene renders childhood innocence problematic from the outset, for it encompasses Diabola *and* Angela. When Diabola's father declares that Diabola is ' "not a little innocent child" ' (p. 55), it might be assumed that Angela is innocent in contrast. However, Angela and Diabola have a parasitic relationship expressed figuratively through an image that young readers are likely to recognize: 'The twins were like two magnets. If you put magnets together, sometimes they attract and rush to each other. If you turn them, they repel and you can't force them to touch. The twins were something like that' (p. 63). The perfectly good Angela loves and cares for Diabola, while the utterly evil Diabola hates and needs Angela. This irresistible attraction-repulsion means that Angela understands far too much about her evil twin to be considered innocent, even so she is not one of Blake's experienced children, informed by social knowledge. Angela's knowledge of evil reaches beyond human experience: 'She was not feeling good. She slowly realised that what she felt was a sort of shadow (but a very dark one) of what Dybo was feeling, up on the roof in the rain' (p. 151). The vicar is perplexed by Angela's unconditional love for her sister, who declares, '"Good cannot love evil! It's against all the rules!"' (p. 58). This echoes Kierkegaard's requirement of love and demonstrates that Angela's love, conceived through an impossible conception of childhood, is overly susceptible to Diabola's evil. In a revision of Kierkegaard, Murdoch observes that the good person can recognize sin, for it is only in truly seeing the other and disregarding the self that we reach goodness: 'Goodness is connected with the attempt to see the unself, to see and to respond to the real world in the light of virtuous consciousness' (2001/1970, p. 91). However, Angela's goodness is not 'a response to the real' world. Angela seems acted upon by her goodness, just as her mere presence seems to act on others, causing a taxi driver spontaneously to 'burst into a rousing hymn' (p. 190). Her goodness is not an example of Murdoch's 'moral discipline' (p. 37), instead her response to Diabola must remain in the immoral realm of the ecstatic.

The climax and closure of *Angela and Diabola* is inevitable, although perhaps not for reasons that may have been anticipated. Readers familiar with Rowling's *Harry Potter* series (1997–2007), for example, might expect the thwarting of evil for – while Harry struggles to accept his affinity with Voldemort (evil) and the moral status of various characters, such as Snape and Dumbledore shifts throughout the series – the triumph of good is finally emphatic. In contrast, the exchange between the twins before Diabola plummets to her death amounts to a refusal of all-conquering goodness. Isolated from other characters in the book, the twins perform a form of Socratic dialogue that works through the book's central philosophical concerns. Diabola fights to maintain the oppositional force of the childhood dualism she represents, but is forced to recognize the reciprocity of good and evil. Angela's goodness will necessarily contaminate Diabola's evil, or as Diabola puts it when Angela says that they need each other, '"You'll try to stop me doing what I want"' (p. 204). Had goodness triumphed, Angela would have saved her sister from falling: 'Angela used every bit of power she had. She wanted – at that moment, she truly wanted – only *not* to let Diabola go' (p. 208). In refusing to accept Angela's salvation, Diabola also rejects the paradox of their conception and birth. Evil must destroy the good that its existence rests on and so strong is evil's hatred of good, that it is willing to destroy itself in order to destroy the object of loathing. In playing out the ideals of childhood in real terms, the dramatic and dark close to this children's book poses questions also framed by Midgley. In her discussion and rejection of Freud's death wish, Midgley asks: 'Can there be a motive which is a pure wish for destruction – not as a means to any good, nor a part of it, but simply for its own sake?' (2001/1984, p. 158); and 'If [the death wish] exists, however, is it really a wish for one's own death, or a wish to destroy others?' (p. 160). Banks invites young readers to respond to these questions by taking the extremes of childhood ideology to its limit. This necessitates the destruction of absolute evil, and also of the goodness that it relates to, thus Angela

> . . . was now an ordinary normal little girl, with good and bad mixed up in her. Her parents adored her and on the whole she made them happy and proud.
>
> But every now and then she would have flashes of bad temper and outbursts of bad behaviour. And at these times, she developed a squint [. . .]
>
> Usually the blue eye would get the better of the green eye.
>
> But not always.
>
> Just like the rest of us. (p. 216)

Squinting through the lens of goodness mixed with bad, it might appear that Angela is ready for the sort of moral agency described by Murdoch, which involves close and careful seeing (an idea that Angela's squint plays out metaphorically). Angela survives to pursue a childhood emancipated from the idealized concepts into which she was born and certainly this can be read in terms of a balanced humanity newly engaged with ethical life and structure. Intriguingly, the vicar – the book's most unreliable character – is left to articulate what seems to be the book's central premise: ' "There is no such thing in this world as pure good or pure evil. For a little while, there was an exception. But it only proved the rule. Perhaps that's why it was allowed to happen" ' (p. 215). Rather than abandoning the church as a relic beyond deliverance, Banks offers the vicar up as a potential philosopher in a tradition reaching back to Saint Augustine (also suggesting that the church ought to take responsibility for the concepts it has imposed so destructively on childhood). Nonetheless, Banks implies that theological explanations are incomplete at best and that good and evil should be conceived, perceived, and received differently in modern society, allowing a return to Baudrillard's notion of a fractal culture in which dualism is dispersed:

> Good is no longer the opposite of evil, nothing can now be plotted on a graph or analysed in terms of abscissas and ordinates. Just as each particle follows its own trajectory, each value or fragment of value shines for a moment in the heavens of simulation, then disappears into the void along a crooked path that only rarely

happens to intersect with such other paths. This is the pattern of the fractal – and hence the current pattern of our culture. (Baudrillard, 1993/1990, p. 6)

In a vision played out through scientific metaphor, Baudrillard assesses the fate of value, mapping its influence in stages until 'there is no point of reference at all, and value radiates in all directions, occupying all interstices, without reference to anything whatsoever, by virtue of pure contiguity' (p. 6). In this fractal radiation ethical structure breaks down, and in Diabola's hyberbolic death lies an implication that evil (and good) have disappeared into Baudrillard's void, prompting the reader to rethink the very foundations of childhood and asking whether ethical life is possible after all.

Touching evil

In its grotesque and hyperbolic realization of good and evil, *Angela and Diabola* takes a panoramic sweep at the dominant images of childhood and invites its reader to witness the results of an absurd experiment and to consider the implications of its ultimate and inevitable failure. Where Banks's novel is excessive and its satiric aim broad, *The Tulip Touch* (1996) is confiding and minutely observed in its demonstration of the human capacity for evil, posing a question articulated by Midgley, 'How does wickedness work in an individual?' (2001/1984, p. 50) or more specifically in Fine's case, how does wickedness work in a child? Anne Fine poses this question through a carefully controlled narrative structure that traces the complex web of human relationships surrounding Tulip Pierce, a disquieting child who appears to be as disturbed as she is disturbing. Fine's realism is rooted in its scrutiny of the ways in which people influence and respond to each other, also weaving into the fictional narrative a discourse of contemporary social anxieties related to well-documented youth crime.

The Tulip Touch is informed by the preoccupations of a British society confronted anew with the knowledge that children are capable of cruelty and of taking human life. Questions permeating *The Tulip Touch*, such as whether Tulip is 'malevolent by nature' or 'deeply disturbed' (1997/1996, p. 153) – tellingly, Tulip's nature is disputed by different voices in a chapter beginning, 'News travels fast' (p. 153) – were also being debated in relation to young offenders in the British press. In 'Lessons of an avoidable tragedy', a 1993 *Guardian* leader comment observes:

No one should be surprised by the public uproar the killing provoked. It unlocked all kinds of primitive fears about the aggressive urges in young children. Was William Golding right? Will children who lack adult supervision – as described in 'Lord of the Flies' – regress into savages? The wish to question a society which produces such a savage act as Jamie Bulger's murder is understandable. But perspective is missing.[18]

Novels such as *The Tulip Touch* offer this missing perspective, in part through the fictionalization of events that echo those debated in the media and also through the opportunity they provide for engaging philosophically with the moral issues raised. Ethically aware books such as this function as an antidote to the moral panic described by *The Guardian* and furthermore they draw young people into debates that concern them, but which frequently refuse them participation. Although *The Tulip Touch* is not based on true events, vestiges of the1968 case of Mary Bell, an 11-year-old girl who was sentenced for the manslaughter of two young boys can be traced in Fine's depiction of Tulip's games. Although details of the case were extensively reported at the time, Mary Bell's crimes did not elicit the press furore and moral panic of 1993 – though public and media interest in the case has grown since, fuelled by the 1995 reissue of Gita Sereny's *The Case of Mary Bell* (first published in 1973) and the controversial[19] *Cries Unheard* (1998). *The Tulip Touch* is not the only book for young people to engage (if only obscurely) with these events, and before moving on to Fine's text I want to consider a novel that approaches childhood evil differently. Anne Cassidy's *Looking for JJ* (2004) is a retrospective narrative that asks how a child might come to kill and whether social reintegration is ever possible for children who commit serious offences. It also scrutinizes the role of journalism in this process – the cut-out newspaper dolls on the 2005 book jacket suggest that the media invests in the construction and de-humanization of child killers.

Cassidy's Jennifer Jones has served a prison sentence for her crime, and the book's shifting chronology confirms that there will be no escape from a murder that has destroyed more than one life. In an article explaining why she was motivated to write *Looking for JJ*, Cassidy acknowledges her need to understand Mary Bell, Robert Thomson, and Jon Venables, children who are 'regularly in the news' and whose 'crimes were dark and incomprehensible' (Cassidy, 2005a). She acknowledges that no matter how many political debates and newspaper articles pore over police reports and trials, it is impossible to know why 'these children and others do kill'. Cassidy admits that she cannot 'answer for Mary

Bell or the boys who killed James Bulger. I can only speak for my own character'. Consequently, *Looking for JJ* offers a detailed familial and social context for Jennifer Jones, suggesting that maternal neglect is the primary factor driving the book's fatal outburst of violence. Cassidy observes:

> These explanations are often the stuff of fiction. Writers can imagine what led to these situations. This is our job. We imagine people and the things that happen to them. Sometimes by doing this we can offer an explanation of sorts ourselves. This is why I wrote *Looking for JJ*. I wanted to imagine a child killing another child. Through that I wanted to try and find reasons. (Cassidy, 2005a)

Cassidy's novel offers perspective through its controlled and unsentimental consideration of motivation, circumstance, and personal history, yet its emphasis on explanation and the drive 'to find reasons' means that *Looking for JJ* does not offer a philosophical approach to the events it interrogates. *Looking for JJ* does raise ethical issues, even so its focus is not on the individual as a moral subject for reasons identified by Svendsen during his discussion of cause:

> We look for the *causes* of evil and these causes are often located outside the discussion of morality. They can be either natural or social, and can range from natural inclination and illness to poverty and traumatic childhood experiences. However, if you attribute all human evil to such causes – causes located outside the individual understood as a moral subject – simply to provide a 'scientific' explanation for evil, you've suddenly reduced moral evil to natural evil, and thereby done away with all moral standards. (2010/2001, p. 23)

Looking for JJ is not quite as reductive at this in moral terms, for moral responsibility is expected of adult characters, including Jennifer's mother, grandmother, teachers, and the journalists that hound the adolescent Alice, nonetheless moral agency is denied to Jennifer whose evil act is located in the sort of childhood trauma described by Svendsen. The evil child is denied as a possibility in Cassidy's text, preserving the notion that children are fundamentally innocent and suggesting that they lack the free will attributed to adults. If this is the case, then at what point does moral agency start? Is the human will liberated at some point in human development? Cassidy does not answer these questions, and political wrangles over *doli incapax* demonstrate how contentious and complex this issue is. Furthermore, *Looking for JJ* does too much thinking for its reader – regularly explaining what Alice/Jennifer thinks or feels – to be considered a book that encourages engagement with a range of *potential* explanations. Many educators and parents would agree that young readers deserve the measured and thoughtful guidance Cassidy offers on the subject, so my observation that it is not overtly philosophical is not intended as negative criticism, rather it seeks to explain how one commanding book on the darkest aspects of childhood differs from another. Notwithstanding, *Looking For JJ* does invite reflection on the ethical responsibility of social institutions such as the courts, the media, and the government when responding to and reporting cases such as this. That response to violent acts is ideologically and culturally bound is exemplified by the contrasting treatment of and reaction to the child killers of a 5-year-old girl in Norway in 1994. Reactions to the case have been compared by several commentators to that of the 1993 British child by child murder, but one of the biggest differences is the public consensus in Norway that the killers 'were victims of their own violence' and deserved the chance to be rehabilitated outside of public view:

> The boys were never named, but most people knew who they were. Their names have never appeared in the media, which shared the feeling of shame and grief and responsibility. Astonishingly, when the community were told that the boys would return to school within a couple of weeks there was no dissent. The boys were accompanied by a psychologist at all times. (Hattenstone, 2000)

Hattenstone observes in his article that the British and Norwegian responses to child murder vary so much because culturally they take contrasting moral positions. The decisions and choices made by British government, courts, and the media shape public moral discourse and this is the point that Cassidy calls on her young readers to consider in *Looking for JJ*.

While *The Tulip Touch* does not explore child murder and its aftermath, shadows of the Bell case overlay *The Tulip Touch*. For instance, several of Tulip's unsettling games resemble those played by Mary Bell, and the friendship between Natalie Barnes and Tulip recalls the reported relationship between Mary Bell and Norma (Mary's 13-year-old accomplice who was acquitted of murder). Character portraits drawn by journalists assessing the Bell case are worth considering at this point, since they illuminate the complexities of childness as explored through Fine's fictional creations:

> Although two years older, [Norma Bell] was deemed to be a passive partner a slow-witted, fragile girl led astray by her quick, devious partner. Her reaction to the trauma seemed normal: she cried, stumbled in her speech, was uncomprehending. Her escorts hugged and comforted her. She was just a little girl.

> Mary Bell . . . stood terribly alone during the trial: tearless, defiant, bandying words with the prosecution, apparently untouched by remorse, certainly not touched by those around her, never hugged and held. With a kind of relief, the public could name Mary Bell as a freak of nature, a sweet-faced chilling monster. Her extraordinarily pretty, heart-shaped face looked out beneath headlines, as it looks out again now: a beautiful icon of evil. (Gerard et al., 1998)

Although she was centrally involved in the murders, Norma's exoneration could be attributed to the fact that her reactions correspond to prevailing expectations of childhood as Gerard et al. suggest, whereas Mary's cold and isolated demeanour refuses them. Of course there is sleight of hand at work here, since journalism makes manipulative use of fictive strategies (as do other narrative forms) – such as emotive adjectives, 'terribly alone', and dehumanizing metaphors, 'chilling monster' – to convince their readership of guilt, to incite hatred, or to evoke pity. Through a mixture of observation and diegesis 'characters' are positioned as pawns in an archaic moral structure of childhood in which they have no moral agency. Judged and accused, these children can have little understanding of the moral and ideological boundaries that confine and define them, boundaries that the implied reader also subscribes to. These are the boundaries that *The Tulip Touch* destabilizes, opening a philosophical space for young people to consider the question of moral responsibility through a related, but different diegetic process.

Tulip Pierce's malevolence is central to *The Tulip Touch*, yet Fine's novel also exposes and explores the moral culpability of those close to Tulip. This involves consideration of human traits, individual actions, and social circumstance, so that readers are invited to think about the cause, conditions, and extent of evil. This is achieved largely though a narrative strategy that brings the reader close to Tulip, while restricting knowledge of her. Natalie's first-person narration is possibly the most important feature of *The Tulip Touch* in terms of *how* it engages the reader philosophically. From the outset, her voice can be identified as a child's:

> You shouldn't tell a story till it's over, and I'm not sure this one is. I'm not even certain when it really began, unless it was the morning Dad thrust my bawling brother Julius back in Mum's arms, and picked up the ringing telephone. (p. 1)

Natalie does not identify herself in these opening lines, still her status as child is suggested by the familial context from within and of which she speaks. The opening sentence appears commanding initially, but this authority is soon undermined by doubts as to whether this story is ready to be told. As Natalie continues, the aphoristic opening begins to sound like an echo of adult wisdom, only half understood. The repeated uncertainties, 'I'm not sure' and 'I'm not even certain', suggest a lack of control of – and perhaps a denial of responsibility for – the story she is about to tell. Just as her telling begins, Natalie draws back from the story, hinting that perhaps it is not her story to relate. In the wavering uncertainty of the opening lines lies the moral interrogative of *The Tulip Touch,* and it is from this very moment that the philosophical discourse of the book is activated. In these moments, Natalie's status as narrator falters, and it is here that Genette's distinction between *homodiegetic* and *autodiegetic* narration becomes useful.

Technically, Natalie's role as narrator is to observe the solitary Tulip and on this level a parallel can be drawn between Natalie and Nick Carraway in *The Great Gatsby* (1926), who observes Gatsby from a comparable distance. Natalie is an outsider, the newcomer in a rural community who meets and befriends Tulip before she can be warned off by those who know that Tulip is different: 'Nobody else would have Tulip in their gang. They knew from experience that she was out of school more often than in' (p. 14). Tulip is unknown to Natalie and to the reader, and so her narration serves to reveal Tulip; to bring a potentially evil child into focus through the telling of her story. This would make Natalie a *homodiegetic* narrator in Genette's terms, playing the secondary character to Tulip's protagonist, established as an observer and witness to Tulip's increasingly uncontrolled and cruel behaviour. In the first two chapters, Natalie is set up as a 'sweet' child, 'dumb with joy' (p. 10) at the prospect of the playground she has been gifted by her father's recent relocation as manager of the Palace. On arrival at the large hotel, Natalie succumbs to the sweeping charms of the Palace in which she can 'somersault endlessly', 'wander at will', and 'bounce on cherry-red sofas' (p. 9); a setting that provides the backdrop for Natalie and Tulip's friendship. Natalie's enthusiastic and energetic response to the Palace fulfils Rousseau's vision of the inquisitive and restless child, eager and excited to explore her new surroundings. In ideological terms, Natalie is presented as a 'normal' child, loved and supported by her busy family and – as a newcomer to her school – openly innocent and eager for friendship. Accordingly Natalie becomes the barometer for what constitutes normalcy and the implied reader is invited to sit on her shoulder, observing Tulip from Natalie's narrative point of view.

Given the narrative perspective, Natalie might seem to be in an ethically neutral position, from which the reader is encouraged to consider the moral implications of Tulip's actions and situation. However, this perspective is unsettled when Natalie first meets Tulip. Natalie mistakes Tulip for a scarecrow, 'still as a statue in the sea of corn', and Mr Barnes corrects her: 'Dad peered against the sudden glare. "No. I do believe that it's a little girl"' (p. 11). Figurative foreshadowing overwhelms Tulip's child identity from the first and hints that Natalie might not be serving the function of *homodiegetic* narrator. Natalie is less interested in Tulip than in the kitten she appears to be nursing and waits, focused on her own gratification:

> So I stood, burning with impatience, while this stranger my age stepped carefully towards us, spreading the corn with her free hand and picking her way so gently that by the time she reached us I couldn't see a sign of the track she had taken. (p. 12)

This might be interpreted in a number of ways, suggesting variously that Natalie's needs are paramount and override any concern she might have for Tulip, the perpetual stranger; Tulip's careful tread is prompted by fear of her father, angry at damaged crops; there is guile in Tulip's gentleness, fooling her new neighbours as to her true nature; Natalie will always struggle to properly 'see' or understand Tulip. Each of these readings is possible and each is left open throughout *The Tulip Touch*. The point I want to establish though is that, although Tulip is introduced here, the focus of this entire chapter is on Natalie's desires, first for a kitten and then a companion: 'She stared at me, and I faltered. The silence between us grew. And then, too embarrassed to come to my senses, I added the really stupid bit. "Do you want to be friends?"' (p. 13). Tulip actually does the observing here and Natalie is forced into uncomfortable utterance; into a friendship that is going to test the boundaries of childhood and her moral integrity. Like Jim Hawkins's attraction to Long John Silver, Natalie's fascination with Tulip will have repercussions for her own moral agency. Just as it is difficult to be certain whether the protagonist of *Treasure Island* is Jim Hawkins or the Sea Cook – for they are united through moral ambiguity – *The Tulip Touch* is as much about Natalie's own involvement in Tulip's 'games' and her own potential for evil, as it is about Tulip herself. In point of fact, the book is not named after Tulip, instead her ability convincingly to embellish outrageous lies, 'That's what Dad came to call the Tulip touch – that tiny detail that almost made you wonder if she might, just for once, be telling the truth' (p. 27); after Tulip's ability to draw people into a world in which the moral boundaries are unclear. 'Guilty', the self-accusing word that closes the book and finally admits moral liability, also suggests that it would be more accurate to label Natalie an *autodiegetic* narrator, revealing more about herself through her diegesis, than the ever-mysterious Tulip.

This narrative complexity unfolds one of the book's most thought-provoking areas of ethical enquiry, as Natalie's normalcy is played out against Tulip's 'downright evil' (p. 154), and hence Svendsen's distinction between the normal and monstrous is helpful:

> Perhaps there really are human 'monsters' in the world – and by that I mean people whose actions are so extreme that we simply can't identify ourselves with them – but there are too few of these to explain the abundance of human evil in general. In the end, it is we – we normal, more or less decent, respectable people – who are responsible for most of the damage. We are the only explanation for all the evil in the world. From this point of view it is 'normal' to be evil. (2010/2001, p. 11)

In *The Tulip Touch,* engagement with this pervasive and 'normal' human capacity for evil is set up by a question demanded of Natalie's father by Tulip: ' "What's the worst thing you ever did, Mr Barnes?" ' (p. 20). The interrogative form indicates a philosophical approach to evil and it halts the flow of the narrative, drawing attention to the book's central concern with evil as a moral concept that is fundamental not just to normal human being, but to childhood. Mr Barnes's clarifying question, ' "When I was a child?" ' (p. 20) emphasizes the unusual nature of Tulip's request, for she points to an aspect of childhood that is frequently hidden by more powerful concepts of innocence, or adult nostalgia. Her question also has a challenging edge to it – suggesting a desire to unnerve or shock – as if she is curious to know whether anyone can better the 'worst thing she ever did'. Mr Barnes's confession points to the power and longevity of guilt and remorse: ' "The thing I feel worst about, even after all this time, is dropping my grandfather's tortoise on the garden path . . . I didn't have the guts to go and tell, so I just shoved it out of sight under the nearest bush" ' (p. 20). Ashamed of dishonesty and cowardice, Mr Barnes demonstrates a mature awareness of moral agency that functions retrospectively, rendering him 'uneasy' at the memory in the present and it suggests that his childhood action is not sealed off and finished; that his actions in childhood have a bearing on his moral status in adulthood. Significantly, his confession also refuses the idea that evil only acts *on* children, revealing that evil (or at least immoral acts) can be enacted *by* children, as Augustine confirms in his anguished cry of boyhood, 'And yet I sinned' (1961, p. 31). In his discussion of theodicies, Svendsen recalls Ivan Karamazov's declaration in *The Brothers Karamazov* (1880) that a child's single tear is enough reason to deny God, and Svendsen points out that Dostoevsky's later attempts to refute this position through Zosima are widely considered unsuccessful because 'Dostoevsky has simply made Ivan's arguments too good' (2010/2001, p. 42). I would add that Ivan's arguments work because the desire for and investment in childhood innocence is so strong that it can blind us – even 140 years on – to the fact that children have done and will do evil; this is the exchange at work between Mr Barnes (the child who has done) and Tulip (the child who does and will do) in this passage. Having suggested that evil is not the preserve of adulthood however, *The Tulip Touch* is equivocal about the precise nature of evil. It is also manifested, responded to, and explicated in different ways, so that the reader is offered glimpses of how evil *might* be conceived, and although Tulip is the locus for evil in the book, evil actions are attributed to (or at least associated with) a number of characters.

The most common way of explaining evil in children's literature is as a supernatural force that must be vanquished for the sake of good; this is precisely the sort of unexamined evil that threatens humankind in Susan Cooper's *The Dark is Rising* (1973) and is rooted in religious (frequently Christian) belief and mythology. Hence, Will Stanton's fury at the disruption of Christmas by the Black Rider: 'It was the first time in his life he had ever felt such rage, and it was not pleasant, but he was outraged that the Dark should have dared to interrupt this his most precious family ritual' (1976/1973, p. 148). The force threatening Will is a supernatural, transcendent entity that has little bearing on Will's moral agency. Will must fight this force because he has been 'born with the gift' which he 'must serve' (p. 52) and because the Dark threatens to destroy him; there is no question of moral agency, rather an investment in good and evil as forces that transcend 'normal' human being and action. It is this conception of evil, so familiar to childhood culture, that leads Natalie's younger brother Julius to ask, ' "Did you know Tulip was a witch?" ' (p. 75), a deduction that allows him to understand, dehumanize, and disassociate himself from the girl who troubles him. Nonetheless, Julius's observation is undermined by the predominantly practical and human nature of the suffering caused by Tulip and by an ironic rendition of the song '*Satan is glad when I am bad*' (p. 155), performed with a wink to Natalie after a dispute as to the source and nature of Tulip's callous behaviour. As Eagleton observes, 'Ideas of evil do not have to posit a cloven-hoofed Satan' (2010, p. 16). Although the reader is reminded that evil can be construed in supernatural terms, Fine encourages a consideration of evil as essentially human and framed by moral responsibility.

For Midgley, wickedness can be recognized in human 'cruelty and related vices' (2001/1984, p. xi), and in a recapitulation of Schadenfreude,[20] Colin McGinn proposes that the 'evil person derives pleasure precisely from someone *else's* pain' (1999/1997, p. 65). Both philosophers describe a category of evil exhibited in Tulip, initially through reaction and attitude to situations and increasingly by way of decisive action; lack of compassion is also exposed gradually via a layering of figurative implication and narrative observation. During the 'tortoise' episode, a fascination with cruelty is hinted at by Tulip, and when she demands of Mr Barnes, ' "Did it smash?" ' Natalie observes, 'The word she chose repelled him, you could tell' (p. 20). Callousness is implied as Tulip becomes excited by the idea of the tortoise having been thrown, but her exaggerated response might equally be attributed to attention seeking. During one of their games, Natalie and Tulip break into somebody's back garden to get at a pet rabbit, which Tulip handles roughly, hauling it out of the hutch by its ears and taunting it, 'She finished up so savagely that I knew I was watching something horrible, nothing to do with the rabbit she was holding, but darker, much darker, and hidden, and coming from deep inside Tulip' (pp. 92–3). Tulip's brutality is not reserved for animals though: Natalie's infant brother Julius becomes a target for one of their games, *Babe in the Wood*, a game that 'used to drive him wild with fear and rage' (p. 46); Tulip ignores a bleeding gash to Natalie's leg (p. 56); and the girls make a young mother cry after jamming the wheels of her pushchair (pp. 89–90). Each of these nasty acts is construed as a game by Tulip and, thus, as a source of enjoyment, which sits squarely within McGinn's notion of taking pleasure in evil: 'It was just "fun", "a good laugh", "something to do" ' (p. 90).

Each of Tulip's sadistic acts builds to a climactic deed of cruelty, which intertextually engages with the media discourse of child evil external to *The Tulip Touch*. When the sister of Muriel Brackenbury (one of their schoolmates) dies, Tulip's reaction emphasizes the public dimension of childhood tragedy, ' "we could sell our stories to the paper" ' (p. 113) and the fact that childhood death is a marketable commodity. Tulip's obsession with the conditions of Muriel's demise, and significantly with the suffering of her relatives, leads her to make 'three little visits to the family of that poor girl who drowned a while back. She keeps coming up to Mrs Brackenbury's door, and knocking, and asking her [. . .] if Muriel would like to come for a walk' (p. 146). In an uncanny fusion of fiction and reality, this replicates the way in which Mary Bell paid 'little visits' to the grieving parents of the children she had murdered.[21] Fine does not suggest that Tulip has murdered Muriel, nevertheless the association raises the possibility that Tulip could be capable of murder and confirms that children like her do exist in the world outside of the book, linking the philosophical discourse of evil in *The Tulip Touch* with documented historical events and the media debate arising from them. This intertextual dialogue is another example of the invitation to reflect philosophically and provides a practical way into deep, focused thinking.

While Tulip's evil is presented as both cruel and intentional, the extent and nature of Natalie's involvement with Tulip's actions provokes consideration of an alternative form of evil. For example, when Natalie joins Tulip on their 'last *Wild Night*', they set light to a shed:

> . . . this time it was Tulip tugging at my arm. [. . .] But, though she pulled at me I wouldn't budge. Why go to all the trouble to raise a fire, and then not stay and watch? [. . .] She tugged so hard at me, I had to go. But as I stumbled after her, still looking back, I knew I was bewitched. *The Tulip Touch* had really got me this time. (pp. 122–3)

Natalie refuses responsibility for her actions here, claiming bewitchment and re-establishing the notion of demonic or supernatural evil. However, given that the notion of transcendent evil is undermined elsewhere, the reader is encouraged to doubt Natalie's proclamation of 'knowledge' ('I knew I was bewitched'). As she moves away from the fire, Natalie recognizes that evil acts have real and tangible consequences, 'all the time I was thinking, people *hide* in sheds' (p. 125). In a moment of epiphany, 'I came to my full senses at last' (p. 124), Natalie realizes that she must reject Tulip and the evil actions into which she has been *unthinkingly* drawn. It is this lack of reflection which helps to identify Natalie's earlier participation in Tulip's 'games' as an instance of Hannah Arendt's 'banal evil', which famously she detected during the 1961 trial of Adolf Eichmann and identified as fundamentally thoughtless – and it is intimately related to the indifference Wiesel encountered in Auschwitz and Buchenwald. In his development of Arendt's theory, Svendsen observes that banal evil involves not only Arendt's thoughtlessness, but also '*conformists* who simply [do] what . . . others [are] doing without pausing to reflect on the morality of their actions' (p. 182). Therefore, Natalie's epiphany marks the transition from banal evil to a moral awareness of her own culpability and of the adults around them who did nothing to prevent their games. Natalie's narration of this awakening is explicit and emphatic, prompting consideration of the moral implications of her past actions; it encourages reflection that Natalie's conformity, 'mostly I took Tulip's line on it' (p. 90), should not be considered a defence, or an indication of innocence. The idea that Natalie's mindless acquiescence to Tulip's schemes is not a lesser, but simply different form of evil from Tulip's is also suggested by the final line of the book, in which Natalie apparently recognizes that she is 'Guilty'(p. 184). This closure, open and provocative, also invites the reader to reflect on the nature and cause of Natalie's guilt. Natalie might be guilty of Arendt's banal evil, but having come to her 'full senses', Natalie might also be guilty of intentional cruelty as she tries to distance herself from Tulip: 'Deliberately, quite deliberately, I let my eyes slide off her face, down her stained pullover to her puckered skirt. And wrinkled my nose' (p. 171). Furthermore, in emphasizing Natalie's struggle towards moral goodness, Fine signals the importance of remorse, which as Svendsen points out 'is an expression of moral self-recognition' (p. 191).

Another source of Natalie's guilt relates to a potential explanation for Tulip's evil, although the book remains ambivalent about the cause of evil, presenting a network of possibilities for the reader's consideration. Natalie reflects, 'I shall feel sorry for Tulip all my life', referring perhaps to Tulip's solitude and a troubled home life that is never substantiated or confirmed. Tulip's world must be pieced together by figurative pointers (such as the metonymic thread of Tulip's drowned kitten), brief glimpses of Tulip's dilapidated home, snatches of hearsay, Tulip's unreliable claims, and a narrative perspective that does not understand fully the causes of adult concern for Tulip: 'What had he [Natalie's father] seen that first day that made him so convinced the Pierces' farm was no place for a daughter of his?' (p. 15). Tulip's mannerisms also point to a child who has experienced far more (or less) than is acceptable to contemporary expectations of home and family life. Tulip's precocious manipulation of those around her signals a sexual knowledge that refuses innocence and lends force to suggestions that Tulip might have been abused by her father: 'She came as often as she could, sucking up to Mum, flirting with Dad' (p. 37). Furthermore, Tulip's excessive claims lead Natalie's father to speculate, ' "Poor little imp. What sort of squashing must she get at home, to think she has to make up all this stuff to impress us?" ' (p. 29), but this sympathy is countered when Natalie's mother decides, ' "There has to be something wrong with her. She's insane" ' (p. 150), and again when one of the hotel guests contends that Tulip is 'malevolent by nature' (p. 153). Each of these explanations – social circumstance, insanity, and essential character – have been used by philosophers to explain evil, though Midgley, Eagleton, and Svendsen concur that none of these explanations is sufficient in isolation. Emphatically different in their philosophical approach to evil, nonetheless they agree that it is essentially human and far more mundane than frequently allowed. Evil is as likely to be located in Natalie's 'normal' childhood as it is in Tulip's uncommon experience, because it is a feature of human being. Fine leaves her reader with a range of possibilities to ponder, but ultimately her reader is left touched by the knowledge that evil actions are possible, and moreover a matter of choice as well as circumstance.

Writers such as Fine and Banks engage in different ways with conceptions of childhood that have incited intense public debate, each drawing its young implied reader into moral discourse that also implicates them. *The Tulip Touch* and *Angela and Diabola* both trust that young readers are able to grapple with ethical complexities, and a range of literary devices at work in these books prompt the implied reader to think through moral dilemmas raised and to reach decisions in relation to them, processes that are essential to moral agency. This sort of investment in the moral faculty of young readers seems urgent following the abolition of rebuttable *doli incapax*; if we are prepared to make our children legally responsible, then it is crucial that they have the tools for moral agency.

The poetry of evil

Stevenson's interest in the moral landscape of childhood experience has left a legacy that can be traced in books for young people that challenge the moral boundaries of childhood through their interrogation of good and evil. As the sociocultural conditions of childhood change and society responds to private, public, and historical events, so the ethical discourse of childhood shifts and increasingly writing for young people can be seen to respond to moral issues directly relevant to children growing up in modern Britain. However, if Long John Silver retains the power to haunt readers with the possibility of a diabolical evil, finally rendered human and eternally fallible, then it is due to the combined figurative force and ethical underpinning of his literary realization. The moral depth and vision of Stevenson's writing verges on the poetic, and this figurative sensitivity to the human conditions of good and evil can also be traced in a range of books written for children, including: *Viking's Sunset* (1960) by Henry Treece; *Elidor* (1965) and *The Owl Service* (1967) by Alan Garner; Vivien Alcock's *The Stonewalkers* (1981); Jan Needle's *A Game of Soldiers* (1985); *Humbug* (1992) by Nina Bawden; *The Stones are Hatching* (1999) by Geraldine McCaughrean; Sally Prue's *Cold Tom* (2001); and *Jackdaw Summer* (2008) by David Almond, a book that returns to and moves forward debates related to childhood, good, and evil, opened in the 1990s.

Opening with the threat of a knife and closing with the tottering laugh of an infant, *Jackdaw Summer* places the extremities of childhood, its savagery and innocence, literally in the hands of its adolescent narrator, Liam Lynch. Liam's discovery of 'Death Dealer', an old pruning knife half buried in the sun-baked earth is balanced by his discovery of a baby in a basket. His liminal adolescent state is poised to explore the moral conditions of human being and to upset the dualism that separates innocence and experience. Good and evil shift and shimmer in the haze of a summer that challenges expectation and discloses evil in the guise of innocence. Gordon Nattrass, Liam's 'blood brother' during early childhood, draws Liam back into the brutal preoccupations of their boyhood. Nattrass has an explicit fascination with evil, taunting wild adders and confronting Liam with his own potential for evil: '"Oh, Liam," he says. "I thought folk like you were all peace and love and joy. But you're a bad bugger just like me, aren't you brother?"' (2009/2008, p. 52). Nattrass poses this question in different ways throughout the book, encouraging the reader to ask whether Liam (and those around him) is essentially good or evil.

Set against the backdrop of Blair's war on terror and in 'the realm of the reivers and the raiders and ancient wars' (p. 195), *Jackdaw Summer* conceives war as unceasing, collective, and essentially human. War is presented as a destructive force of evil, but the concept of war is distinguished from the notion of soldiering. The reader is encouraged to look beyond the soldier and see the moral agent; to see the person with a conscience and a need to be healed by the goodness promised by political ideology, and so frequently denied on the battlefield. Almond turns his characters inside out in *Jackdaw Summer*, exposing the performative bravado of Nattrass's aestheticized devil and stripping innocence from Oliver (once Henry), the orphaned victim of war in Liberia: '". . . I became a very good boy soldier. I took part in slaughter. I went into villages and rounded up children like me and showed them how to become like me. Can you imagine *that*, Nattrass? *Can* you?"' (p. 202). Oliver's relentless stream of questions, posed to Nattrass at knifepoint, draw the reader into the philosophical conundrum of the boy soldier; the ultimate victim-perpetrator. It is here that the backdrops shifts from Blair's war on terror to Blair's war on childhood and we are back to the territory of the child murderer and the question of whether such a child can be considered evil: '"You are not me. I am Henry Meadows. I am the one who raises the knife. I am the one who screams and who plunges it deep into her heart"' (p. 204). Oliver's confession offers no easy answers to the question of child evil and implied readers are left to think carefully about where good and evil can be located and about how they might react if they were to find a dagger that led to a baby. As Liam thinks back to his childhood, he reflects, 'We used to talk . . . about what we'd do if the worst things happened, if the awful things out there in the world arrived in Northumberland' (p. 14). Of course, the 'worst things' do come to Northumberland during that ground-baking summer, yet only because Liam is ready to see them. He has 'woken from childhood wonder' and is confronted with the 'awful things' that have always been there.

Jackdaw Summer finds poetry in this discovery, demonstrating that through art and creativity – art and literature as process is a central theme of the book – evil can be reckoned with in order that goodness, at the very least, can be made visible. When Liam's mother protests that Nattrass's art instillation is ' "voyeuristic trash" ' and asks, ' "What about loveliness.? . . . about beauty? Where's the stuff that'll touch the heart?" ' (p. 137), she takes Murdoch's position that art has the potential to express goodness; that it has value for moral agency. As Murdoch observes, 'Art then is not a diversion or a side-issue, it is the most educational of all human activities and a place in which the nature of morality can be *seen*' (2001/1970, p. 85). Nattrass and his confrontational artistry can be defended from Wiesel's position though, because Nattrass's virtual rendition of torture cannot be accused of indifference: ' "We've got a title for it all now," he says. "Should've had it from the start it's so obvious. The Human Beast, we're calling it. What d'you *think*?" ' (p. 153). Nattrass invites Liam to think, and his invitation extends to a wider audience; an audience that he tries to upset and unsettle with his art. Indifference is refused in Almond's repetitive articulation of an ethical challenge, 'What did you *think*?'; 'What d'you *think*'; 'But doesn't matter what *you* think, Liam. *They* think it's great' (p. 153), and in this mantra the implied reader is also invited to *think*.

Nattrass's anger might be rooted in a source quite different from Wiesel's, nonetheless his challenge to indifference is valid because in his artwork inheres a provocation to respond. Wiesel explains that creativity can have a source in anger, resulting in great art inspired by injustice, but 'indifference is never creative . . . Indifference is not a response' (Wiesel, 1999). Moving beyond Gordon Nattrass and David Almond's novel, it is clear that writing for young people can offer and encourage a response to good and evil that negates indifference.

3

Moral Ammunition: Growing Out of Dissatisfaction through Ethical Life

The family, as the immediate substantiality *of spirit, is specifically characterized by* love, *which is spirit's feeling of its own unity. Hence in a family, one's disposition is to have self-consciousness of one's individuality within this unity as the essentiality that has being in and for itself, with the result that one is in it not as an independent person but as a* member.

Hegel, 2008/1821, p. 162

Fighting for right

Family constitutes for Hegel the first moment of membership into ethical life; the point at which moral unconsciousness shifts into a conscious awareness of the moral arena. In *Outlines of the Philosophy of Right* (1821),[1] Hegel distinguishes between the *abstract right of morality* and the *ethical life*, and in so doing he describes a phenomenological exchange between self and other and a process by which the subjective will is free to take moral actions and to participate in an objective ethical life. He also argues that education should encourage children's 'feeling of dissatisfaction with themselves as they are' and their 'longing to grow up' (p. 174), for this longing is a manifestation of the inherent readiness for ethical life in human beings. Since literary childhood is frequently represented in the context of social institutions – such as family, school, and state – Hegel's systematic approach to the agent's coming into the 'philosophy of right' is useful when thinking about how the morally active child comes 'rightly' to relate to social institutions. Hegel's notion of ethical life involves a process through which both child and institution are morally engaged. Svendsen argues that

Hegel's view of history as 'rational' is essentially optimistic and that it should be viewed with a degree of scepticism (2010/2001, p. 61); certainly this optimism can be detected in Hegel's dependence on the ethical integrity of family and state, though he accepts that not all institutions are ethically sound and only certain institutions fit his model. Conceding this reservation, Hegel's notion of ethical life remains important due to its integrative acknowledgement of individual and society, shaping separate entities that come together in ethical life in a manner that is not always allowed for in discussions of morality and childhood. Midgley's observation about external cause helps to explain a prevalent imbalance in the ethical arena, 'There is at present a strong tendency for decent people, especially in the social sciences, to hold that [wickedness] has no internal causes in human nature – that it is just the result of outside pressures which could be removed' (2001/1984, p. 2). Cassidy's *Looking for JJ* takes this position, for example, demonstrating that an act of murder is caused by the malfunction of family life. Cassidy makes an important political point, demonstrating that institutions can destroy individual lives, yet this stance assumes the child to be morally impotent and powerless to act freely. Moral discourse that focuses solely on the ethical context of childhood posits that the individual child is at the mercy of social institutions and that actions and choices are forged by accident of birth rather than free will, thus abnegating the child's moral responsibility.

Since 1945, a large number of British children's books have appeared that refuse this abnegation, investing instead in the idea of the child as moral agent and exploring the ethical dimensions and nature of their social engagement, or *member*ship in Hegelian terms. Family is an obvious starting point for a discussion of ethical life as represented and explored in children's literature, since for most children ethical life begins with family membership, however that family might be composed, and literary ethical discourse in this area is rich and varied – exemplified by Mary Norton's *The Borrowers* (1952); *The Eagle of the Ninth* (1954) by Rosemary Sutcliff; Alan Garner's *The Owl Service* (1967); *The Peppermint Pig* (1975) by Nina Bawden; Jan Needle's *My Mate Shofiq* (1978) and *Wild Wood* (1981); Vivien Alcock's *The Cuckoo Sister* (1985) and *A Kind of Thief* (1991); *Junk* (1996) by Melvin Burgess; Aidan Chambers's *Postcards from No Man's Land* (1999); *The Noughts and Crosses Trilogy* (2001–5) by Malorie Blackman; Siobhan Dowd's *A Swift Pure Cry* (2006); and *Just in Case* (2006) by Meg Rosoff – reflecting a cultural preoccupation and varied approach to the ethical foundations and conditions of familial and social life during the late twentieth and early twenty-first century. It is not surprising that in the wake of two world wars that engaged thousands of young people in ethical life at its most extreme and challenging, writers for young people should explore and challenge the moral contract between child and social institution.

Although this chapter focuses on family, it is evident that family cannot be separated from other social institutions and experiences comprising the system of ethical life. For example, this system inevitably encompasses war according to Hegel: 'It follows that if states disagree and their particular wills cannot be harmonized, the matter can only be settled by *war*' (p. 313). War is typically understood in terms of international conflict – and Hegel deals with it in terms of 'International Law' – but this is frequently filtered through the moral agent's familial contract in children's literature: Nina Bawden's *Carrie's War* (1973), *A Game of Soldiers* (1985) by Jan Needle, and Robert Westall's *Gulf* (1992) demonstrate the child's moral agency in the ethical context of family and war (which are linked inextricably in these novels). Each book deals with British involvement in conflicts (even if only via the media) during the twentieth century – Second World War, The Falklands War, and the Gulf War respectively – and in some way deals with 'A whole war inside one small body' (Westall, 1993/1992, p. 85), bringing Hegel's objective international law, civil society, and family to bear on the child as morally active subject. Moreover, they all situate the child within a clearly defined, if problematic, familial life, providing the basis for moral engagement. In Peter Dickinson's *AK* (1990), this moral engagement is more complex, since child soldier Paul knows no other family than war. Consequently he is thrown into moral turmoil on 'The day the war ended' (2001/1990, p. 5).

Dickinson's novel is an ethically charged and politically aware imagining of what it might be like to experience from within the devastating African civil conflicts that have ravaged the continent since the 1970s; conflicts that have recruited child soldiers, often through brutal means, in increasingly significant numbers since the early 1980s. Unlike David Almond's *Jackdaw Summer*, which deals with the psychological aftermath and moral implications of child soldiering through the eyes of a Liberian refugee in Northumberland, *AK* is set in the (semi) fictional state of Nagala, 'It is on no map of Africa, but it is there, this vast, poor country' (p. 1) and places Paul in the middle of an ongoing power struggle. This convention[2] of 'inventing' countries in books that do not otherwise depart from the realist mode is a method of dealing sensitively with current or ongoing conflicts and situations, allowing for an ethical consideration of child soldiering in the African context that remains undisturbed by specific political circumstance. Indeed, *AK* demonstrates that child soldiering is an issue full of ethical complexity and poses difficult questions for its implied reader to ponder. In 'Child Soldiers: The Ethical Perspective', Jeff McMahan asks:

> What can moral philosophy contribute to the resolution of the problem of child soldiers? It obviously has nothing to say about the urgent practical problem of preventing unscrupulous recruiters from forcing children to fight their unjust wars for them. That is a question of political and legal policy on which philosophers have no special competence to pronounce. But the problem of child soldiers does have a normative dimension and raises questions that philosophers are specially qualified to address. (2006, p. 1)

It is this normative dimension of child soldiering that Dickinson draws on and thus *AK* relates the tale of a typical (rather than actual) combatant, facing hypothetical events that pose a range of morally focused questions. Paul's search for paternity, purpose, and peace is part of this hypothetical framework, allowing Dickinson to explore and raise issues related to child soldiering from an ethical, rather than a political perspective. Indeed, the technique of employing a 'hypothetical and non atypical' example is also employed by McMahan as he hypothesizes a scenario for his imagined (but typical) child soldier. McMahan suggests a range of questions that 'philosophers are specially qualified to address', such as, 'Can [child soldiers] be seen as morally responsible agents? Can they deserve punishment, or blame?' (p. 1). *AK* certainly poses these questions, while also asking questions that begin with the child soldier and then extend beyond him/her, such as: Can war that employs child combatants ever be just? Can war ever be just? Furthermore, the themes that drive Paul into action – paternity, purpose, and peace – are ethically structured, each illustrating a process whereby the moral subject negotiates or accepts membership into ethical life; and ethical life in *AK* is figured primarily in terms of family.

AK opens at a moment of liminal crisis for Paul, whose experience of war has come to define him; on 'the day the war end[s]' he loses purpose and his journey to re-establish motivation begins in this moment (paternity and peace are also significant, although Paul has yet to recognize their worth). Paul seeks to reassert identity in reaction to this loss, a process hampered by a displaced memory that he cannot reconcile with life in the bush:

> In his dream there'd been a hut made of grass and mud, a girl chanting at the door as she pounded mealie in the bowl cradled between her knees. He had known her . . . he remembered . . . he tried to hold on to his dream of her . . . she was gone. And the dreamer who had belonged to that world . . . he was gone too. (p. 5)

Coming to Paul 'In the dawn of that day' (p. 5), figuratively this memory alludes to the dawn of life and to a childhood that has been denied him. Evidently an early childhood memory, this dream life evokes home and family, a configuration that Paul comes to value through his relationship with Jilli – who is first mentioned in the familial context, 'Jilli's family' (p. 33) – and which shapes choices made later in the book. In its summoning of a 'known' other, Paul's vision captures the essence of Hegel's notion of family, 'characterized by *love*, which is spirit's feeling of its own unity' (p. 162). The love that defines family for Hegel is the conscious awareness of 'my unity with another' (p. 162), and self-consciousness can only come with a renunciation of independence that leads to family membership. For Hegel, ethical life is not possible without this familial union of self and other, and *AK* also demonstrates that moral responsibility is a product of familial belonging. Furthermore, the familial focus of *AK* offers Dickinson's readers a *familiar* frame of reference through which to consider issues raised by child soldiering in Africa that are likely to be outside of their own experience.

That Paul is not yet ready to renounce his independence is affirmed by his need to assert selfhood, although his inchoate sense of being soon becomes apparent. As the dream fades, Paul reaches for the certain and 'cold touch' of his gun: 'Automatically he moved his left hand an inch and closed it round the night-chilled metal of his AK' (p. 5). There is an unexplained gap here between Paul's dream of home and family and his clutching of an AK. These antithetical images and the action that links them – a reach towards an object for reassurance – recall Donald Winnicott's theory of transitional objects and phenomena in *Playing and Reality* (1971), which helps to explain the centrality of the child-gun trope in *AK* and how it leads into the ethical domain. Winnicott posits that the young child's attachment to objects, such as teddies or dolls, indicates 'an intermediate area of *experiencing*, to which inner reality and external life both contribute' (2005/1971, p. 3). The object of attachment allows the child healthily to separate from maternal bonds in infancy and to develop independence; in Winnicott's terms, a clear sense of self (me) and other (not me). Winnicott suggests that this use of transitional objects is universal and that although the types of objects used by children differ, it is the use of such objects that is important rather than the objects themselves. Nevertheless, when Winnicott does give examples of transitional objects, he mentions toys (often hard toys for boys), but never an AK-47. The image of Paul holding a loaded gun is provocative and incongruous because Paul treats it as most children might a teddy and draws comfort from it as many children do from their blankets or dolls. This image of child and gun is commonly employed by charities aiming to highlight the plight of children in war-locked countries; these images imply a universal recognition of the incongruity between conceptions of childhood and violent associations with the lethal capacity of guns. Dickinson conjures this image repeatedly, prompting reflection on the significance of the relationship between boy and gun as it changes throughout *AK* and consideration of the moral consequences of arming young children.

Winnicott's theory presupposes a child-mother relationship, which Paul's dream suggests has been ruptured. So while Paul's transitional object replicates the familial bonds necessary for healthy development (and ethical life), the gun also represents a brutal breach between child and mother. Winnicott observes that 'an infant may be so disturbed in emotional development that the transition state cannot be enjoyed, or the sequence of objects used is broken. The sequence may nevertheless be maintained in a hidden way' (p. 6). The gun is then an ambivalent motif, simultaneously destructive (of recognizable childhood) and constructive (relocating an 'intermediate area of experience'), suggesting that a child soldier such as Paul might not by default be prevented from healthy maturation (Winnicott) and entry into ethical life (Hegel). Paul's gun therefore facilitates a defensive and necessary articulation of self, '... he knew exactly who he was, Paul, Warrior, of the Fifth Special Commando of the Nagala Liberation Army ... Who he was, what he was, all he was. Paul. Warrior. A boy with his own gun' (p. 5). The fragmented syntax is important here, for although Paul confirms membership of the Nagala Liberation Army, the sequence of incomplete sentences emphasizes his isolation and belies the unity which Hegel suggests is a condition of membership and ethical life; he is not yet a member of a family, instead a lone child with only a gun for comfort.

Paul's status as Warrior is morally and conceptually significant in terms of childhood: 'Michael said that they must be called Warriors, not boys, because what they were doing was no business for a child' (p. 6). The voice of authority here, Michael Kagomi, serves as a guide to the nature of duty and moral responsibility throughout *AK* – for Paul and the implied reader – and here Michael's words echoes the War Child slogan: 'Child soldier. Some words just don't belong together.' However, while War Child has a political and ideological agenda that would put an end to child soldiering, *AK* does not commit to this position, nor is the reader told what to think. Michael's point does not reject the idea of child soldiering – though this position is opened as a possibility here – for Michael has after all trained boys to be soldiers. Rather he implies that the idea of armed combat does not sit with conceptions of childhood, especially those that emphasize childhood innocence, for the notion of *jus in bello* (law in war) innocence differs from that related to childhood. McMahan explains that one of the fundamental concepts of just-war theory states that 'because noncombatants threaten no one . . . they are not legitimate targets' and further:

> This view is reflected in the language of just war theory, which endorses the venerable principle that it is wrong intentionally to kill the innocent, but interprets innocence in accordance with the etymology of the term. In Latin, the innocent are those who are not *nocentes* – that is, they are not those who are injurious or threatening. (p. 2)

As McMahan points out, this interpretation of innocence clearly denies protection to child soldiers because they *are* 'injurious or threatening' to other combatants. The related point *AK* makes through Michael is that child soldiers are denied childness; they cannot be children if they are not innocent (though children are not typically considered innocent because they are not *nocentes*). In Western culture, childhood innocence more commonly implies a proximity to God (in theological terms), or a state of inexperience, and ignorance about human being and social conditions, and these more familiar conceptions of innocence (as related to childhood) are drawn on later in the book when Paul observes children who have not been nurtured by war: 'Paul and Francis and Kashka were exceptions in their class, because they'd actually fought in the war, lived the life of a Warrior, known that kind of tension, that kind of horror and triumph. It set them apart' (p. 38). Child soldiering lends these boys a knowledge that denies them childness; they are children, yet they know nothing of childhood. *AK* repeatedly makes the point that childhood is constructed, relative, and not essential to being a child, but in making this point so forcefully, *AK* asks whether any war that denies childhood to its child combatants can be considered just.

In order that Michael Kagomi can fulfil the role of moral guide in *AK*, he must be presented as a positive moral agent. The inherent problem with this in an accurate (if idealized) depiction of child soldiering is suggested by the narrator's vague account of how the children have been recruited to the Fifth Commando: 'The Warriors were boys whom the commando had picked up, one way or another, during the war' (p. 6). The narrative implies that these boys have been rescued by their commando, rather than violently abducted as is often the case (McMahan's scenario of brutality, cruelty, and indoctrination confirms this), even so the non-committal 'one way or another' leaves the precise circumstance of recruitment open. This means that Michael can be developed as an agent for good, without being rendered incredible. Established as a character with no desire for war, and with a sense of ethical and political responsibility that leads him to take a role in a new administration seeking to topple a corrupt regime, Michael becomes a figure for resistance and moral freedom in *AK*.

Michael continues to take responsibility for Paul after demobilization, and it is in their moment of paternal and filial undertaking that the conditions of ethical life described by Hegel can be identified. Michael wants Paul to attend school, and before he can insist on this, he must claim paternity, given that Paul has been orphaned, or permanently cut off from his family (Paul's past is never fully revealed). When Paul responds, ' "Your wife mightn't like it" ' (p. 23), Michael replies with one of *AK*'s central refrains: ' "I'll tell her she's my second wife," ' he said. ' "My first wife was the war. She was a cruel bitch but she gave me a son, and then she went and died. Good riddance" ' (p. 23). Configured in crude language as wife and mother, war is presented as a perversion of the ethical life envisaged by Hegel. Michael's marriage is not the 'substantial' and '*immediate ethical relationship*' Hegel describes, which involves total involvement, 'life in its totality' (2008/1821, p. 163), nor is there any sign of familial unity here. Hegel gives examples of societies that fail their children through laws that deny the freedom to will and there is no doubt that any war involving child soldiers earns Hegelian disdain: 'One of the blackest marks against Roman legislation is the law whereby children were treated as slaves', and he pronounces this law an 'offence against the ethical order in its innermost and most tender life' (p. 174). When Michael bids 'Good riddance' to his wife and war, it might seem that *AK* articulates a pacifist agenda, where actually the conditions of an unjust war are refused, not the basic concept of war. As Michael explains to Paul:

> 'Don't tell yourselves it is only one of those things that happens in a war. Don't argue this way – we have right and justice on our side, so we must act, we must fight. This is true, but the next part of the argument is false. We are right, but that doesn't make everything we do right also. It wasn't right for this man and this boy to die. When your enemies are strong and you are weak you mustn't say to yourself "I cannot striked [sic] them directly, so I will strike elsewhere." Next step after that you'll be putting car-bombs into crowded markets and burning villages whose people are too scared to help you and executing foreign aid workers. And soon the rightness that was on your side is dead.' (pp. 118–19)

I quote this passage at length, for it is central to the Hegelian stance taken on war in *AK* and also serves as a lesson in moral thinking for Paul and the implied reader. Given that Dickinson is dealing with ethically complex conditions, it seems that an account of right in war needs to be articulated, providing a guiding moral framework for the implied reader. Paul consciously refers to this advice as he comes to difficult choices and situations, prompting the reader to consider the right and wrongness of actions/events independently.

Michael recognizes that freedom (to choose and will) is inherent in the various forms of ethical life such as family, 'Ethical life is the *Idea of freedom*' (Hegel, 2008/1821, p. 154), and that in order for Paul to gain 'freedom of personality and . . . come of age' (Hegel, p. 175), he needs to achieve family membership. When Michael asks that Paul accept him as a father and attend school, he affords Paul the opportunity to enter into Hegel's third phase of family life, which is concerned with '*the education of children and the dissolution of the family*' (p. 163). The dissolution of family is not a rejection of family, rather an aspect of human-social development and progress, allowing sons to become fathers (and daughters mothers) in their own right and for civilizations to grow. Michael presents the idea of attending school in Tsheba as a choice:

> 'If you were my actual son,' he said, 'I would simply tell you to go to Tsheba, whatever you thought yourself. As it is I can only ask you. You must choose.'
>
> Paul didn't hesitate.
>
> 'My name is Paul Kagomi,' he said. 'I *am* your son. I will go to Tsheba.' (p. 30)

In accepting his filial duty, Paul acts freely in himself in Hegelian terms, and his first utterance of the family name that he will come to use with pride confirms that he is prepared to accept the 'subjective' and 'moral character' (Hegel, p. 173) of paternal discipline and education. Dickinson makes it clear that accepting filial duty is only one aspect of ethical life and that Paul has some way to go before he is able to find a way of fighting a just war and letting go of the gun to which he clings in early childhood. Paul cannot yet reject his mother, as Michael can his wife, for still he lacks the requisite moral education and experience. However, when he reflects, 'It's not my fault that I loved her,' (p. 23) Paul is cognizant of the moral implications of this misplaced maternal love; like Natalie's declaration of guilt in *The Tulip Touch*, Paul's defensive tone implies acceptance that he is culpable for his actions as a Warrior. As McMahan suggests of child soldiers, 'even if they have been brutalized and brainwashed, they are still, it might be argued, sufficiently morally responsible to be able to recognize that indiscriminate killing is wrong' (2006, p. 6). Clearly, such children are not partaking in Hegel's ethical life, but McMahan and Dickinson alike suggest that given the opportunity for *member*ship, freedom of will could be theirs. Hope in the nature of human being and in the social structure of freedom to will that essentially shapes *AK* and in this inheres its idealism, yet *AK* also accepts that hope can be disappointed. The freedom of responsibility and choice is finally handed to the implied reader of Dickinson's novel, for *AK* offers two endings; two potential consequences of a crisis in childhood and ethical life, one that envisions the possibility of lasting peace, and another that denies progress and refuses the family entry into civil society:

> He rounded a corner and stopped. A child stood in the path, a boy about ten, naked except for a loin-cloth, staring at him. Thin, but not starving. Not a bush-child either. No water nearer than the river.
>
> The man understood all this in the instant of seeing but for another half-second didn't move. Something about the child held him, the nakedness, the harmlessness, the clear gaze. (p. 229)

In this version of Paul's future, death is delivered by the child soldier, arresting and lethal in his 'harmlessness'. This pessimistic vision is only one way of imagining how the world might be, and in offering conflicting possibilities for the future, Dickinson makes it clear that ethical life must deal with and allow for good *and* evil. Although there exists a peaceful future in which Paul realizes Michael Kagomi's dream of running a National Park and achieves Hegel's 'ethical dissolution of family', the shadow of death meted out by the child soldier remains to stimulate the implied reader into moral agency.

AK deals with issues that most British children and young adults are likely to encounter at a geographical and sociocultural distance, either through news reporting of events in Africa, work done by charities to raise awareness of child soldiers, or related circumstances such as the 1984–5 Ethiopian famine which led to the divisive[3] Band Aid recording of 1984 and Live Aid performances in 1985. The era of the celebrity appeal brought international affairs to the attention of the British public, and young people in particular, although the philanthropic drive of such appeals relies on emotive reporting to encourage financial aid – uncomfortably mixed with sanctimonious posturing of stars entrenched in the capitalist machinery – and the focus is primarily on giving, rather than thinking or acting. Of course while financial aid is important, so too is a deeper understanding of the problems involved, as many 1980s commentators pointed out. In his book charting the history of protest music, Dorian Lynskey remarks, 'One thing Live Aid did was to remove the risk from protest. The cause was so uncontroversial that everyone could appease their consciences without the slightest risk of ruffling feathers' (2010, p. 485). Conversely, books such as *AK* and *Jackdaw Summer*[4] explore consequences of government corruption and colonial exploitation, offering a philosophical space to consider the human experiences ensuing from political instability and injustice. These books afford young people the opportunity to engage thoughtfully and imaginatively with issues of moral complexity that are outside of their immediate experience, yet within the realm of ethical life common to human being.

Genre and the radicalization of family

Where *AK* reflects the tumult of contemporary African warfare and politics, Susan Price's *Twopence a Tub* (1975) and *On the Edge* (1984) by Gillian Cross draw on prevalent areas of social anxiety and conflict in 1970s and 1980s Britain; a period that Arthur Marwick labels 'the time of troubles' in his social history of Britain and observes of the public mood, 'Apart from a general sense of a worsening economy and declining living standards, the special doom-laden features which contemporary commentators singled out were the outbursts of militancy, violence, and terrorism' (1996/1982, p. 184). These 'outbursts' affected directly many children's lives – families from mining communities, or those living in Belfast or Derry – and the understandably grim tenor of commentary will have coloured childhood at least for those more distanced from disruptive and violent events. Perhaps as a partial consequence of this, youth culture became increasingly engaged with political issues through literature, film, television, and popular music. In common with millions of children growing up in 1970s Britain, my knowledge of national and world events was mediated in part through *John Craven's Newsround*. Launched by the BBC in April 1972, *Newsround* (as it later became known) proved willing to introduce children to weighty topical issues and as Olly Grant observes:

> This raises an interesting question. Is it appropriate for a children's show to cover the more traumatic headlines? Craven thinks it is. The world can be a 'confusing place,' he argues, and young people need a trusty hand to guide them through it. 'There were critics,' he admits. 'I remember one person wrote to me, saying, "You're destroying the garden of childhood." But I don't think that was true at all. What we were doing was putting a ladder up against the wall of the garden, and letting children climb up to see what was going on in the outside world – with a familiar friend there to explain what they were seeing.' (Grant, 2011)

Craven's ladder analogy accords with my sense of how I was introduced to events and issues outside of my limited school and family life (and I would frequently wait for the later 'adult' news if an item on *Newsround* had intrigued me). In its first year of reporting, *Newsround* covered the aftermath of Bloody Sunday (30 January 1972), bringing violent clashes between the army and protesters to the attention of young people, and later followed the miners' strikes which, preceded by a decade of strike action, reached a pitch of violence in 1984. Another source of political commentary came from protest music, which was popularized during the 1980s by artists such as Paul Weller and Billy Bragg and broadcasters such as Andy Kershaw. My memory of news reports from Merthyr Vale colliery is superimposed with Billy Bragg's ardent performance of 'Between the Wars' on *Top of the Pops* in 1985, a song that looks for peace through the language of discontent: 'I looked to the government to help the working man.'[5] Bragg became an iconic voice of miners' strike, travelling the country with his guitar, staging benefit concerts, and articulating socialist views through which he sought to mobilize his audience; he was a young man with moral and political conviction and as such he was a focus of inspiration. In common with writers such as Jani Howker, whose *Isaac Campion* (1986) is steeped in a tradition and history of working people, Bragg talks to the present from a historically informed perspective; as Bragg reflects:

> I was now part of a tradition that stretched back to the Diggers and that historical perspective opened up in front of me. There then came a moment when I felt I should recognise that by showing that I do have a knowledge of folk music and 'Between the Wars' was a manifestation of that. (Lynskey, 2010, p. 514)

Bragg's music forged ideological and political links to the past in order that his audience might be inspired to think, act, and change the future, for Bragg invests hope in those who listen to him: 'Only the audience can change the world – not performers' (Lynskey, p. 524). This direct address to young people is also evident in *Isaac Campion,* a poetic and philosophical tale of family life tested by the violent forces of economy and social change. Its *autodiegetic* narration speaks to a reader directly with an urgency that seeks for purposeful understanding: 'This is what I'm trying to tell you. When you look back over all those years, you think that what happened was bound to happen . . . They've got this notion about the past, about history – they forget that folks lived in it . . .' (Howker, 2003/1986, p. 9). The shift from second- person to third-person plural personal pronoun indicates an audience beyond the implied reader and to a general misconception of how contemporary society came to be, 'I have a notion in my head that children weren't invented until after the Great War' (p. 124), and how things once were, 'Me father's hand was hard.'

It could come whistling out of nowhere, but he stood between that world and me'
(p. 112). Howker captures shifts and changes in social structure at the dawn of the
twentieth century – by opening a window into a dying horse-trade – as they come
to bear on the individual and on family life, working ideas through a figurative
layering that leads to philosophical reasoning and understanding. *Isaac Campion*
encourages reflection on the justness of paternal correction, framing through
metonymy and metaphor Foucault's point in *Discipline and Punish* (1975):

> Discipline 'makes' individuals; it is the specific technique of a power that
> regards individuals both as objects and as instruments of its exercise. It is not
> a triumphant power, which because of its own excess can pride itself on its
> omnipotence; it is a modest, suspicious power, which functions as a calculated,
> but permanent economy. (1991/1975, p. 170)

In Foucault's terms, the discipline meted out to Isaac by his father recognizes
him as an object within the economic structure of family and work; Isaac is as
much a part of his father's trade as the horses he loves and fears, and his father
is bound to discipline him in accordance with the demands of the trade. The
question underlying *Isaac Campion* is whether there could have been another
way of doing; another way of living through the moment; another pattern,
such as that sought by Billy Bragg and the young protagonist of Susan Price's
Twopence a Tub. Indeed, cultural links forged through media or song, via the
cultural phenomena of childhood, can draw attention to complex and alienating
aspects of social experience, preparing the way for a deeper consideration of
ideological and ethical issues offered in books such as *Twopence a Tub* and
On the Edge. Price and Cross confront topical issues – industrial strikes and
terrorism respectively – through generic conventions that precipitate ethical
engagement.

   Twopence a Tub presents ethical life as a continuum that unites historical
periods and its narrative impetus advocates ethical and political activity, which
are linked and differentiated in Price's novel. Set in the nineteenth-century Black
Country, *Twopence a Tub* explores issues raised when individuals, families, and
communities attempt to challenge the power structures that compromise or
refuse individual freedom. Such challenges prove divisive in Price's depiction of
an unsuccessful and gruelling colliery strike and the ethical and political issues
thrown up by the historical representation of a striking community establish
a framework for considering a contemporary sociopolitical landscape marked
by industrial action. Through the focal lens of Jek Davies, a pugnacious and

ruminative protagonist, *Twopence a Tub* explores the extent to which will can be free when the state is insecure in Hegelian terms:

> The state is actual only when its individual members have a feeling of their own selfhood and it is stable only when the aims of the universal and of particular individuals are identical. It has often been said that the end of the state is the happiness of the citizens. That is perfectly true. If all is not well with them, if their subjective aims are not satisfied, if they do not find that the state as such is the means to their satisfaction, then the footing of the state itself is insecure. (2008/1821, p. 240)

Hegel argues that in order for the individual to be free and successfully partake of ethical life, the state must support the individual's aim for satisfaction and happiness. Indeed, this conviction underlies Jek's discontented protest, '"We ain't all right!"' (p. 12) and the wider negotiation of historical moment in *Twopence a Tub*, demonstrating how life *should not* be within the ethical framework and asking how satisfaction and happiness *could* be achieved.

Price's novel adheres to the authenticity typical of much historical fiction for children, which serves the didactic purpose of realizing historical period and this is achieved through a range of devices familiar to the realist mode, including: temporal markers, 'Shanny had been born in the last week of December 1840, Jek in the first week of January, 1841 . . . going down the pit on the same day, April 2nd, 1851' (1991, p. 8); material description, 'The colliers had built themselves a lavatory, called a "boggin-hole" . . . It was a rough shack with a piece of sacking hung over the door; inside, a trench, and a plank with a hole cut in it, balanced over the trench on bricks' (p. 13); or historical register and dialect, '"I don't play tha saft games"' (p. 21). The extradiegetic narration is full of explanatory detail, helping to orientate the reader historically and to establish the material conditions of the mining community that precipitated the strike. The historical register and diegetic detail serve to distance the reader and simultaneously to build an empathetic bridge between past and present, though as Geoffrey Hartman warns,

> When empathy becomes conventional, and the new or alien loses its aureole of scared danger, it is increasingly difficult to admit transcendent personality or real difference. But art retains its power of making room for the strange, the different, and even the divine. It is the familiar world that must now be saved – from familiarity. Only in this light does impersonal narration find its reason. [. . .] A great novel does not breed familiarity; a bad novel is simply one that betrays the mystery, rapes the past, and lets us possess too quickly another person or mind. (2004, p. 163)[6]

Read at the extradiegetic level, it could be argued that *Twopence a Tub* gives too much to its implied reader, expecting empathy and achieving no more than a lesson in how history repeats itself; the familiar rendered overfamiliar. However, it is in the modal nature of its past-to-present philosophical discourse that *Twopence a Tub* challenges and eschews familiarity. Jek's function as focal character is interrogative, constantly questioning the conditions of his existence and challenging the complacency or conviction of those around him. The novel opens with ostensible certainty, yet Jek's declaration that '"We ain't all right!"' soon takes on an ambiguous doubleness that permeates the entire novel; 'He thought that there was beauty in it, but only because the ugliness took the breath away, and it was wrong. Wrong, wrong, wrong'(p. 14). It is soon evident that Jek refers to the unsatisfactory conditions in which he and his family are forced to live and work – accommodation is unsanitary and insufficient wages are exchanged for excessive and treacherous labour – and that his assertion points to an awareness of political and ethical life. Jek's notion of *right* is uncertain and he seeks the views of those around him until, 'He felt that his head was crammed to bursting point with ideas and conflicting opinions, and that the thin chain of thought that *was* Jek, was being pushed under and smothered by all the others' (p. 35). As Jek begins to question his own assumptions and convictions and they are challenged by those around him, the implied reader is also drawn into the interrogative process of a narrative that is as much about the negotiation of ethical life as it is about a specific period in history.

Jek's initial response to the decision to strike is full of elation and political idealism, trusting in the power and financial robustness of the union, believing that strike action will achieve its goal of 'twopence a tub' and optimistic that the needs of himself, his family, and community will be met. Doubts about the success of the strike surface immediately though, '"Meself, I don't think we'll win, because we never do. I never heard tell of anybody like us who beat the Gaffers"' (p. 25) and consequently Jek feels 'cheated', 'The announcement of a strike, to his way of thinking, should have parades and trumpet-blowing, and angels on high. There had been none of these things and now it didn't seem real' (p. 26). This lack of reality points to a modal shift that lifts the book out of historical authenticity and into the modal region of possibility and moral philosophy as Jek begins a journey into what 'can', 'may', 'might', 'would', 'should', and 'could' happen as result of the strike. Jek's entry into modal possibility comes through a conversation with his grandfather who contends that '"Strike's against God and it's against man. It ain't right no way thee look at it, and thee can't win"' (Price, 1991, p. 22). The modal phrasing of Jek's interrogative challenge to this position, ' "Would He really send us to Hell for going on strike, Grandad?" ' (p. 27) casts doubt on the power of the church, for in the use of modal auxiliary his grandfather's position is weakened. Jek's question marks a shift from 'blind faith' to ideology and offers a (Marxist) political challenge to religious dominance. As Louis Althusser argues, 'In the pre-capitalist historical period . . . it is absolutely clear that *there was one dominant Ideological State Apparatus, the Church*' (2008/1971, p. 25),[7] and this subversion of church authority becomes part of the challenge to state in *Twopence a Tub*. Although the ideological sympathies of the book are difficult to read against, Price leaves her reader to consider the answer to Jek's question and humorously points to the complexities of the issues it raises in Jek's hedging: ' "I don't believe in God," he told himself aloud. But that was rash – who knew? There was certainly, undoubtedly, a force for evil – so why not a God? And if there was a God, then He wouldn't take kindly to such remarks. "There might be a God," he added to make amends' (p. 35). Once again, Jek's use of the modal auxiliary, 'might', refuses certainty, revealing one of the book's prevalent strategies in encouraging the implied reader to think and question alongside Jek.

Although Jek's position can be identified as political idealism at the outset, this outlook is undermined both by the political challenge mounted by 'Gaffer' and church and by Jek's shift into ethical awareness; a shift that shakes his political conviction. Jek's idealistic vision of the strike is mounted in (im)possibilities that are foreshadowed in the repetitive use of 'would' here: 'They would strike, and the Gaffers would have to give in; they would get higher wages and all the better ways of living that went with higher wages, and everybody would be happy' (p. 34). As he witnesses the suffering caused by the strike though – intolerable privation; increased and often abusive familial tension; the negative impact on 'topside' workers who indirectly rely on the coal industry – Jek wonders whether striking is a morally right action after all. He is especially troubled by the treatment of 'blacklegs':

> Some strikers were even saying that if there was an accident at the Pit – and Timothy Russel was still talking of making one – they would leave the 'breakers to rot, not make any effort to rescue them at all. This was bad. It went against all the basic laws that Jek had taken in without their being spoken. You didn't leave a man to struggle by himself, over anything. If a man forgot his snap, everyone in his work-gang gave him some of theirs. If he lost his wages, then his friends made a contribution from their own pay . . . The rule was as strong as any law, and the idea of breaking it was shocking. (p. 86)

Jek's fight shifts ground as a result and *Twopence a Tub* becomes an effort to perceive and embrace the ethical life envisaged by Hegel as the consequence of a just society. Evil can no longer be directed at the Gaffers alone and although Marxist theory might argue that the striking miners are compelled to fight state repression with force, Jek is uncomfortable with an abnegation of moral responsibility. Increasingly he wonders whether a fight from the side of poverty and depravation necessarily equates to right, and thus ' "We ain't all right!" ' echoes through the book. It also seems important that Jek is not a sympathetic character – he is petulant and aggressive – thus the reader is encouraged to engage with the questions he poses, rather than to relate to him empathetically. Jek also displays the violent tendencies of his father and when he hits his young sister Nellie – a sibling to whom he is particularly attached – Price leaves the reader to consider where responsibility lies for his action. Much of Jek's interrogative dialogue and free indirect discourse seems intent on drawing the reader into the ethical issues raised by the strike and to consider where responsibility might be located. When Jek meets Rachel, a girl who thinks and reads (a rare creature in Jek's world), she reminds him of his political stance and repeatedly goads him into thinking about his political position as distinct from the moral values he refuses to relinquish:

'So,' Rachel said, 'thee'd pack in the strike for them? Thee'd give up all hope o' winnin' an' gettin' higher wage for blacklegs and childer an' top-side workers?'

Another silence. 'I think we ought to,' Jek said quietly.

'I think,' Rachel said, 'as thee should make up thy mind whose side thee'm on.' (p. 119)

Jek's attraction to Rachel is grounded in her ability to make him think deeply and to (re)consider his beliefs and values, though just as significant is her ability to lead Jek calmly into the ethical life: 'Rachel had given him an argument to stop the arguments inside him. It was like a poultice' (p. 154). Jek's growing attachment to Rachel marks his proper growth into just family life, a crucial aspect of Hegelian freedom that has been denied him due to a state instability that permeates every aspect of life. Jek's experience of family life thus far is metonymically represented by his brutal father and although Jek feels a duty to protect and support his family, this duty is a burden, rather than the sort of freedom supported by the 'right' family life.

Although *Twopence a Tub* closes with a failed strike and the prospect of an arduous working life stretching into the future, it is the promise of familial dissolution through Rachel that lends a vestige of hope to underwrite contemporary struggles in which the implied reader is embedded socially and culturally:

> But now he had to work through the next days with as little thought and as little feeling as possible, until Sunday.
>
> Then he could see Rachel.
>
> And on Monday he would submerge into work and dim existence again – until Sunday. Then he could see Rachel.
>
> And on Monday . . . (p. 173)

The elliptical close to *Twopence a Tub* reaches out of the 1850s into the early 1970s, drawing together periods of political turmoil and economic struggle through a recognition that capitalism leaves little space for humanity: 'the characters who appear on the economic stage are but the personifications of the economic relations that exist between them' (Marx, 1999/1867, p. 51). The historical conventions at work in *Twopence a Tub* offer young readers a secure platform of didactic contextualization and they position the text politically – the book is quite transparent in its antagonism towards the ruling classes, for example – and this allows for a comparative reading of past-present. However, the interrogative framing of dialogue and narrative structure prompts the reader to ask questions, to consider deeply, and to form opinions in a movement towards ethical life. Price does not offer economic certainty, nor a conviction that the struggle of working people is likely to imminently cease, but it does place faith in young people's ability to think their way into the future and into new formations of family and state that are more just than those they leave behind them.

A young adult thriller is not the most obvious place to look for a philosophically rich consideration of Hegelian and Marxist social philosophy, nonetheless *On the Edge* is such a thriller and it makes use of a pivotal thought experiment to ask whether individual rights can ever outweigh social/collective rights. This question is framed thematically, politically, ideologically, and ethically in relation to family and although the thought experiment is not articulated until late in the book, issues and dilemmas raised early on feed into it and expose the political and moral conditions of family structure. *On the Edge* relates the kidnapping of Liam Shakespeare (known as Tug) by 'The Free People', a group of terrorists being investigated by his mother Harriet Shakespeare. When Harriet uncovers a campaign to kill several prominent people, the Free People kidnap Tug in order to purchase her silence:

> 'If I tell – they will kill Liam and point out that he's had to suffer for my stubborn principles. And that's what being in a family does for you. If I *don't* tell,' she

gripped the edge of the table, 'there will be several deaths this afternoon, less important to me, but much more sensational. And Free People will be able to announce that being in a family is corrupting. That my love for my son has interfered with my passion for truth and justice. The passion that I have foolishly boasted so much about.' (Cross, 1987/1984, pp. 151–2)

This dilemma might seem easy to resolve for a mother, yet Harriet implies awareness of the consequentialist resolution to this which would have her son die in order that the most people survive. This experiment also gets to the essential nature of ethics, shaping human being as a social experience requiring consideration of self (and our entitlements) in relation to others (and their entitlements). *On the Edge* is especially interested in how the family forms self-other relationships, and in the process demonstrates that moral agency is contingent upon social relationships (as it asks readers to consider what they might do in Harriet's situation).

Cross's thought experiment is articulated through a dialogue exchange and comes at a climactic moment in the plot when only hours remain before the terrorists' deadline. Pressure applied by the terrorists is a conceptual aspect of the story content, and the narrative structure of *On the Edge* contributes to the framing and urgency of decision making, so that characters and implied reader are drawn into the workings of moral agency. Several aspects of the narrative structure feed into this urgency, usefully described by Genette in terms of duration. *On the Edge* takes place over ten days, from the moment prior to Tug's kidnapping to that of his escape. Each chapter recounts the events of one day – chapters are headed 'Day One, Sunday 7th August' and so on – and temporal demarcations are further broken down in subheadings that mark time, thus Day One begins at 11.00 a.m. As Genette points out, it is impossible actually to measure the duration of a narrative with any sort of precision, but the temporal markers of date and time serve as a means of measuring '*steadiness in speed*', which Genette defines as the 'relationship between a duration (that of the story, measured in seconds, minutes, hours . . .) and a length (that of the text, measured in lines and in pages)' (1983/1972, pp. 87–8). Consequently, the narrative slows down when focused on Tug's incarceration over several pages in a single time slot, giving a sense of the drawn-out agony of his isolation and captivity. It then accelerates when the terrorists' deadline approaches, due to an accumulation of time slots, several of which are short in length relative to other sections. The momentum of the thriller is achieved through variations in speed, and these variations are also a method of engaging the implied reader in moral dilemmas thrown up by the plot elsewhere; as characters think quickly, so this forward impetus is passed to the implied reader.

Genette points out that spatial (in addition to temporal) breaks also contribute to variations in speed, allowing for the measurement of story-time and spatial shifts are an important aspect of tension building and pace setting in *On the Edge*. The chapters alternate between a focus on Tug, incarcerated in the internal space of the cottage in which he is being held, and on Jinny Slattery, a local girl who witnesses the kidnappers' arrival at the holiday cottage and who guesses Tug's true identity after hearing news reports about the kidnap. Jinny moves about in the world external to Tug's cottage, piecing together clues and the spatial exchange between captive and liberator builds tension, especially since these shifts are also marked in time, encroaching on the terrorists' deadline as the narrative proceeds. Tug and Jinny also partake in extraordinary familial experiences during the duration of the narrative and the regular spatial exchange encourages a comparative assessment of these experiences. Tug's kidnappers force him to address them as Ma and Doyle and to treat them as family members, disorientating him and making him doubt and question the foundations and nature of his relationship with his mother. In seeking to rescue Tug, Jinny is forced to challenge and break rules imposed by the strict regime of her family's working life on their farm, and she too comes to question the familial conditions imposed by her parents' decision to opt out of the bourgeois system. Consequently, the teenagers come to question the values underlying familial relationships and the political and moral choices made on their behalf by their parents. The structure of Cross's thriller influences tension and speed, and also emphasizes central ethical and political issues.

The familial dissolution contained in the terrorists' threat is literal – and antithetical to Hegel's system of freedom – its extreme conditions prompting the reader to engage closely with the implications of its political position. Where for Hegel 'ethical dissolution' embraces the fulfilment of filial relationships brought freely to bear on new roles of responsibility in society, the dissolution called by the terrorists in *On the Edge* seeks to 'break the tyranny of the blood tie and abolish the out-dated family unit' (p. 76) through a fanatical and destructive agenda. The call for the 'Abolition of the family' (Marx and Engels, 2002/1848, p. 239) is a familiar element of *The Communist Manifesto* and the Free People imitate Marxist philosophy in their argument that '*The family is a primitive institution that gives the rich an excuse to exploit the poor and prevents the poor from resisting*' and in their call to '*Help build the revolution NOW*' (Cross, p. 82). The apparent call for a revolution to unify people is belied by the tactics of terrorism and brutality employed by the Free People though, and the reader is left to consider their justification of murderous means: ' "Bombs went off on six beaches at once.

Blew about twenty families to bits and sent a shocking number of people scurrying away without their parents or their children. Free people claimed they had been 'exploding the myth of the happy family"' (p. 81). The Free People's rationale problematizes the designation of evil to such an act and as Tug comes to doubt his allegiance to his mother and forms emotional bonds with his captors, so too the reader is encouraged to consider whether, as deontological ethics would have it, killing is always wrong. In Eagleton's view, '... such terrorism is wicked[8] rather than evil', because 'it is theoretically possible to argue with those who use unscrupulous means to achieve rational or even admirable ends', whereas the evil are not rational and cannot be persuaded out of their actions (2010, p. 157). Similar issues are raised by the IRA bombing campaign carried out from the 1970s to the 1990s and more recently the Islamic terrorism that destroyed the World Trade Centre in 2001 and instigated the London bombings of 2005, so young people are offered the opportunity to consider the moral complexity of events witnessed during their own lifetime. Moreover, this fact of historical violence (the beach bombing revelation) confers tension on the kidnapping suffered by Tug and lends moral force to choices confronting characters seeking his rescue – for example, Jinny's resolve to disobey her parents' rules and Harriet Shakespeare's decision to inform the police about the terrorist plot she has uncovered – underlining the point that moral decisions are often difficult and not without sacrifice. The conventional tension underlying the thriller emphasizes the weight and significance of moral agency.

The Free People isolate their determination to destroy the family from other areas of human experience, hence their focus on the family appears radical and obsessive. In politically segregating family, it misrepresents Marxist thinking, which links each element of its theoretical discourse in Hegelian fashion. Marx's theories are not diametrically opposed to Hegel's, but constitute a deeply considered response to the Hegelian philosophy of right that evolves and unfolds – just as Hegel's ideas evolve and unfold into each other – in the direction of the practical and material, rather than remaining in the theoretical realms of Hegel's *Idea*. The Free People refuse the structural *unity* of Marxist discourse, nonetheless the drastic position articulated by the terrorists provides Cross with the hypothetical conditions for her thought experiment and makes visible the institutions that shape modern British society, as emphasized in this exchange between Ma and Tug about the motivation behind Doyle's terrorist activities:

'He doesn't think it's any use just telling people things. Because they can only see what's straight ahead of them. The things they've *always* seen. If you want to get them to look at something new, you've got to *make* them see.' (p. 124)

Figuratively, this works as a way of understanding a central agenda of *On the Edge*, which exposes the relative, political, and constructed nature of institutions that shape human experience – in this case the family – in order that young people might 'look at something new'. Each of these positions, responding to and refining each other, makes visible Louis Althusser's 'Ideological State Apparatuses' (ISAs) – such as church, family, school and trade unions – which Althusser distinguishes from '(Repressive) State Apparatus' (SAs) – such as government, army, police, and prisons. Althusser argues that ISAs function in the *'private* domain' through ideology that is difficult to detect, while SAs belong in the *'public'* domain and function 'by violence' (2008/1971, pp. 18–19). Cross suggests that Althusser's Marxist view of family is only *one* way of approaching and seeing family life, though she makes ideology visible though the narrative structure, central themes, and plotting of *On the Edge* as Althusser does through theory. It is also telling that the Free People seek to draw the family out of the private domain in order to eradicate its ability to function on behalf of the state, but in so doing they replicate the violent strategies of the Repressive SAs. It can be argued then that the Free People are replacing one unjust state with an equally unjust state, each enforcing policy through violence. As a result, Cross makes it possible to see that terrorism can be defended on moral grounds, while also demonstrating that the foundations of such defences are insecure. Of course the issue is complicated by the fact that Cross also provides the kidnappers with backstories revealing potential emotional and psychological reasons for joining the Free People. Doyle appears to have suffered an abusive childhood at the hands of an aggressive father, and it is implied that Ma has lost, or possibly killed, her own child, so (as in *The Tulip Touch*) the reader is left to consider whether moral responsibility is relinquished as a result.

Returning to the call for unity that underlies Marxist philosophy and structures its discourse, it is evident that another of the families in *On the Edge* responds to the bourgeoisie in reactive, rather than revolutionary terms. Instead of severing the bonds of family, the Slatterys seek to resist bourgeois materialism through a dependence on blood ties unfettered (at least ostensibly) by the constraints and values of a capitalist society, which in their view generates '"Lots of money to buy trash"' (p. 72). The Slatterys's decision to move out of the city and support themselves through farming is a reaction to Joe Slattery's suffering under the pressure of market forces, but rather than uniting with others in a common struggle, they seek to isolate themselves and sever the bonds of humanity. Jinny's mother explains, '"We came here so that we could be in control of our own lives and not tangled up with anyone else. We *chose* this life"' (Cross, 1987/1984, p. 72). The tight threads of Cross's plotting demonstrate through story structure that such tangles are impossible to avoid though and that the choice they made is not the type of moral choice leading to ethical life and freedom of will. As the Slatterys are forced to engage increasingly in the affairs of others, their way of life appears to be an unattainable ideal reminiscent of the socialist aspirations rejected by Marx and Engels:

> ... this form of Socialism aspires either to restoring the old means of production and of exchange, and with them the old property relations, and the old society, or to cramping the modern means of production and of exchange, within the framework of the old property relations that have been, and were bound to be, exploded by those means. In either case, it is both reactionary and Utopian. (2002/1848, p. 248)

In this view, the reactionary Utopia of the Slatterys's farm is limiting, backward looking, and essentially impossible. The Slattery family aims to liberate its members; instead it operates another form of social incarceration, neatly mirroring Tug's imprisonment. Jinny's social isolation causes her to yearn for human contact, 'to lead a normal life, like anyone else of my age' (p. 73), even if this means embracing bourgeois values. A clue to the fact that the Slatterys's chosen lifestyle might not be as morally sound as it might seem is provided in the opening scene in which Jinny poaches a hare with her father Jim Slattery – witnessing unwittingly the kidnappers' arrival with Tug – an act that she clearly feels uncomfortable with, '*I can't do it*, said the voice in Jinny's head' (p. 12). Jinny does not explain why she feels unable to kill the hare, and the reader is left to decide whether it is the taking of a defenceless life that unsettles her, or the illegal act of theft that constitutes poaching.[9] The image of the hare resonates through the book, for Jinny comes to see Ma as 'the Hare-woman', observing that 'there *was* something hare-like about the woman she was staring at. The elongated face. The long legs. And an odd, sharp alertness, as if those eyes watched for pursuers' (p. 23). Figuratively and morally, the Slatterys's poaching is linked to the kidnapping and the images encourage the reader to ask whether Ma is as much victim as predator. Jinny understands her family's justification for poaching, 'It was part of life. Part of survival and winning your own food. *Never rely on anyone else*, Joe said. *Make sure you can do everything yourself.* Only – suppose you couldn't?' (p. 12). Jinny's question is not answered directly, nonetheless it does point to the impossibility of the ideal of insularity and the issues raised of living outside of the law and the social structures binding other people in the village are left for the reader to ponder. In challenging, if not quite refusing an impossible and unsustainable way of life, Jinny's disobedience finds vindication – blindly following an unjust regime can lead to Arendt's thoughtless evil, or Wiesel's indifference after all – and this is just one way in which Cross probes the conditions and rules of social life.

Although *On the Edge* questions the social validity and possibility of independence, encouraging the implied reader to consider the ethical conditions of severing ties from community and civil life, it promotes the sort of autonomy Hegel identifies as being part of the subject's freedom to will. In order to truly function as a member of a family, or other related institutions, the subject needs to think for herself and unify with the other while retaining a complete sense of self. When Jinny objects that she has not chosen the life her family has provided, her mother observes, '"You're like all children. You get the kind of life your parents choose until you're old enough to choose for yourself. And when you are, you'll be well-grown and independent. Twice as independent as most girls of your age"' (p. 73). This approaches the sort of family dissolution Hegel speaks of, although the 'twice independent' points to a double remove and suggests that Jinny and her family have some way to go before Hegelian membership can be achieved. It is Tug, forced under duress to focus on the conditions of his familial relationships, who achieves the unity envisaged by Hegel. Having struggled with confused memories of Hank (his mother) throughout the book, Tug is finally able to draw on her wisdom, reaching a point of ethical dissolution:

> Suddenly, without trying he knew what the *real* Harriet Shakespeare would say. With a fierce look on her tough, plain face. *For Heaven's sake, Tug, do I have to decide everything for you? You've got to rely on yourself. Be a person of your own.*
> (p. 166)

Tug's epiphany does not amount to a rejection of the maternal care and education he has received from Hank, rather this is the liberation of self, being 'a person of your own' that comes though family membership; in ceasing to be reliant on Hank, Tug moves into a new and liberated phase of being that contradicts the terrorist's claim that '*The blood tie strangles the true brotherhood of mankind*' (p. 82). Like Susan Price, Gillian Cross leaves the reader to consider the implications for ethical life of Tug's final call to the mother he lost and the mother he has recently found: '*This is me. Here I am, Hank. Here I am, Ma. This is me. This is who I am*' (p. 170).

Hegel argues that 'in duty the individual finds his *liberation*' and that the conditions of duty inhere in the transactions between self and an '*ethical community*' (2008/1821, p. 157). Moreover there is a fluidity in Hegelian thinking that allows for a range of different conceptions of community and for the fact that not all communities (from family to state) are ethical, as each of the books discussed in this chapter reveal. Consequently, Hegelian thinking offers a useful framework for thinking about how the young person might engage morally with family and the wider community and for considering the issues arising from social structures that impinge on their freedom. This Hegelian fluidity allows for consideration of a range of philosophically open books that engage with the ethical conditions and implications of family and social life. Jan Mark's bleak and provocative *Divide and Rule* (1979) shows how individual freedom can be worn down by the corrupt guardians of power as Hanno's repeated question, ' "What will become of me?" ' (1979, p. 139) reverberates through the book; while Jenny Valentine's *Broken Soup* (2008) borrows from the conventions of mystery writing to engage with the ethical power of community to prevent a family collapsing beneath the burden of grief, allowing Rowan to think 'about us being a family again' (2011/2008, p. 247).

Stop the Train (2001) by Geraldine McCaughrean depicts the growth of a community of settlers in 1893 Oklahoma and asks whether it is possible to fight the forces of capitalism from within. The vision of family and civil life in *Stop the Train* rests on a notion of ethical rules and structures founded in trust and a conviction that individuals grow into families, moving on into society and that the rules binding them are liberating in Hegelian terms. Cissy's father is saved from financial ruin by the banker with whom he deposited his meagre savings on arrival in Florence: ' "On the first day we got here, you trusted me, Mr Sissney. Trust. It is a critical factor in banking. Well, in any line of business, come to that . . . A critical factor in friendship, also, I find" ' (2007/2001, p. 167), and in this trust are sown the seeds of family and communal development. Crucial to the reader's ethical engagement in this book are the children who populate the town, forging friendships and solving problems that seem set to destroy Florence before it has had a chance to establish itself as a town at all, let alone a prospering town with any chance of a future. Ultimately in *Stop the Train*, it is in the children's ingenuity and faith that ethical life is facilitated, ingenuity and faith that is also accorded to the implied reader who is charged to work thoughtfully and reflectively to pull together disparate narrative strands. McCaughrean's novel, along with each of the books discussed in this chapter, reflects on the social structures that form human experience and presents them through the lens of ethical enquiry. Such books for young people invest in children as free individuals ready to engage in unity with the world around them: 'Children are free *in themselves* and their life is only the immediate existence of this freedom. Consequently they are not things and cannot be the property either of their parents or others' (Hegel, 2008/1821, p. 173).

4

Midnight Philosophy and Environmental Ethics

But thou, my babe! shalt wander like a breeze
By lakes and sandy shores, beneath the crags
Of ancient mountain, and beneath the clouds,
Which image in their bulk both lakes and shores
And mountain crags: so shalt thou see and hear
The lovely shapes and sounds intelligible
Of that eternal language, which thy God
Utters, who from eternity doth teach
Himself in all, and all things in himself.
Great universal Teacher! he shall mould
Thy spirit, and by giving make it ask.

Coleridge, 'Frost at Midnight', 1798,[1] 54–64

A land ethic in the making

Coleridge's 'Frost at Midnight' articulates an environmental ethics in which the 'eternal language' of nature is united with the being and expression of humanity. Ethical concern for human and environment is encapsulated in childhood reminisced and potentialized; hence the temporal shift between 'I dreamt of my sweet birth-place' and 'all seasons shall be sweet to thee'. In part a meditation on the process of philosophical thinking, 'Frost at Midnight' situates 'Abstruser musings' in the exchange between the natural world and human consciousness open to the solitude of a reflective moment; an exchange which for the philosopher involves retrospection – represented by the poet's spent childhood – and anticipation – figured in his infant's future and unified in the midnight present. The philosophical vision perceives a childly spirit, open to learning, who 'shalt wander like a breeze/ By lakes and sandy shores' and will be stimulated intellectually by a deep understanding of God and nature: 'Great Universal Teacher! he shall mould/ Thy spirit, and by giving make it ask'. Proximity to and learning through nature foster the interrogative spirit of the philosopher; the child who is stimulated by nature to ask will come to think deeply and reach for the workings of human being. Although 'Frost at Midnight' is not expressly concerned with moral philosophy, there is an ethical mandate in the paternal-philosophical care that draws together 'Dear babe' and 'ancient mountain' into a reciprocal relationship of deep understanding, 'so shalt thou see and hear'.

The environmental ethics expressed in 'Frost at Midnight' falls upon the ear as 'a wild pleasure', identifying a spiritual harmony in which nature and humanity care for each other. Human concern shapes 'Frost at Midnight' and it does not entirely counter Routley and Routley's charge – for charge it is in their view that 'human chauvinism' dominates ethics – that 'popular Western thought and most Western ethical theories assume that both value and morality can ultimately be reduced to matters of interest or concern to the class of humans' (1995/1979, p. 104). Nonetheless, although reflective emphasis rests on the (human) personal pronoun in 'me to that solitude', the ethical value in 'Frost at Midnight' does not privilege humanity with the dominance and colonialism typical of moral humanism. A mysterious nature – 'The frost performs its secret ministry' – enfolds humanity, and human consciousness is presented as one aspect of a much broader, deeper natural world. Limitless is the natural world that draws on eternity, where limited humanity is cradled by the temporal markers of child and fatherhood. Balance in the human-nature relationship is located in the poetic imagination though, for it is here that nature is *man*aged and earthed. As Geoffrey Hartman puts it, 'poetry, like the world, can only house an imagination which is a borderer, which will not disdain earthly things. Whatever the imagination's source, its end as poetry is the nature all recognize, and still a nature that leads beyond itself' (2004, pp. 88–9).[2]

Considering the conditions of ethical environmentalism in children's literature and literary images of childhood – such as those rendered seminally in 'Frost at Midnight' and renovated in Barry Hines's *A Kestrel for a Knave* (1968) – in this chapter, I proceed from the idea that through the figurative expression of poetry and literature the human reader is offered a moral engagement (albeit uneasy and challenging) with the natural world that leads to and beyond her/himself. 'Frost at Midnight' identifies something more than affinity between child and nature and is not especially interested in advocating a Rousseauian upbringing for children. Certainly there are echoes of Émile's (1762) invective on overcrowding in 'the foul air of the town', which eventually will 'devour' and 'degenerate' the human race, thus, 'it needs renewal, and it is always renewed from the country. Send your children to renew themselves, so to speak, send them to regain in the open fields the strength lost in the foul air of our crowded cities' (1911/1762, p. 26). However, Rousseau mounts a challenge to industrial development and urbanization not evident in 'Frost at Midnight', postulating an unlikely return to an arable society: 'Men are not made to be crowded together in ant-hills, but scattered over the earth to till it' (p. 26). This regressive philosophy seeks to reconstruct a 'lost' environment and is precisely the ethical vision articulated in Michael Foreman's 1972 picture book *Dinosaurs and All That Rubbish*.

Published three years after the first crewed moon landings, through under-lit and densely filled watercolour, *Dinosaurs* visualizes the ruin inflicted on Earth by the human desire for 'unnatural' advancement (and it is in Foreman's pictorial juxtaposition of drear, factory-lined landscapes against the lush colour splashes of a rediscovered paradise that philosophical potential is located). That such scientific endeavour is deemed unnatural is suggested by the proximal comparison of a bowler-hatted man in a tree with birds who can fly naturally: 'The trees filled with birds which flew still nearer the star. "I must fly," said the man' (Foreman, 1974/1972, p. 6[3]). For many young children of the early 1970s, this sort of challenge to a space race celebrated in *Airfix* models, and hyperbolic news commentaries must have been thought-provoking. *Dinosaurs* makes Joseph DesJardins's point that 'largely through human activity, life on Earth faces the greatest mass extinctions since the end of the dinosaur age sixty-five million years ago' (1997, p. ix), yet Foreman's text falls short of expressing a coherent environmental ethics, through muddled moralizing that resurrects dinosaurs as implausible saviours and guardians of an earthly paradise that is 'to be enjoyed and cared for' by everyone (p. 28); indeed its overbearing closing message is difficult to read against or beyond.

Dinosaurs takes Rousseau's concept of renewal to extremes, and this notion of renewal is common to Rousseau and Coleridge, though 'Frost at Midnight' bypasses a dichotomous battle between urban (adult) and rural (child) via an ethical endeavour that identifies and reinforces a conceptual alliance between childhood – growing into the philosophical maturity of adulthood – and environmental ethics; an alliance that unites the natural world and humanity in a communal vision. The community anticipated here is subtly different from the humanist community – of which the Hegelian community is a particularly fluid and phenomenological version[4] – described by J. Baird Callicott, with 'duties and obligations to family and family members, to municipality and fellow-citizens, to country and countrymen, to humanity and human beings' (1995/1980, p. 29). Rather, Coleridge's poetic vision is philosophically compatible with Aldo Leopold's land ethic, as proposed in the influential and eloquent *A Sand County Almanac* (1949): 'In short, a land ethic changes the role of *Homo sapiens* from conquerer of the land-community to plain member and citizen of it. It implies respect for its fellow-members, and also respect for the community as such' (Leopold, 1968/1949, p. 204). Just as Coleridge's faltering poetic exertion reaches philosophical depths that bring him, and frail humanity, into communion with the natural world, so Leopold's attention to 'winds and sunsets' weaves a living philosophy that combines (or more rightly communes) poetry, ethics, naturalism, and environmentalism. Furthermore, as Callicott points out, 'The biotic community and its correlative land ethic *does not replace* our several human communities and their correlative ethics . . . Rather it *supplements* them' (1995/1980, p. 29). Leopold recognizes, as does 'Frost at Midnight', that for those who cannot live without wild things, experience brings both 'delights and dilemmas' and, for Leopold, those dilemmas result in a forceful land ethic, arguing that 'the chance to find a pasque-flower is a right as inalienable as free speech' (1968/1949, p. vii).

Notwithstanding the looming shadows of imperialist domination, the complex history of British children's literature marks a trail heralding Leopold's notion of a communal land ethic. Glimmerings of his ethical approach can be found in: Captain Frederick Marryat's *The Children of the New Forest* (1847), wherein historical period is drawn through a naturalistic detail attending to and respecting an environment that reciprocally sustains and protects; or Richard Jefferies's *Bevis* (1882), which though firmly marked by colonial enterprise builds the natural environment of Bevis's existence with the same detailed care that styles Bevis's urgent boat-building: 'Where there were streaks of white sand sifted by the stream from the mud, he could see the bottom: under the high bank there was a swirl as if the water wrestled with something under the surface: a water-rat, which had watched him coming from a tiny terrace, dived with a sound like a stone dropped quietly in' (Jefferies, 1989/1882, p. 12); and Arthur Ransome's *Swallows and Amazons* (1930) in which the blurred borders of the imagined and actual lakeland reflect the children's emotional, physical, and changing relationship with and perception of a landscape that their cultural traditions once taught them to colonize. The land ethic is ideologically and more visibly reflected in early twentieth-century books, such as *Tarka the Otter*

(1927) by Henry Williamson, Alison Uttley's *The Country Child* (1931), and B.B.'s *Brendon Chase* (1944); although such books depict a natural history and environment filled with flora and fauna alien to the skunks and chipmunks of Leopold's *Almanac*, they mirror an ethical enterprise that counters mechanization and desires accord and balance-shift between human and natural world.

British literary tradition heaves with books that draw children into a relationship with the natural world and many of these convey some sort of ecological message or imperative, yet the child-nature relationship is not necessarily a mark of ethical discourse, community, or harmony. The image of child in nature persists partly due to the conceptual affinity between childhood and a natural world imaginatively rendered as benign, instructive, inspirational, comedic, diverting, and physically nourishing, as manifest in poetry and literature written for children from *The Butterfly Ball and the Grasshopper's Feast* (1807) by William Roscoe, to Burnett's *The Secret Garden* (1911), or to John Lawrence's woodcut picture book for young children *This Little Chick* (2002). This Rousseauian and quasi-Romantic affinity[5] between child and natural world retains its influence in children's literature of the twenty-first century and it can also be detected in a social environmentalism that draws on this conceptual relationship between child and nature. From the mid-twentieth century, the child-nature alliance took on an increasingly politicized[6] aspect as momentum grew to highlight environmental issues through propaganda that specifically targeted young people. For example, the Royal Society for the Protection of Birds (RSPB) – first established in 1889 to protest against the fashion for wearing feathers in hats – founded the Junior Bird Recorder's Club (JBRC) in 1943, to be replaced by the Young Ornithologists Club (YOC) with its magazine *Bird Life* in 1965; the British group of Friends of the Earth was established in 1971; and the Young People's Trust for the Environment was founded in 1982. Of course, international movements also had an impact on British youth culture during this period and most environmental groups – such as the World Wildlife Fund established in 1961; and Greenpeace founded in the early 1970s – have active youth sections. It seems reasonable to suggest that many charities and movements have found their way into the culture of childhood because they appear to validate prevailing concepts of childhood; if children have an affinity to the natural world then they have a vested interest in preserving it and appeals to their 'nature' are likely to have impact even on immature humans not widely recognized as moral agents. Furthermore, appealing to a protectionist paradigm of childhood, such sociopolitical interventions promote 'safe' ways of alerting children to the conditions of the world in which they live; thus adults are encouraged to buy stuffed toys, or to 'adopt' creatures under threat of extinction for their children.

Tucking up children with plush pandas though can be seen as a manipulative evasion, working against the impulse of conservation and environmentalism. The conceptual alliance between child and nature can make it difficult honestly to deal with the issues concerning key thinkers in environmental ethics; most obviously the rapacious and barbarous human treatment of the natural world. Recalling the profound relationship between child and land envisioned in 'Frost at Midnight', John Passmore's cautionary response to the Romantic perception of nature is worth sounding:

> It is the great importance of Romanticism that it . . . encouraged us to *look* at nature, to see it otherwise than as a mere instrument. But we do not need to accept the Romantic identification of God with nature in order to accept this way of looking at the world. Indeed, the divinization of nature, even apart from the philosophical problems it raises, dangerously underestimates the *fragility* of so many natural processes and relationships, a fragility to which the ecological movement has drawn such forcible attention. (1995/1975, p. 141)

Fragility then can be located in the natural world and also in the child's relationship to it, a point powerfully made in *A Kestrel for a Knave* when Billy finds the kestrel hawk he has trained with such care '"in t'bin"' (Hines, 1969/1968, p. 150). When Billy charges his mother with a lack of concern over the demise of Kes, her response expresses a sociocultural negation of the child-nature trope that also underscores its impossibility: '"Course I'm bothered. But it's only a bird. You can get another can't you?"' (p. 151). Running to escape from the horror of this moment, Billy dives into a narrative rewind, reeling through the violent memories that define his short life until, abruptly and finally: 'He buried the hawk in the field just behind the shed; went in, and went to bed' (p. 160). A complex web of moral responsibility weaves around the kestrel's death and Billy's brutal upbringing, yet it is clear that child and bird are fiercely savage and easily damaged by the desires of humanity that tether them. Ideals embedded in pastorals of childhood[7] can mislead and adult memories of childhood lost are forged frequently in the union of child and landscape or creature, evading (though not truly forgetting) the knowledge that nature is not always benign; hence the concept of natural evil discussed by Mary Midgley and Lars Svendsen in their investigations of evil. Robert Elliot takes this idea a step further, conceding that not 'all natural phenomena have value in virtue of being natural'; he points out that disease is 'natural in a straightforward sense' and 'is certainly not good', and that 'Natural phenomena such as fires, hurricanes,

volcanic eruptions can totally alter landscapes and alter them for the worse'
(1995/1982, p. 82). Elliot stresses that environmental ethics is not grounded in an
idealization of nature which would undermine its pursuit of a right consideration
of the natural world and this emphasis forges links between environmental
positions that might seem opposed.

In his deft piece of philosophical (re)positioning that situates Leopold's land
ethic between the concerns of animal liberationists and moral humanists, Callicott
points out that animal liberation/rights seemed to overshadow environmental
ethics 'in the late 1970s and early 1980s', when 'many people seemed to conflate
the two' (1995/1980, p. 29). I shall go on to reveal through contemplation of
moral questions posed in novels such as *Watership Down* (1972) by Richard
Adams and *The Cry of the Wolf* (1990) by Melvin Burgess that it is possible to
trace alliances and distinctions between these movements. Before moving on to
explore ethically aware books for children though, I pause to consider one of the
most persuasive voices calling for animal rights in the 1970s, since many writers
for children from Captain Marryat to John Burningham respond to related
concerns. In his confrontational *Animal Liberation* (1975), Peter Singer makes
his case with an ethical force that is difficult to ignore:

> The tyranny of human over non-human animals . . . has caused and today is
> still causing an amount of pain and suffering that can only be compared with
> that which resulted from the centuries of tyranny by white humans over black
> humans. The struggle against this tyranny is a struggle as important as any
> of the moral and social issues that have been fought over in recent years.
> (1991/1975, p. i)

Singer's comparative use of an ongoing human struggle – which has brought
about ideological and social change – draws the implied reader to his position
from a point that s/he can relate to as a human 'speciesist',[8] for *Animal Liberation*
asks its reader seriously to reconsider the very foundations of moral goodness
(which for Singer precludes any practice that involves animal cruelty, whether
it be eating meat or wearing fur coats). Singer's thorough evaluation of the
animal rights movement and of human processes that involve animals, such
as farming and scientific experimentation, leads him to an ethical model in
which non-humans are accorded the same rights as humans. Accordingly, 'We
ought to consider the interests of animals because they have interests and it is
unjustifiable to exclude them from the sphere of moral concern' (p. 244). Of
particular relevance here, Singer discusses the childhood influences directing
'our attitudes to animals', that 'begin to form when we are very young, and . . . are

dominated by the fact that we begin to eat meat at an early age' (p. 213). Singer asserts that any aversion that children might feel to eating meat is typically quashed by parental persuasion, additionally pointing to cultural shifts that are increasingly evasive about the animals we eat.

Singer argues that 'not so long ago' in a literary diet of nursery rhymes such as 'Three Blind Mice' 'there was no inconsistency between what [children] were taught and what they ate' (p. 214). Whether nursery rhymes are received in the literal manner suggested by Singer is debatable, yet his point seems valid in relation to a book such as *The Children of the New Forest*, involving detailed descriptions of deer hunting and preparing venison for the table: ' "This is a fine beast, and the venison is now getting very good. Now you must see me do the work of my craft." Jacob then cut the throat of the animal, and afterwards cut off its head, and took out its bowels' (Marryat, 1994/1847, p. 43). In common with many early works of children's literature in tune with the natural world, *The Children of the New Forest* advocates a hunting ethic based on human sustenance and requirement, although there is a colonial pleasure taken in hunting game discordant with Singer's notions of species equality. Marryat's historical novel is precise and practical in the details of survival, serving the conventions of its historical endeavour. *Bevis* also belongs to a hunting history of children's literature, although the relish, regularity, and brutality with which the boys dispatch waterfoul, rabbits, and an otter far exceeds their requirements for survival on New Formosa. Alternatively, B.B.'s *Brendon Chase* presents the natural world into which the boys escape through a philosophical poeticism that encourages deeper reflection on the human relationship with the environment. B.B.'s paean to a vanishing landscape and changing human-nature relations accords with Leopold's land ethic which allows for the respectful hunting of game. Leopold's 'sketches here and there' in *A Sand County Almanac* (1949) contain a sustained eulogy on fly fishing, for example, in which 'I sit in happy meditation on my rock, pondering, while my line dries again, upon the ways of trout and men' (1968/1949, p. 39). Callicott accepts that Leopold's validation of hunting could seem contradictory in a communal land ethic (1995/1980, pp. 33–4), but careful examination of Leopold's ethic (and the 'sketches here and there' that lead into the ethical proposal) reveals that hunting can be necessary to the sustenance of a healthy biosphere concerned with communal health, rather than the requirements of human or non-human individuals, though hunting is only permitted with reservations related to safeguarding the balance of species in the preservation of the biosphere. So, although Singer's moral vision does not allow for the hunter's communion with nature espoused by B.B. and Leopold, there is an ethical integrity in their approach that Singer claims is not typical of books for the youngest readers:

> British books, like *The Farm* in the best-selling Ladybird series, convey [an] impression of rural simplicity, showing the hen running freely in an orchard with her chicks, and all the other animals living with their offspring in spacious quarters. With this kind of early reading it is not surprising that children grow up believing that even if animals 'must' die to provide human beings with food, they live happily until that time comes. [. . .] To alter the stories about animals that we read to our children will not be so easy, since cruelty is not an ideal subject for children's stories. (1991/1975, p. 215)

Singer was writing in 1975, and similar books have replaced Ladybird's *The Farm* (now a collectable piece of childhood nostalgia), John Lawrence's *Little Chick* among them; Lawrence's beautifully rendered woodcuts are unlikely to escape Singer's accusation of dishonesty. In the United States, the Humane Farm Association produces books for children that seek to demonstrate how animals *should* be treated and to show that not all farms are idyllic, though books that deal with the realities of animal slaughter for the youngest readers are rare.

A range of books published recently target the child as conservationist, taking a pedagogic approach, such as David Bellamy's *101 Ways to Save the Earth*[9] (2008), Charlotte Voake's *A Little Guide to Trees* (2009), and *Carbon Monster* by Katherine Wheatley (2011). Informative publications such as this fit within a wider paradigm of environmental education that has found its way onto the UK National Curriculum via Key Stage 2 Science and Geography and they link to 'Sustainable Schools', initially a government initiative following the first 'Education Sustainable Development Action Plan' published in 2003. These books emphasize prominent environmental issues, but still they lack the philosophical impetus of picture books for young children that seek to highlight and challenge the cultural evasion described by Singer, such as Anthony Browne's *Zoo* (1992) or Alexis Deacon's *Slow Loris* (2002). Both deal with zoological captivity, echoing Singer's ethical concern that animals should be treated as individuals; Browne and Deacon propose in different ways that the rights accorded to humans to live outside cages should also be conferred upon animals. In *Practical Ethics*, Singer's problem with Leopold's land ethic and the deep ecology[10] that values ecosystems 'as a whole' is grounded in the fact that these ethical systems do not allow for or recognize individual rights: in Singer's view 'ethics of deep ecology thus fail to yield persuasive answers to questions about the value of the lives of individual living beings' (1993, p. 282). In his subtly powerful observation of zoo life, Deacon presents the zoo as an institution akin to Foucault's prison in which the individual – both human and non-human – is controlled and diminished for the sake of social and political systems.

Slow Loris allows itself to sink into the reading consciousness without making any explicit reference to its central ethical concerns; this is philosophy by stealth. Deacon's perceptive and witty picture book directs fun at speciesism, in Singer's terms, that seeks to trap animals, suggesting that systems can be evaded and that the 'wild' can be recovered through covert means. *Slow Loris* tells the tale of a particularly slow Loris who turns out to have a secret: 'At night, when all the other animals were sound asleep. Loris got up and did things . . . FAST . . . until he was so tired he couldn't do another thing' (2002, pp. 15–19[11]). The other animals discover his secret and recognize that 'Loris wasn't boring at all. He was really wild' (p. 31). This idiomatic reference to Loris's partying lifestyle employs a covert use of punning to make a more serious moral point about the rights of 'really wild' animals in captivity. When the other zoo animals join in with Loris they also find an alternative way to be wild and undermine the human value of the zoo: 'The next day all the animals were slow. "Boring," said the visitors. But, like Loris, they didn't care, now they had a secret too' (p. 37). This final verbal observation subverts the value system of zoos; zoos are designed to give something of value – such as stimulation, entertainment, or education – to human visitors, however the animals refuse this by evading the behavioural conventions of zoological conditioning.

The subversive subtext of *Slow Loris* is not commented on by the narrator, yet it is conveyed in a number of ways to encourage an ethical engagement with the book: page layout; use of colour; narrative understatement; verbal and visual humour each contribute to the book's ethical awareness and reconsideration of value. A close reading of the opening pages suffices to demonstrate the playful depth of this deceptively simple and concise picture book. The opening line of *Slow Loris* is understated, and it is the only line to make verbal narrative comment on Loris's opinion of the zoo that contains him: 'Slow Loris lived in a zoo though he didn't care for it much' (p. 5). Verbally, there is no explanation for Loris's lack of enthusiasm for zoo life, but the illustration on this page depicts Loris and a zookeeper in a bare room unmistakably modelled on the interrogation room of a prison or police station (Figure 4.1). The zookeeper is hunched at a table over a pile of written notes and is watching Loris move over the table towards a tangerine beside his notes. The monochrome wash of greys and muted greens mirrors the lethargy of the zookeeper's posture and the ennui suggested

Figure 4.1 Docile bodies interned (p. 5).

Source: Image taken from *Slow Loris* by Alexis Deacon, published by Hutchinson. Used by permission of Alexis Deacon and The Random House Group Limited.

by Loris's expression; both appear trapped and shaped by their environment. Human and creature call to mind Foucault's notion of the docile body in *Discipline and Punish* (1975), whereby society holds 'the body . . . in the grip of very strict powers, which imposed on it constraints, prohibitions or obligations' (1991/1975, p. 136). In the case of *Slow Loris*, physical control is produced by incarceration, as is the case for Loris, and by the discipline of the zoological institution that also appears to affect the zookeeper and render him docile. *Slow Loris* asks where the value comes from in zoos if human and animal are stripped of individual rights and controlled by the demands of the institution.

The visual evocation of dampened human and non-human spirit serves as moral comment alone, still there are further clues on the opening spread to the ethical emphasis of this picture book. Although Loris is caught mid-movement and it is impossible to measure his speed across the table, there is energy in his bearing that contrasts with the zookeeper's inertia, hinting that Loris is not quite the slow creature exhibited to human visitors. Furthermore, a little pencil sketch positioned beneath the publishing information and opposite the (ostensible) first page depicts Loris holding a satsuma and gazing intently – as suggested by his large, intensely black eyes – at a tortoise on a rock beside him (Figure 4.2). Juxtaposed, these images suggest that the slow, slowness of this particular Loris – revealed on subsequent pages – is not an aspect of his nature, instead an evasive ploy to manage the apathy induced by the zoological environment. In this peritextual revelation, the slow tortoise appears to inspire Loris and this translates Loris's excruciatingly slow movement over the subsequent pages – where strip images and full-page spreads are used to draw out time – into a ploy to distract the public from the knowledge that Loris's secret allows him to express and satisfy his wild nature. Alternatively, it could be that in the tortoise's slow movement, Loris sees reflected his own exhaustion (as a result of wild nights) and ennui (a reaction to life in captivity) and that his gaze is one of empathy. However these pages are interpreted, they raise a series of questions about the position of animals in captivity. Loris is forced to 'fake nature' in Robert Elliot's terms,[12] for his behaviour can only ever approximate wild behaviour and the value to be found in his wild state is compromised or negated by zoological conservation. The philosophical subtext to this picture book is radical in nature, but its playful narrative strategies and visual-verbal interplay makes a near secret of its philosophical challenge, covertly asking a number of questions of the reader which might ask what exactly is being conserved by zoos.

Slow Loris is one of a number of philosophical picture books – other examples include *Oi! Get Off Our Train* (1989) by John Burningham; Dyan Sheldon and

Figure 4.2 Slow contemplation (p. 4).

Source: Image taken from *Slow Loris* by Alexis Deacon, published by Hutchinson. Used by permission of Alexis Deacon and The Random House Group Limited.

Gary Blythe's *The Whales' Song* (1990); and *Dear Greenpeace* (1991) by Simon James – that take their momentum from the humane moralism rooted in the animal liberation movement. Malorie Blackman's novel *Pig-Heart Boy* (1997) offers a unique approach to Singer's concern with animal rights, asking directly whether the death of a pig for the life of a boy is a 'fair exchange' (2004/1997, p. 59), and Blackman presents her young readership with an array of divergent ethical positions on the issue of cross-species organ transplantation. Environmental ethics covers wide-ranging moral terrain that can be confrontational and contradictory as positions taken and considered in *Watership Down* and *The Cry of the Wolf* suggest. Such literature feeds into and out of the burgeoning field of ecocriticism. Drawing together environmentalism with the concerns of literary and cultural analysis, ecocriticism spans different academic and social disciplines as anthologized by Glotfelty and Fromm in *The Ecocriticism Reader* (1996) and traced by Greg Garrard in *Ecocriticism* (2004), much of which draws on the early influence of environmental pioneers such as Henry Thoreau, Aldo Leopold, Rachel Carson, and Arne Naess and borders on related domains such as feminism in the work of Kate Soper and Val Plumwood, or Marxist theory in the writing of Mary Mellor or David Pepper. Such interdisciplinary diversity, often motivated by political and ideological conviction, inevitably involves discord, as signalled by Callicott (whose own environmentalism is grounded in Leopold's land ethic) when he makes a plea for unification :

> Moralists of every stripe . . . must make common cause against the forces that are often simultaneously destroying human, mixed, and biotic communities. The differences between human, humane, and environmental concerns are real, and sometimes conflictive. But just as often they are convergent and mutually reinforcing. And all our ethical concerns can be theoretically unified, I am convinced, by a communitarian moral philosophy, thus enabling conflicts, when they do arise, to be adjudicated rationally. (1995/1980, p. 30)

Callicott's philosophy posits that there is much to be gained from drawing together overlapping concerns of ethical environmentalism, while recognizing the serious differences between branches of ethical enquiry. Callicott further acknowledges the priorities of humanist ethics, albeit suggesting that if ethical endeavours must begin with human concerns then they should not end there. Singer observes that up until the early 1970s, 'discussions of equality and rights in moral and political philosophy were almost always formulated as problems of human equality and human rights' (1991/1975, p. 237) and argues that this formulation must be challenged as a matter of urgency. Callicott's communitarian vision allows for human interest to be served from within a wider biotic or 'mixed community', as described by Mary Midgley in *Animals and Why They Matter* (1983) that penetrates 'species-barriers' (p. 117). Evidently Callicott, Singer, and Midgley offer different solutions to human dominance over the natural world, yet they share a conviction that ethics should not proceed from human interest and this conviction shapes the ethical framework in *Watership Down* and *The Cry of the Wolf*.

Biotic communities

Leopold's notion of a land ethic that brings together the biotic sphere into a community of ethical concern can usefully be applied to Richard Adams's *Watership Down*, which represents the natural world with ethical purpose and utilizes anthropomorphism to pull its reader into the land and consequently into the sphere of environmental ethics. *Watership Down* also considers the interests and duties of individuals in a Hegelian (essentially human) notion of community, permitting individuals to challenge bad or unjust societies such as that represented by General Woundwort's *Efrafa*; ethical duty can only be expected of the individual when integrated into a fair and just society, such as that represented by Hazel's warren at the end of *Watership Down*. This concern with human individuals and the social structures that bind them in a web of duty might seem to refuse a land ethic that is holistic in focus and can dispense with the individual in a way that Hegelian – and indeed utilitarian and animal liberationist – theory cannot. These positions inform each other in *Watership Down* though, so the reader is asked to consider the individual rights of animals *and* humans alongside the importance of preserving natural landscapes and biospheres that reach beyond the individual. This mix of ethical perspectives, drawing on the land ethic, ethical humanism, and humane moralism[13] is reflected in the literary traditions informing *Watership Down*; it relates to the naturalism of Jeffries and Williamson, and also descends from the anthropomorphism of Kipling's *Jungle Books* (1894 and 1895) – in its mid-level anthropomorphism – and Beatrix Potter's *Peter Rabbit* books (1902–30[14]) – in its detailed rendering of the British countryside through humanized species.[15] Consequently, *Watership Down* supports a range of ethical positions for the reader's consideration, suggesting that the questions it poses might be answered in a number of ways.

The invitation to see the world (as if) from the perspective of rabbits requires an imaginative leap aided in the opening pages by *external focalization*[16] that allows for a shifting point of view, from the wide focus available to human observation of a scene to a perceptive position closer to the height and ground level of rabbits. The opening passage is broadly sweeping:

> The primroses were over. Towards the edge of the wood, where the ground became open and sloped down to an old fence and a brambly ditch beyond, only a few fading patches of pale yellow still showed among the dog's mercury and oak-tree roots. On the other side of the fence, the upper part of the field was full of rabbit-holes. (Adams, 1973/1972, p. 15)

The object of external focalization here is the landscape, though this is not merely an exercise in scene setting for character interaction. The land represents a point of experience shared by the observing (human) implied reader and the rabbits who evidently reside in the field. The poetic, naturalistic expression of the environment suggests cultural value, developing into an ethical environmentalism as the narrative proceeds. Introducing the 'rabbit-holes' (and by association the rabbits) through this distanced, external focalization, the narrative preserves the reflective distance of 'Frost at Midnight', rendering the woods and fields a human concern at the outset; a concern that nonetheless is connected to rabbit life through the notion of habitat, or home. This is the sort of linking necessary to Leopold's biotic sharing and it is forged as the narrative moves closer to the rabbits themselves, 'nibbling at the thin grass near their holes' (p. 15), eventually describing two rabbits externally before they are identified and named through dialogue. This process of drawing together woodland, rabbits, and human (narrator) moves the implied reader to the position advocated by Leopold in his articulation of land relations free of economic considerations: 'As a land-user thinketh, so is he' (1968/1949, p. 225).

It is a short narrative statement on the first page of *Watership Down* that confirms the ethical impetus and central focus of the narrative, 'The warren was at peace' (Adams, p. 15). The novel's central ethical drive is the conviction that all creatures have a right to habitat (figured in the search for an ideal warren) suited to their species and requirements. The entitlement to peace is also important, but this proceeds from the notion of land, habitat, and community. The land ethic accepts that the environment gives rise to natural dangers and that peace (in the sense of tranquility) can only ever be temporary, hence the rabbits 'avoid close woodland, where the ground is shady, damp and grassless and they feel menaced by the undergrowth' (p. 34), for 'elil'[17] lurks in the darkness. The humane moralism of *Watership Down* renders the human threat to the rabbits' peace and habitat unnatural though, and consequently humans are predators of a different order and are not embraced by the term 'elil'; this is the point at which it is impossible to read *Watership Down* solely as an allegory of human experience (such as military regimes in general, or specifically the Second World War in which Adams served).

The representation of different warren formations and hierarchies in *Watership Down* can be read in allegorical terms as a reflection of human social structure, just as it is true to say that the rabbits' ability to reason and speak anthropomorphizes them and allows for reflection on human behaviour and experience. Nevertheless, it is inaccurate to suggest that stripping away the rabbit skin of Adams's rabbit characters reveals no more than boy-scouts on a journey of survival, bonding, and discovery. The central theme of community is crucial to the ethical structure of *Watership Down*, which explores the possibility of biotic communities – not restricted to human enterprise and endeavour – so the anthropomorphic distance (and relation) between human and non-human is important to understand in terms of the land ethic, or deep ecology posited in Adams' novel. Accordingly the leporine aspects of the rabbits' behaviour are observed and explained in detail by an informed narrator:[18]

> The truth was that every one of them was tired. Many rabbits spend all their lives in the same place and never run more than a hundred yards at a stretch. Even though they may live and sleep above ground for months at a time, they prefer not to be out of distance of some sort of refuge that will serve for a hole. They have two natural gaits – the gentle, lolloping, forward movement of the warren on a summer evening and the lightening dash for cover that every human has seen at some time or other. It is difficult to imagine a rabbit plodding steadily on: they are not built for it. (p. 36)

Aspects of these characters are human, yet they are recognizably rabbits – in their gait, for example – so that they are a rabbit-human fusion and not simply humans in disguise. The level of anthropomorphism employed in *Watership Down* serves to draw human being into the rabbit world and community, from which otherwise humans have excluded themselves. This opens an important space morally for the implied reader, for it suggests that through the communal vision of the land ethic there is a means by which humans might come to live in harmony with the creatures they have persecuted historically. The narrative position of this passage is also worth comment, for the implied reader shifts from observing creatures who reason and talk like her/him – in the sequence of dialogue between Hazel and Bigwig preceding this passage the implied reader is proximal to the characters – to observing creatures with species-specific behaviour via an expositional sequence that distances the implied reader. The narrative position oscillates in such a way that human and rabbit come to partake of common territory – hence sharing an ethical sphere of rights – without being equivalent – ergo having different requirements to satisfy rights. The rights expressed in *Watership Down* are varied, though most stem from the entitlement to a home protected from immediate danger, such as that envisaged by Fiver: '"I know what we ought to be looking for – a high, lonely place with dry soil, where rabbits can see and hear all round and men hardly ever come. Wouldn't that be worth a journey?"' (p. 45). The modal emphasis of 'ought' posits something that should be – were it not for the interference of humans – and Hazel's doubt as to whether there is – or will continue to be – such a place is justified by the destruction of the Sandleford Warren. Related to the basic entitlement to habitat is the right for rabbits to breed freely, as Hyzenthlay asks: '"Shall we mate with whom we choose and dig our own burrows and bear our litters alive?"' (p. 336). The rights called for here – and which are directed to the implied reader as well as to Bigwig, via the shifting focus of Adams's anthropomorphism – fall within the remit of John Rawls's tentative acceptance of humane moralism in *A Theory of Justice* (1971). Although Rawls argues that animals do not fall within his notion of justice because animals do not have the capacity for justice, he concedes:

> . . . it does not follow that there are no requirements at all in regard to them, nor in our relations with the natural order . . . The capacity for feelings of pleasure and pain and for the forms of life of which animals are capable clearly imposes duties of compassion and humanity in their case. (1999/1971, p. 448)

Of particular significance here is that humans might have 'requirements' to animals, and *Watership Down* certainly asks the reader to rethink her/his relation to the natural order through the posing of questions such as those articulated by Fiver and Hyzenthlay. A further question from Bigwig directs attention beyond that which is right, '"It looks as though we really are going to live a natural life again at last, doesn't it?"' (p. 414). Bigwig's emphasis on that which is natural is key to the ethical framework of the book, for any moral threat to the rabbits' entitlements have come from that which opposes nature and might thus be deemed unnatural.

As Kate Soper points out in *What Is Nature?* (1995), the complexity of the term 'nature' is 'concealed by the ease and regularity with which we put it to use in a wide variety of contexts. It is at once both very familiar and extremely elusive' (p. 1), so it is important to establish the way in which Adams's novel defines nature if we are to draw a consideration of the natural and unnatural into the book's ethical framework. John Passmore's tight definition of 'nature' in 'Attitudes to Nature' is helpful, for it reflects an important aspect of the human-nature world balance visible throughout *Watership Down*: 'I shall be using the word "nature" in one of its narrower senses – so as to include only that which, setting aside the supernatural, is human neither in itself nor in its origins' (1995/1975, p. 129). In line with Passmore's definition, that which is unnatural in *Watership Down* has its source in humanity. For example, rabbits displaying characteristics which are not typically leporine have been contaminated by interaction with humans. The megalomaniac General Woundwort is 'not like a rabbit at all' (p. 370) and obsessively avoids human contact after his father, who 'thought nothing of living close to human beings . . . paid dearly for his rashness' (p. 310). From the first chapter, the rabbits' primary enemy is identified as human, although it is the human propensity to dominate and develop land in an environmentally destructive manner that is the main target of ethical concern. That humans are aligned with the unnatural and as a threat to environmental equilibrium is confirmed by the discovery of the notice board:

> Heavy posts, reeking of creosote and paint, towered up as high as the holly trees in the hedge, and the board they carried threw a long shadow across the top of the field. Near one of the posts, a hammer and a few nails had been left behind.
>
> The two rabbits went up to the board at a hopping run and crouched in a patch of nettles on the far side, wrinkling their noses at the smell of a dead cigarette-end somewhere in the grass. Suddenly Fiver shivered and cowered down. (p. 18)

The notice board represents the destructive potential of humankind, and the hard, menacing language – reek, tower, and throw – used to describe its presence contrasts negatively with the opening passage of tangled shrubbery and disordered plant life. The material objects of human industry and indulgence – creosote, paint, hammer, nails, and cigarettes – serve to disturb the tranquility of the warren and to justify Fiver's unease. The rabbits can only sense that the board's presence is somehow other and threatening, but the implied reader is expected to recognize its full implication once the wording on the sign is revealed as advertising for a new housing development. This shift in focalization from rabbit to human perspective and perception draws the reader into the book's ethical framework, encouraging her/him to engage with the implications of human dominion over the natural world. The question being asked of the reader is whether it is morally right to champion the needs of one species over another and whether it is justified to slaughter animals and destroy their habitat in order to accommodate humanity. The full force of human moral responsibility is held back until Holly's graphic description of the careless – ' "The men had done their work badly . . . Either they didn't know about the wood holes or they couldn't be bothered to come and block them" ' (p. 164) – and cruel destruction of the warren. There is no doubting the narrative position when Fiver observes that ' "There's terrible evil in the world" ' and Holly responds:

> 'It comes from men . . . All other elil do what they have to do and Frith moves them as he moves us. They live on the earth and they need food. Men will never rest till they've spoiled the earth and destroyed the animals.' (p. 159)

Holly's distinction between categories of elil is important, since it locates evil in that which acts against nature. Natural predators are not evil because they 'do what they have to do' and so the notion of natural evil is refused here; foxes and badgers hunt, winters starve and summers drought, yet this accords with the harmony of the biotic sphere and the resulting trauma or privation must be accepted. (Although there are hints throughout *Watership Down* that the biotic sphere might not be as 'natural' as it might appear. Human presence is peripheral, devastating, and associated with mechanism, technology, and industry. The recurrent, chemical smell of cigarettes metonymically represents human endeavour and implies a negative impact on the environment that could alter the pattern of predatory behaviour of elil mentioned by Holly. As Leopold points out, 'man-made changes are of a different order than evolutionary changes, and have effects more comprehensive than is intended or foreseen' [p. 218].) Evil is located in that which surpasses need and takes more from the Earth than is necessary and humans are the only creatures, in the terms articulated here, to consume at the expense of all other creatures. That evil is primarily a human phenomenon recalls Svendsen's point that it is caused by the sort of people described by Holly, going about their jobs without seeming to consider or care about the consequences: 'In the end it is we – we normal, more or less decent, respectable people – who are responsible for the most damage. We are the only explanation for all the evil in the world' (2010/2001, p. 11).[19]

The mythical framework of *Watership Down* is also significant at this point, for it allows a challenge to the Christian myth that dominated human-animal relations for centuries in Europe, an influence which even enlightenment philosophy was unable to shed; as Singer points out, there is little in the history of philosophical endeavour prior to Bentham to challenge the Old Testament position, 'laid down in Genesis, that the human species is the pinnacle of creation and has God's permission to kill and eat other animals' (1991/1975, p. 188). In replacing God with Frith, the mythological structure of the book strips humanity of permission to dominate the natural world; Frith has not required humans to behave as they do and as a result they must take responsibility for their actions. Not only is evil human then, it is also 'primarily a moral category and effects a person's every actions' (Svendsen, p. 37). Elil cannot be held responsible for the mythological (or evolutionary) developments that require them to kill other creatures in order to survive, and when humans exceed their needs they enter into the bounds of immorality. Holly's attribution of evil is supported by the narrative structure and stance of *Watership Down*, though this is not to say that Holly's word on the matter is final.

Watership Down is more broadly philosophical than Holly's charge of human evil might suggest, but in order to establish this it is necessary to show that the book is not remorselessly misanthropic. This is partly intimated by the demonstrated level of anthropomorphism, fusing human and animal behaviour; an indication that relations between humans and non-humans can be sympathetic and mutual. The chapter in which Hazel is rescued by the farmer's daughter Lucy is pivotal in introducing the possibility of a land ethic in which humans can be 'biotic citizens' (Leopold, p. 223). 'Dea ex Machina' is the only chapter in which narrative focalization switches to a human, and in spite of Adams's wry acknowledgement that this is a plot contrivance to extract Hazel from a difficult situation, it is crucial to the opening of philosophical possibility or hope. Lucy is established as a girl in tune with the natural world – as she wakes and recognizes that 'A wood-pigeon was calling in the elms' and wonders whether there would be any mushrooms in the field (p. 458) – and this is confirmed by Doctor Adams,[20] a locus for adult and professional authority with whom Lucy is cultivating friendship, who 'thought of her as a proper farm girl – a country girl' (p. 460). This human sensitivity to nature is important given the unnatural qualities of humanity pursued elsewhere. Lucy's musings on a future for herself require the approval of Doctor Adams and her vague ambitions involve her knowledge of and affinity for the natural world: 'When she showed him things she had found – a goldfinch's egg, a Painted Lady fluttering in a jam-jar . . . he took her seriously and talked to her as he would to a grown-up person' (p. 460). Lucy's father eventually agrees to let her show Hazel to Doctor Adams because he is proud of their relationship – 'Doctor had said once or twice she was real sensible with these things she picked up' – and of a daughter bound for the grammar school 'so they told him' (p. 460). Lucy has potential, as yet undefined, seemingly linked to her interest in and desire to help Hazel.

Lucy responds to Hazel's cry as he is attacked by the cat, recognizing that his cry suggests pain or terror, feelings denied to animals by Cartesian philosophy which argues that since animals do not have souls they are not conscious; as Voltaire playfully summarizes: 'Descartes affirms that the soul is the same thing as thought' (Voltaire, 1980/1734, p. 68). The Cartesian position must be countered if a land ethic is to be proposed and take root, for Descartes approves the human dominion over animals and Earth, and also (even if inadvertently) denies creatures the care and sympathy towards animals advocated variously by Hume and Voltaire (and a range of philosophers who challenge Cartesian conclusions).[21] Hume observes, 'Animals are found susceptible of kindness, both to their own species and to ours; nor is there, in this case, the least suspicion of disguise or artifice' and goes on to ask, if we 'admit a disinterested benevolence in the inferior species, by what rule of analogy can we refuse it in the superior?' (1975/1751, p. 300), while Voltaire comments, 'How pitiful, how mean, to say that animals are machines without feeling or consciousness, who always do things the same way, never learn anything, never perfect anything, and so on' (2011/1764, p. 41). Voltaire's opinion is also echoed by the 15-year-old writer of a pony story published in the 'Young Rider's Section' of *Riding*: 'A lot of people say that animals have no souls and that they have no Heaven. Apparently only humans have these advantages. But I don't believe that' (Weddell, 1940, p. 282).

Voltaire (and Weddell) attests to the feeling in animals that Lucy has responded to and Hume argues for human benevolence based on the fact that it can be observed in animals, so drawing animals into the sphere of moral concern; and he even hints at moral agency in animals. Lucy calls on this agency when she admonishes her cat for being cruel, though it is her farmer father who must point out to her that making a pet of Hazel would be more callous and that ' "Cat was doin' 'is job then. Did oughter've let 'im finish be roights" ' (p. 460). Father and daughter each recognize that the rabbit has rights, while expressing this entitlement differently. The farmer's pragmatic view seeks to end the creature's suffering, whereas Lucy's view is less clear. Her reaction to paternal disapproval is to cry, though these tears are misleading and might seem to hinder an ethical consideration of animals for the reasons expressed by Midgley:

> A sense of unreality often blocks our attempts to understand our moral relations with animals. The whole question is hard to fit into our ethical system. Arguments for taking it seriously tend to be dismissed rather than met, to be stigmatized wholesale as perverse, sentimental, emotive, childish, impractical, superstitious, insincere – somehow not solid. (1983, p. 9)

Lucy's involvement with Hazel could seem an unwise strategy for opening a path to ethical possibility and consideration, for she is a child responding to the situation before her with an emotional outburst of tears; her role might then be dismissed by anyone who argues that emotion negates reason and obstructs the practical considerations of morality. Lucy's behaviour might better be described as childly, rather than childish, for she brings with her the pastoral tradition of Romantic childhood and also the knowing edge of the philosopher articulated in 'Frost at Midnight'. Furthermore, as Midgley points out, emotional responses such as disgust and revulsion can be crucial in motivating ethical concern: 'Real scruples, and eventually moral principles, are developed out of this kind of raw material. They would not exist without it' (1983, p. 43). Lucy's reaction to Hazel neatly illustrates Midgley's point as it shifts from an emotional to a considered response in which Lucy balances Hazel's needs – '"No good to keep 'im, though, Doctor, would it? In 'utch, I mean"' – with those of her father's farm, '"Dad'd be ever s'woild, though, if I was to let 'im go anywheres round 'ere. 'E always says one rabbit means 'undred an' one"' (p. 462). In considering the consequences of her actions at this point and assessing the moral claims of farmer and rabbit, Lucy acts in line with Mill's vision of 'Utility', which 'holds that actions are right in proportion as they tend to promote happiness, wrong as they tend to produce the reverse of happiness' (Mill and Bentham, 1987, p. 278).[22] Additionally, in considering that which produces happiness, Bentham observes that benevolence to animals can result in 'the pleasures of good will, the pleasures of sympathy, or the pleasures of the benevolent or social affections' (Mill and Bentham, 1987, p. 92).[23] Lucy's actions, laughing and skipping (p. 462), express the pleasure gained from her resolution to the problem before her, but her benevolent act in returning Hazel to the wild also moves beyond a utilitarian concern for the happiness of the most individuals, for in this act she inadvertently ensures the future of Hazel's warren and the surrounding community. In a car journey that symbolically shortens the distance between human farm and natural space, the concerns of Leopold's land ethic that considers the well-being of the entire biosphere begin to be met.[24] As Lucy and Doctor Adams watch Hazel dash 'away over the grass' (p. 463), their action might seem to satisfy Leopold's conviction as he considers the outlook for human relationships with the land (in the broadest sense):

> It is inconceivable to me that an ethical relation to land can exist without love, respect, and admiration for land, and a high regard for its value. By value, I of course mean something far broader than mere economic value; I mean value in the philosophical sense. (1968/1949, p. 223)

Hazel's release sets the tone for the final two chapters in which the rabbits settle into a present transcribed with future prosperity and survival, investing the land with a value recognized in the ethical relation to land Leopold describes. *Watership Down* reaches towards this metaphorically in the alliances forged between rabbits, mice, and birds. Hazel's leadership envisages a community of mutual support and exchange among species, insisting that '"If anyone finds an animal or bird, that isn't an enemy, in need of help, for goodness' sake don't miss the opportunity. That would be like leaving carrots to rot in the ground"' (p. 171). This is not Hume's disinterested benevolence, rather a recognition that ethics can be forged on the requirements of community. This notion of community underscores the thematic focus on habitat in *Watership Down*, drawing together human and non-human in the search for land and an egalitarian social structure that can be read in terms of human and non-human relevance and consequence.

In a book which on the whole renders humanity an acquisitive and brutal enemy of the land it seems significant, considering that editions continue to be published for children, that hope is carried by a human child. In the 1970s, the drive towards a more pessimistic outlook had yet to establish itself in children's literature, an ideological journey explored by Hollindale in his essay, 'Hope against Hope' (2011). To some degree Lucy fulfils a Romantic vision of childhood, yet she is also envisaged in Leopold's outlook for the future as a being who values the land through philosophical and thoughtful care, allowing the implied reader to take a moral position distanced from the predatory men with 'shining wire' and 'white sticks'. Though much more brief,[25] a similar invitation to ethical agency is offered in *Tarka the Otter*, an ethical predecessor to *Watership Down*. As the hunt pursues Tarka to the kelt pool of the River Torridge, lookouts are employed to glimpse the otter:

> . . . a scarlet dragonfly whirred and darted over the willow snag, watched by a girl sitting on the bank. Her father, an old man lank and humped as a heron, was looking out near her. She watched the dragonfly settle on what looked like a piece of bark beside the snag; she heard a sneeze, and saw the otter's whiskers scratch the water. Glancing round, she realized that she alone had seen the otter. She flushed, and hid her grey eyes with her lashes. Since childhood she had walked the Devon rivers with her father, looking for flowers and the nests of birds, passing some rocks and trees as old friends, seeing a Spirit everywhere, gentle in thought to all her eyes beheld.
>
> For two minutes the maid sat silent, hardly daring to look at the river. (Williamson, 1963/1927, p. 234)

I cite this passage in full for its import in terms of moral agency outweighs its relative brevity in *Tarka the Otter*. Agency is enabled by this temporary shift in narrative focalization, expressing a communion with nature essential to a land ethic and philosophical contemplation as beholding shifts to 'gentle' thinking. This is the gentleness of consideration and benevolence, as expressed by Bentham and its rightness seems to be confirmed in Tarka's escape from the hunt; his escape is not expressly attributed to 'the maid', but the two minutes of silence mourns creatures lost to an unnatural death and envisages a more gentle future for them.

Epiphany in green

The intervention of the child protagonist in naturalistic writing can be seen as a motif for a forward-thinking through of environmental ethics, and in Melvin Burgess's (1990) *The Cry of the Wolf* this motif takes on a different emphasis from that in *Watership Down* and *Tarka*. *The Cry of the Wolf* is not a piece of naturalistic writing, rather a modern fable imagining that English wolves remain on British shores and that a relentless hunter seeks their extinction by his hand. Naturalistic fiction for young people in Britain is bridged by *Watership Down*, a landmark text that links the naturalism of the early twentieth century with later environmental fantasies – such as *The Duncton Chronicles* (1980–93) by William Horwood, or *The Gnole* (1991), Alan Aldridge's venture into ecological fantasy – that are indebted to Tolkien's high fantasy in *The Hobbit* (1937) and the naturalistic vision of *Watership Down*. In fact the tradition of fusing narrative and sustained naturalistic writing in prose for young people faded from the forefront of children's publishing after the 1970s. This is not to suggest that environmental concerns vanished from children's literature, instead that they are pursued through different narrative techniques and genres – such as the meta-fictive play of Gillian Cross's *Wolf* (1990); the dystopic fantasy of Philip Reeves's *Mortal Engines* quartet (2001–6); or Michelle Paver's Mesolithic quest, *Chronicles of Ancient Darkness* (2004–9) – and different literary forms, such as poetry and the picture book in the latter part of the twentieth century, moving into the twenty first.

The ethical core of *The Cry of the Wolf* expresses in fictive form the moment of epiphany described by Leopold in his sketch 'Thinking Like a Mountain' during which Leopold observes, 'Only the mountain has lived long enough to listen objectively to the howl of a wolf' (1968/1949, p. 129). Leopold relates the tale of when he came upon a wolf and her pups during an expedition into Arizona's White Mountain, 'What was literally a pile of wolves writhed and tumbled in the center of an open flat at the foot of our rimrock' and he explains, 'In those days we had never heard of passing up a chance to kill a wolf. In a second we were pumping lead into the pack' (p. 130). Confounding for some readers perhaps, Leopold's direct tone and honesty is important if the shift in his thinking is to be understood:

> We reached the old wolf in time to watch a fierce green fire dying in her eyes. I realized then, and have known ever since, that there was something new to me in those eyes – something known only to her and to the mountain. I was young then, and full of trigger-itch; I thought that because fewer wolves meant more deer, that no wolves would mean hunters' paradise. But after seeing the green fire die, I sensed that neither the wolf nor the mountain agreed with such a view. (p. 130)

In this moment, Leopold recognizes that the drive to rid the American wilderness of wolves is actually to destroy wilderness itself; elsewhere he points out, 'Wilderness is the raw material out of which man has hammered the artifact called civilization' (p. 188) and that nothing more than 'wild spots' remain. Leopold's moment of revelation is not driven by sentiment, rather by a profound sense of loss reflected in the eyes of a wolf which he (and humankind) had killed through a misguided sense of wisdom, right, and dominion. This loss is rendered poetically by Ted Hughes as he observes, 'The Howling of Wolves/ Is without world',[26] though Hughes also conveys the supernatural (and thus the wolf is at a double remove from humanity) quality of the wolf's howl; the wolf's howl conveys physical loss and epistemological lack. Leopold argues that policies to strip the 'wilderness' of predators such as wolves, lions, and bears have split the wilderness to build cars for hunters brought in to manage big-game herds of elk or deer and that this is just one away in which the environment is falling out of balance (p. 191). In Leopold's view, human civilization is robbing the mountain of its ear and voice. For all that conservation strategies attempt to reclaim areas of wilderness, their fauna will have been damaged beyond repair, for 'Wilderness is a resource which can shrink but not grow' (p. 199).

A related observation informs the ethical structure of *The Cry of the Wolf*, as evinced in the narrative description of Greycub 'stalking and walking unseen through the man-made countryside' (Burgess, 2011/1990, p. 76) and eventually making 'the wilderness of Scotland' his territory, 'the only place in the British Isles where he could feel truly remote from human kind' (p. 113). In *The Cry of the Wolf*, humanity has encroached to such an extent that nature is starting to disappear – reflected in the Hunter's extermination of all but one English wolf – and its point of origin obliterated by human development and mechanization; the description of the space travelled by Greycub, the last English wolf, mirrors his search for another member of his own species and his point of origin. Deprived of species and community (in the biotic sense) membership, Greycub's fruitless journey confirms that something precious has been lost to the world, 'He was a relic, in whom wolf culture had never blossomed. The society that had given his kind a way of life for so long was already extinct. He was a ghost whose narrow life had no hope of widening' (p. 113). Although Greycub survives his final confrontation with the Hunter, his future has already been denied him through the human destruction of environment and origin; in space and time, the wolf ceases to exist. Readers are asked to consider whether any amount of 'man-made countryside' can compensate for that privation and the reader's ethical agency is prompted in *The Cry of the Wolf* by an act of restoration that triggers a thought experiment.

In 'Faking Nature' (1982), Robert Elliot defends and builds a case for ethical resistance to restoration conservation. Building a thought experiment to bolster his argument, Elliot hypothesizes a mining company offering to restore to its original condition a dune area of beach sands after the extraction of minerals which will destroy the landscape: 'In other words they are claiming that the destruction of what has value is compensated for by the later creation (re-creation) of something of equal value. I shall call this "the restoration thesis"' (Elliot, 1995/1982, p. 76). In Elliot's view, the 'restoration thesis' is used to undermine environmental protest, and he demonstrates that 'there is at least a prima facie case for partially explaining the value of objects in terms of their origins, in terms of the kinds of processes that brought them into being' and that natural landscapes (for example) are valued in part for 'a special kind of continuity with the past' (p. 81). The narrative contempt implied in Burgess's 'man-made countryside' is supported by Elliot's argument. Elliot refutes the restoration thesis through philosophical reasoning, while *The Cry of the Wolf* invalidates it through narrative imagining; in each case, thought experiments are employed to show why restoration is fundamentally flawed.

Restoring the English wolf to British shores, the fabulous premise of *The Cry of the Wolf* demonstrates the avaricious spread of humanity – represented by the polarized extremes of adult evil (the Hunter) and child ignorance (Ben Tilley) – postulating that the nature of human civilization refuses the existence of the wolf. The presence of Burgess's English wolf in an otherwise realist narrative is unsettling (and consequently thought provoking) precisely because this long-extinct[27] creature seems a credible and (un)familiar part of the British landscape through which Burgess allows it to roam once more; its presence is uncanny and points to the impossibility of restoration. The English wolf takes on the modal provocation of philosophy, since the narrative makes it clear that it *should* not be a creature of fantasy; still it is an anomaly in contemporary Britain. That the English wolf *ought* to exist is confirmed by paean in prose – Greycub's 'coat was a shimmering field of silver flecked with gold' (p. 107) – yet the impossibility of its existence is confirmed by the brutal directness[28] of dispatch: 'The first bolt took Conna directly through the neck. His spine was not severed, but the central artery to his head was cut, and he was able to crawl a few meters into the undergrowth before choking on his own blood' (p. 78). The relentless hunt to exterminate the wolves, the diminishing space in which they have to flee, and the brutality of each execution emphasizes the finality of species extinction and shrinking land mass, confronting the reader with an accumulation of stark images designed to arouse ethical engagement. Burgess is writing during a period in which conservation was visibly on public and political agendas, with campaigns arguing for the reintroduction of lost species gaining momentum during the 1990s;[29] *The Cry of the Wolf* enters this debate via a thought experiment in species restoration, asking what might happen were English wolves to roam the British Isles once more and how humans might respond to them.

Once again, narrative focalization is central to the engagement with the philosophical framework of the book. *The Cry of the Wolf* employs variable focalization, which changes narrative focus from chapter to chapter, alternating between: Ben Tilley (a young boy who betrays and befriends the wolves); the Hunter; and the wolves/wolf (for plural is hunted into singular). Each chapter is limited to a single point of external focalization with a (slightly variable) restriction of field[30] that builds suspense as the wolf-man hunt proceeds. During the chapters focused on the Hunter, the threat posed to the wolves by his relentless ambition is evident:

> To kill the very last remaining one. Someone had killed the last bear in England; someone had killed the last beaver. If you did something first, it could be done over and over again after you; but to do something last made you unique, and the Hunter wanted that more than anything. (p. 13)

As the English wolves diminish the Hunter's resolve becomes increasingly fierce (even pathological), so when the narrative returns its focus to the wolves, the

Hunter becomes a hidden menace, striking the wolves (and reader) unawares, disrupting descriptive passages closely focused on the wolves. When Silver (pack leader at the outset) gives birth to her cubs, the intimate description of pups suckling and tumbling is interrupted abruptly, 'She heard the soft and violent thud ahead of her twice . . . The sound of another bolt in the air came in the same second and there was a sickening bloody thud on her own shoulder' (p. 31). The narrative pace does not allow the reader to settle into a smoothly flowing story, for direction and pace are altered as focalization shifts and the plight of the wolves becomes desperate. The narrative structure mirrors the erratic changes in direction taken by the wolves as they flee the Hunter, conveying a sense of deep disturbance that reaches beyond the wolves represented on the page.

Perhaps the most significant narrative intervention comes during the chapters that focus on Ben Tilley whose involvement with the wolves engages with traditional concepts of childhood,[31] while also shifting the direction of hope offered by the benign and innocent child motif in naturalistic writing. On the opening page, Ben Tilley is situated in a Romantic space that plays midday to 'Frost at Midnight':

> Ben Tilley lay on the banks of the River Mole keeping very quiet. It was a still, hot day. The river moved silently below him, and around him in the grass there were tiny rustlings and scratches from insects about their business. A robin was singing nearby and the sun beat down, baking into his back, pressing him into the dry mud. (p. 1)

The child located in natural space offers a familiar and comfortable vision of childhood; a vision disrupted immediately by the presence of a gun in his hands, described in some detail. This is not the gun deployed by the boys in *The Children of the New Forest, Bevis,* or *Brendon Chase,* for ideological shifts since the early twentieth century have rendered hunting – and Ben is hunting water rats – deeply controversial; the 2004 Hunting Act outlawed fox hunting, deer hunting, and hare coursing in England and Wales[32] after years of protest and political wrangling. Inexperienced and anxious – he has stolen his father's air pistol – Ben struggles to hit his quarry and his movements attract the attention of the Hunter who demonstrates his skill by shooting at a sparrow and then a bird in the bushes invisible to Ben's novice eye: 'Ben looked down at the bird. Its beak was open and stained with blood . . . Its breast was red too, but not with blood. "But it's a robin," he said' (p. 5). Ben is not able to explain his distress at the death of a robin over a sparrow or a rat and the Hunter sneers at his hypocrisy. Fleetingly, this moment confronts innocence with evil and innocence quails in its presence; but to read

Ben's reactions in terms of innocence is to misunderstand the direction of hope articulated through Ben in *The Cry of the Wolf*. Unlike Lucy in *Watership Down* or the maiden in *Tarka the Otter* – characters who render human evil adult – Ben does not represent hope that a future generation might live in communion with animals and the wider environment. The hope vested in Ben is that future generations will take moral responsibility and recognize that human evil is not the preserve of adulthood.

Embedded in theological and cultural traditions which Ben's grief suggests that he is subliminally aware of – robins are present in at least two classics of children's literature, *Peter Rabbit* and *The Secret Garden* – the robin's death marks the end of childhood ignorance and a rousing of ethical awareness. The Hunter's derision of sentiment is rooted in callous resolve and, coming from a polar position, Singer argues that hypocritical and 'sentimental appeals for sympathy toward "cute" animals' are problematic because they have 'the effect of excluding the entire issue of our treatment of nonhumans from serious political and moral discussion' (1991/1975, p. iii). Ben's robin is equivalent to Leopold's wolf in this moment and no longer will Ben wield his gun with the same youthful 'trigger-itch'. The Hunter's goading confounds Ben momentarily though and he responds with boastful retaliation, exclaiming: ' "You could hunt the wolves" ' (p. 6). In this pronouncement, Ben alerts the Hunter to the wolves' existence and betrays the creatures he comes to love when they seek sanctuary on his father's farm; in this reckless moment of self-regard, Ben becomes eternally accountable for the wolves' demise, whispering to Greycub at their final parting: ' "You wouldn't lick me if you knew what I'd done" ' (p. 108). *The Cry of the Wolf* demonstrates that as a human child Ben is no less entangled in the social structures and cultural traditions that privilege humanity over 'wolves' than the Hunter who makes a trophy of his conquests, 'The room was full of dead wolves – their skins, their skulls, their teeth. [. . .]There were heads mounted on the wall, blind things, worse than dead, that no longer even smelled like wolf, gathering dust on their dry teeth and black gums' (p. 116). Ben's culpability draws him closer to the Hunter, and it seems that the Hunter might not represent human evil, rather civilization as humans have fashioned it. In this formulation, the Hunter is not an aberration; he is a material product of the evil Svendsen recognizes in the 'normal' people who populate a diminishing wilderness; people like Ben and his parents. If the child Ben is charged with hypocrisy and guilt, where does this leave the implied reader? At the very least, moral awareness is expected of the reader in the very first chapter.

The friendship that develops between boy and wolf when Greycub returns to High Pond Farm is culturally charged and can only claim a future in an imagined space beyond physical experience, nonetheless optimism also lies in the persistence of literary tradition – reaching from mythical versions of 'Romulus and Remus' to Kipling's *Jungle Books* and on to Ted Hughes who recognizes that the 'crying of a baby . . . Brings the wolves running' – rooted in goodness and moral balance. In *Savage Girls and Wild Boys* (2002), Michael Newton explores historical cases of feral children reared in the wilderness; impossible children in terms of Burgess's wilderness-free fable and Leopold's sketches. Tracing the cultural fascination with feral children, Newton ponders the Roman reception of the Romulus and Remus myth, observing that in a tale riddled with the discreditable and forbidden, it is remarkable that 'the transgressive element that most scandalized the Romans was precisely the one that concerns us here; that is, the twins' suckling from the she-wolf' (p. 5). Later versions of the tale transformed the wolf into a prostitute, eradicated the wolf who had sought to counteract the consequences of evil, and consequently robbed the myth of a moral lesson about the positive balance between humanity and nature. As Newton points out, the she-wolf's act of kindness is crucial to understanding the story: 'Nature's mercy admonishes humanity's unnatural cruelty: only a miracle of *kindness* can restore the imbalance created by human iniquity' (p. 5). In his reinvention of this myth, Burgess demonstrates the consequences of human cruelty and iniquity in the Hunter's persecution of the wolves and the wider destruction of wilderness, leaving the child to succour the wolf (inverting the motif) and the wolf to serve justice on the Hunter (and humankind). The child is then the source of kindness once enacted by the she-wolf and in showing compassion to Greycub, Ben achieves hope for humanity, if not a restoration of balance (which Burgess has shown to be impossible). Ben is not innocent, still his acceptance of this renders him a moral agent with the potential to make amends for his childhood betrayal; just as Leopold makes amends through his honest ability to reconsider his own convictions through philosophical engagement. The hope endowed in Ben is limited though – and this is the cultural shift towards pessimism that Hollindale traces – for having demonstrated that the restoration thesis is flawed, it is clear that loss recovery is not an option; consequently Burgess leaves his reader (through Ben) with a complex ethical conundrum to resolve.

Watership Down and *The Cry of the Wolf* engage with a range of ethical positions, inviting the implied reader to consider the rights of animals and humans, the welfare of the land and biosphere and the human encroachment into wilderness. Burgess and Adams address their readers with the honesty demanded by Singer in the early 1970s, confronting them with images that inform and provoke rather than protect. In each novel, the presence of the child beckons to the implied reader in an opening of ethical discourse, suggesting that it is in the area of moral engagement and agency that the questions they raise can be deliberated. Published almost 20 years apart, these novels reveal that in the development and growth of environmental ethics during this period, so too the child figure is wrought with fainter hope, and the shift to a more pessimistic rendering of the world seems an important tool in the provocation of deep thinking.

Paper-makery

Hope remains nonetheless in the environmental impetus of the British publishing industry, evinced in a range of different ethically aware books produced for children and teenagers in the last five years. In *Can We Save the Tiger?* (2011), Martin Jenkins and Vicky White address the youngest readers in their deletion of the modal qualification in Rawls's observation that 'the destruction of a whole species can be a great evil' (p. 448). The educative approach of the verbal text assumes that species extinction is bad and that the reintegration of extinct species is good, which Holmes Rolston III argues in not always the case in 'Duties to Endangered Species' (1995/1985). In the final lines of *Can We Save the Tiger?*, Jenkins observes: 'the chances are that pretty soon we'll end up with a world where there are no tigers or elephants, or sawfishes or whooping cranes, or albatrosses or ground iguanas. And I think that would be a shame, don't you?' (p. 51). There might seem little space for philosophical debate in the directed interrogative here, yet having provided young readers with facts that they might not be aware of, the detailed illustrations use space, colour, and tone[33] to engage the reader and move beyond the facts into creative consideration of extinction and restoration. Books that reach beyond a contemplation of animals and species extinction also engage young people in ethical issues relevant to a society altering rapidly about them. Sharing ground with *The Baby and Fly Pie*, Andy Mulligan's *Trash* (2010) employs the compelling pace of the thriller (and a varied narrative that shifts in voice and tone) to draw young British readers into a childhood built on the excreta of capitalism:

> Most of those people live in boxes, and the boxes are stacked up tall and high.
> So, when you use the toilet, you do it on a piece of paper, and you wrap it up and
> put it in the trash. The trash bags come together. All over the city, trash bags get
> loaded onto carts, and from carts onto trucks or even trains – you'd be amazed

at how much trash this city makes. Piles and piles of it, and it all ends up here with us. (2011/2010, p. 3)

As the mystery behind a trash bag discovered by Raphael (one of the book's teenage protagonists) is revealed, so the structures of power are implicated in corruption, murder, and betrayal of those most in need, involving the young reader in a process of moral implication, discovery, and condemnation. The authorial notes further entice readers into an engagement with the boundaries of fact and fiction, asking them to imagine what it might be like to live on a trash heap in Manila and to consider the biotic price of such consumption: 'Behala dumpsite is based loosely on a place Andy visited while living in Manila. There really is a school there, and there really are children who will crawl through trash for ever.'[34] In another form of thought experiment, the author creates a fantasy world, only to reveal it as close to someone's reality. What the reader might do with such a discovery is beyond the scope of this discussion, but if the reader's mind accepts the invitation to travel it might just challenge the statement that these children will 'crawl through trash forever'.

In a picture book published on FSC paper[35] that neatly draws together the concerns of this chapter, *The Great Paper Caper* (2008) by Oliver Jeffers deals with rubbish of a different nature. Living in a communal space beneath a forest, a pig, duck, fox, beaver, and boy notice that tree branches are disappearing mysteriously and they decide to investigate because 'Branches, they agreed, should not disappear from trees like that' (p. 6[36]). The modal insistence here confirms an ethical position uniting the animals, who are prone to squabble. That vanishing wood is considered an ethical issue is confirmed by the penal and judicial process undertaken on discovery that the bear has been stealing branches in order to make paper planes now littering the forest. The bear admits his guilt before a jury of forest creatures and confesses that 'he hadn't meant to do so much harm' (p. 32). Jeffers treats the bear's offence with a comic gravity, drawing attention to the environmental issues being raised and the bear is rewarded for his acceptance of moral responsibility with a paper plane recycled from those he had scattered round the forest (in his attempt to win the 112th Paper Plane competition that his ancestors had won before him). The communal efforts of the forest creatures to locate environmental harm and to restore balance embrace Leopold's vision of a philosophy that challenges prevailing attitudes: 'We shall hardly relinquish the shovel, which after all has many good points, but we are in need of a gentler and more objective criteria for its successful use' (1968/1949, p. 226). This shift is figured in the wordless image that closes the book in which the bear appears to have given up his (wooden) ancestral home in exchange for a small caravan and is watering a sapling, rather than pushing logs through the sort of mechanized, polluting monstrosity (as depicted earlier in *The Great Paper Caper*) so abhorred by Leopold.

Garrard observes, ' "Pollution" has seeped into our culture in many areas and on various levels of representation' (2004, p. 12), and in its refusal of pollutants, specifically litter and fumes, Jeffers's picture book takes its place in a cultural tradition looking back to Charles Dickens's *Hard Times* (1854) and Rachel Carson's *Silent Spring* (1962). Garrard warns, 'Pollution has become a spectacle that is almost detached from any real sense of threat thanks to the ubiquity of such images' (p. 13), but Jeffers counters this Baudrillardian vacuity through the gap created by a wordless illustration. The silence of the final image (Figure 4.3) is key for, like Deacon in *Slow Loris*, Jeffers never articulates the environmental messages at work in *The Great Paper Caper*. Ethical language and a playful parody of judicial process points the reader in the direction of thoughtful engagement with issues raised and hope rests on its vision of land used by human (boy) working from within the land and alongside the non-humans that inhabit it; as Leopold observes, 'Conservation is a state of harmony between men and land' (1968, p. 207). A 'secret recipe' hidden beneath the cover of Jeffers's book might well dispute the moral position that books should not be defaced, but the active invitation to 'paper-makery' could produce in the reader Coleridge's midnight philosopher. Paper-makery cannot and does not seek to undo the advance of technology, even so it involves a change of pace in the shift from machine to man-made; from mechanization to creative recycling.

Books such as *The Great Paper Caper* are part of the cultural crop envisaged by Leopold when he maintains: 'That land is a community is the basic concept of ecology, but that land is to be loved and respected is an extension of ethics. That land yields a cultural harvest is a fact long known, but latterly often forgotten' (1968/1949, pp. viii–ix). Writing in the late 1940s, Leopold identifies a social amnesia that works of children's literature explored in this chapter address directly. The environmental awareness precipitated by the global success of *Watership Down* in the 1970s has receded somewhat, yet children's books continue to shape ecological thinkers in the readers they imagine as other commentators have pointed out. During his discussion of narrative strategies employed in recent children's texts that parallel eco consciousness with cathetic relationships,[37] Stephens remarks, 'While, as Booth conceded, there is no hard evidence that a particular story can be the cause of moral transformation in a reader, as critics we will judge a work's potential moral or ethical efficacy

Figure 4.3 Sprouting paper-makery (p. 38).
Source: Reprinted by permission of HarperCollins Publishers Ltd. © 2008, Oliver
Jeffers, The Great Paper Caper.

according to how ethically framed actions are realised' (2010, p. 206). Making a
related point in 'The Darkening Green',[38] Hollindale observes that while 'There is
no profit in making silly claims for children's literature . . . Children's books are
not going to change the world, or perform any rescue acts', it is true that 'they
can help some children to think radically about their own species and the global

habitat it should but does not care for' (2011, p. 94). Hollindale evokes his own memories of television programming and books that effectively awoke in him moral agency and which 'had a decisive effect on my own beliefs, the colour of which is the very darkest green, shading into black' (p. 79). The self-reflective impetus to Hollindale's eco-critical readings bolsters my view that children's literature can stimulate a process linking ideas or images to thinking through, and that it can alter the way in which young people perceive, respond to, and engage with the human and non-human world ethically.

The Making of Monsters: Duty, Gender, and the Rightness of Wrong

*Now the moral law in its purity and genuineness (and in the practical this is
what matters most) is to be sought nowhere else than in a pure philosophy;
hence this (metaphysics) must come first, and without it there can be no moral
philosophy at all.*

Kant, 1998/1785, p. 4

Patience is a virtue,
Virtue is a grace;
And Grace is a little girl
Who doesn't wash her face.

Traditional[1]

*A revolution in thought and ethics is needed if the work of sexual difference is
to take place. [. . .] Man has been the subject of discourse, whether in theory,
morality, or politics. And the gender of God, the guardian of every subject and
every discourse, is always masculine and paternal, in the West. To women are
left the so-called minor arts: cooking, knitting, embroidery, and sewing; and,
in exceptional cases, poetry, painting, and music. Whatever their importance,
these arts do not currently make the rules, at least not overtly.*

Irigaray, 2004/1984, p. 8

Law breaking

Between Kant and Irigaray lies a refusal of the conditions of virtue demanded
of pure philosophy and moral law, together with a manoeuvre from abstract

(morals) to physical (mores) that opens a space for the female body (of thought). Kant might identify the parodic target of this traditional rhyme as the 'marvellous mixture' of morality that parents hand their children in accordance with 'attempts at morality in that popular taste' (1998/1785, p. 22), for Kant is scornful of approaches to education that prepare children for '*possible*' concerns in the future through teaching '*a great many things*', yet 'commonly neglect to form and correct their children's judgement about the worth of the things that they might make their ends' (p. 26). The unwashed ends articulated in this playful rhyme are precisely those that Kant considers irrelevant, because 'when moral worth is at issue, what counts is not actions, which one sees, but those inner principles of actions that one does not see' (pp. 19–20). Proper attention to moral principles when teachers bring their 'concepts to purity' can be conveyed to 'children of moderate age' in Kant's view (p. 23). Conversely, Irigaray might identify in the shift from grace to Grace a playful denial of the 'status quo values' and 'imperialism that fails to consider the living subject' (2004/1984, p. 7). In her challenge to the centrality of 'first philosophy' (p. 7), Irigaray calls for 'a revolution' that will 'reinterpret everything concerning the relations between subject and discourse' (p. 8) and in the rhyme's subversive 'admonition of adult authority' (Opie and Opie, 1992, p. 142) can be located the seeds of Irigaray's revolution and a childly expression of moral grievance.

Separating Kant and Irigaray is a void from which the concerns of this chapter rise to unsettle the sunshine of a childhood pastoral: 'The world looked so warm and cosy and safe. Monsters did not belong in this bright suburb, with its neat gardens rich with roses and lavender and cats' (Alcock, 1999/1988, p. 28). Alcock's creature is raised to challenge the guardians of subject and discourse in which the duty of care confronts Kant's moral law, because 'I wanted to show my father that girls are as good as boys any day of the week' (p. 5). Frankie renders sexual difference an ethical issue in *The Monster Garden* (1988), although here she seems unaware of the moral colouring of her comparative phrasing 'as good as'; this realization comes to Frankie as she battles the 'purity' of Kantian duty and law. Not only does Frankie confront the dominance of her brothers and father, but also of Western traditions that render morality paternal and fraternal; and in Mary C. Rawlinson's (2006) view, fraternity is especially problematic from a feminist perspective. Alison Jaggar points out that 'Western philosophers have often constructed moral justification as the attainment of "the moral point of view", a grandiose expression that hints heavily at a transcendent moral reality' (2000, p. 239). Each of the books discussed in this chapter – through their concern with the duties of boyhood and girlhood – problematize the transcendent and objective stance typical of philosophical discourse. Kant's underlining of the 'purity' of philosophy from which moral law derives, 'completely cleansed of everything that may be only empirical and that belongs to anthropology' (1998, p. 2), is exhaustive to the point of defence, for in *Groundwork of the Metaphysics of Morals* (1785), Kant seeks to bury that which women and children have long known: duty and moral justification are contingent on conditions laid down by an *other* law. Kant's deontology is persuasive and pervasive, still its normative stance causes problems for those who are not embraced by the centre and who must surely ask what it means to be good when respect for moral law seems to be wrong.

In her discussion of the ways in which literature (specifically mystery and detective fiction) calls into question 'the concepts and project of moral philosophy', Rawlinson observes that

> ... this literature demonstrates that moral agency is not only poorly represented by the concept of fraternity, but that it is often impossible within the institution of fraternity. Moral urgencies are, in fact, rarely conflicts of rights between equals. Almost any morally charged relation – parent/child, teacher/student, doctor/patient – is a relation among *unequal* subjects, and the concept of fraternity cannot capture its asymmetry. (2006, p. 131)

This asymmetry is identifiable in a range of quite different books for young readers, such as *Ask Me No Questions* (1976) by Anne Schlee, *The Monster Garden* by Vivien Alcock, and Nina Bawden's *The Real Plato Jones* (1994), since each wrestles with fraternity in a series of challenges to the purity of moral law and deontological ethics. Implied readers are invited to consider the possibility of moral agency that is not ideal or centred; a moral agency that justifies itself from a position of alterity, breaking down the binary coding of female-male. Concerns about duty are also prevalent in these texts and it is revealing to consider Kant's moral law as a site of battle; for although not expressly engaged, Kantian ethics are so pervasive that they have come to configure – a sometimes debilitating – moral identity. This notion of a morality that shapes identities is especially relevant to children's literature, since girlhood and boyhood is often validated or commended when girls or boys conform to related moral conditions. As evident in many books for children, moral conditions are frequently different for boys and girls, problematizing Kant's insistence on a 'completely cleansed' morality. Before exploring the books that move towards asymmetry, however, I want to consider a book that works out its masculine duty from the centre of male dominance, yet challenges Kant's assertion that in order to be morally good, '*I ought never to act except in such a way that I could also will that my maxim should become a universal law*' (1998/1785, p. 15).

Alone about The Chase

B.B.'s *Brendon Chase* (1944) is a woodland Robinsonnade set loosely in the early twentieth century at a time when 'motor cars were not as common as they are today' (2000/1944, p. 164). Its temporal narrative placement rejects an increasingly mechanized civilization in line with Henry Thoreau and Aldo Leopold. Indeed B.B.'s forest is rendered in detailed, elegiac terms, and *Brendon Chase* can be seen as a swan song for a natural world in decline, echoing his contemporary's observation: 'Like winds and sunsets, wild things were taken for granted until progress began to do away with them. Now we face the question whether a still higher "standard of living" is worth its cost in things natural, wild and free' (Leopold, 1968/1949, p. vii). *Brendon Chase* recounts the great adventure of the Hensman brothers, Robin, John, and Harold, who run away from their surrogate home, the Dower House – they have been living in the care of their maiden Aunt due to their father's posting abroad – to live as outlaws for nine months in the 11,000 acre forest, Brendon Chase. Advocating a boyhood of survival and education in nature, the novel partially invests in John Locke's position that moral and scientific knowledge are learned through experience, thus '. . . he that from a child untaught, or a wild inhabitant of the woods, will expect these abstract maxims and reputed principles of sciences, will I fear, find himself mistaken' (2004/1690, p. 73). Even so, the masculine coding of *Brendon Chase* draws through the narrative a commitment to duty that recognizes Kant's notion of a priori values shaping moral agency. These ethical contradictions set the tone for a tale in which the pivotal act of running away ruptures the ground of moral certainty.

Brendon Chase lingers on the threshold of change, looking back to and investing in long-standing constructions of boyhood at work in novels such as *Tom Brown's Schooldays* (1857) and *Bevis* (1882), while anticipating an uncertain future as B.B.'s boys become men; a future and manhood that must be embraced (un)willingly in the name of duty. As in *Brendon Chase*, concerns are expressed in Hughes's novel about the restrictive dangers of 'petticoat government' and the young Tom Brown is prepared for his schooldays by experiences of fishing and fighting with a male companion. However, while the muscular Tom Brown is grown in a mould identical to that of the Hensman brothers, his boyhood masculinity develops a spiritual aspect typical of the muscular Christianity promoted in many nineteenth-century boys' stories, exemplified by Ballantyne's *The Coral Island* (1858) or Marryat's *The Children of the New Forest* (1847). Furthermore, these muscular Christians embrace their duty and future with a faith that suggests manhood will be just as rewarding as boyhood; as confirmed by Tom Brown's 'glimpse of the glory of his birthright' on the steps of Dr Arnold's tomb at the close of the book (1989/1857, p. 376). Unlike these precursors, *Brendon Chase* shares with *Bevis* an almost secular vision of boyhood, though it retains the muscularity of *Tom Brown*. The poetic rendering of the natural world approaches the spiritual in its devotion, and Robin reflects on the powers of the creator during his frequent lone journeys into the heart of Brendon Chase: 'These fishes in miniature were truly fascinating. The Creator must have had eyes like a watchmaker, thought Robin' (p. 101). A theological shift is evident here, retaining something of the Romantic in Robin's appreciation of the land, although the Romantic emphasis on divinity[2] is downplayed in favour of a more grounded present that worships a creative force configuring the land rather than an identifiably Christian God. Robin's musings pre-empt Philip Pullman's notion of a republic in *His Dark Materials* (1995–2000) and match the poetic awe of Leopold's *A Sand County Almanac* (1949): '[Robin] loved best to be by himself in the woods, he liked to hunt on his wild lone and wander just like this, for a whole day, in some leafy secret place where nobody bothered to come. It was his idea of Heaven' (p. 101). Accordingly, though Robin's masculinity is forged in the deontological fires (overlaid with Kantian purity) of Tom Brown's Christianity – and he responds to the duty invested in this ethical outlook – a shift in ethical emphasis can be located in Robin's harmonic concern for the land.

The moral structure of *Brendon Chase* is conflicted and complex, but deontological ethics emanating from paternal authority forms the basis of moral law at the outset, offering justification for fleeing those impostors who seek to usurp moral governance:

'Oh, it's all right, don't worry about them, women, women, women, that's the whole trouble. I'm just about sick of petticoat government . . . If Father and Mother were here it would be all different and we shouldn't want to cut school and run away to the forest and live like Robin Hood. Anyway, Father told me once that when he was a boy his people let him go off every holiday with a gun and a tent and he walked all round the coast of Scotland living on what he shot and fished. But Aunt throws a blue fit even if we get our feet wet and we can't even ride the pony Father gave us, for fear we should fall off.' (p. 15)

Aunt Ellen's 'petticoat government' is positioned as a threat to the masculinity upheld as crucial to boyhood and subsequent manhood. Aunt Ellen's law opposes the patriarchy driving this passage; an opposition metonymically conveyed in the observation 'we can't even ride the pony Father gave us'. The boys cannot respect their Aunt's law, claiming deference to a patriarchal law that endorses the pursuits anticipated in running away to Brendon Chase and provides a model of boyhood – survival in the outdoors and independence, styled on Bevis and Mark's adventures on New Formosa in *Bevis* – that the boys aspire to and which the narrative supports. However, Aunt Ellen's law is denied less by this familiar trope of patriarch in absentia – *Swallows and Amazons* (1930) also employs this trope, another book in which patriarchal law is less centred than it might initially appear – than it is by the fraternal triumvirate that grows in strength as *Brendon Chase* progresses. It is in fraternity that the boys come simultaneously to accept their moral responsibilities and to question the direction and basis of their ethical groundwork.

Aunt Ellen's law is consistently undermined by the narrative point of view – encouraging the implied reader to reject her moral position – for example, she is described as 'a maiden aunt who knew nothing of children, and never understood boys' (p. 12), and this narrative complicity with the boys is compounded by their pivotal act of running away. A convention of adventure stories and a perennial dream of childhood – as imprinted on the cultural unconscious by *The Water Babies* (1863), *Bevis*,[3] and *Peter and Wendy* (1911) – running away is a conceptual hook likely to draw young readers into the story and into its ethical framework:

> 'My idea is,' [Robin] said, 'that we should run away to Brendon Chase!'
>
> 'Run away!' exclaimed John, 'and not go back to school on Thursday?'
>
> 'Exactly. Why shouldn't we live in the forest like Robin Hood and his merry men?'
>
> For the moment there was dead silence. The boldness of the idea was shocking.
> (p. 14)

The modal challenge of Robin's rhetorical question 'Why shouldn't we?' points to a philosophical shift from 'is to ought' and underscores the moral integrity of Robin's suggestion. Robin's 'shockingly bold' idea establishes his leadership (as does the name he shares with Robin Hood) and a muscular masculinity that is daring and confrontational. References to Robin Hood are ubiquitous and B.B. playfully explores the notion of what it might mean to be an outlaw – an epithet he frequently gives the Hensman boys and one that reinforces fraternal allegiance. Rawlinson argues that philosophical notions of justice have 'confidence in fraternity as a regulative ideal' (2006, p. 131), and the Hensman boys' act of running away cements their fraternal relationship, affording them a moral supremacy that overrules other categories of law.

While focusing mainly on the boys' experience in the woods, the narrative shifts perspective periodically in order to show the impact of the boys' absence on those left to uphold social laws, such as Aunt Ellen, Bunting the policeman, and the Whiting, the local vicar. Aunt Ellen's response to the boys' actions is stirred by 'family pride' and a 'lack of a sense of humour' (p. 192); consequently her government is focused on ends and inclination (in Kantian terms) rather than a volition that is good in itself. Similarly, Bunting's motivations are base and antithetical to moral law and fraternity for 'His pride had suffered, his self-respect had suffered, no wonder that he cried for vengeance!' (p. 214). The boys repeatedly humiliate Bunting, and the theft of his uniform when they catch him swimming in the Blind Pool symbolically eradicates any threat that the local constabulary might represent, suggesting that his civil law has no essential relationship with moral law. It is in this rejection of female and civil law that *Brendon Chase* confirms the legislative authority of fraternity and demonstrates that fraternity is exclusive, unsettling Kant's notion of universal moral law. Moreover there are hints that the fraternal sphere is disempowering to those outside it:

> 'I suppose we *are* doing wrong running away from the Dower House and Aunt Ellen; of course, it's wrong when you come to see it from their point of view. But as I say, if our parents were here we shouldn't have done it. We may have missed a good slice of Banchester, but we've been learning other things.' (pp. 154–5)

The boys concede that there are other modes of rectitude external to fraternal law and the various law-giving agencies in the book confirm Rawlinson's view of crime fiction – and *Brendon Chase* is certainly interested in the criminal status of running away – which 'demonstrates the *specificity* of agency and suggests the idea of singular universals, multiple figurations of the universal' (2006, p. 132). This specificity is evident in the wrangles between Aunt Ellen, Bunting, and the fugitive boys, nonetheless it is clear that fraternal law sits atop a moral hierarchy linked to the conditions of boyhood and masculinity. The boys recognize that social law demands punishment for their 'crime', though their willingness to accept punishment actually accedes to fraternal justice and contributes to the masculine ideal of muscularity. Discussing Peter's camomile tea punishment in *Peter Rabbit,* Perry Nodelman observes that it 'is not really a punishment at all' and that Peter is a 'hero, having undergone a male initiation, confronting the enemy on his own territory and prevailing. Seen in these terms Peter's illness is merely a continuation of the test, something more he must suffer to demonstrate and celebrate his tenacity' (2002, p. 4). Withstanding punishment is an attribute of masculinity and the fact that the nature of the boys' punishment is not revealed when their father arrives to remove them from the forest suggests that their willingness to face chastisement is crucial, rather than the penalty itself: 'whatever happened, whatever punishments were coming to them, this wonderful adventure would have been worth while, it would never, never be forgotten!' (p. 296). Such masculine codes feed into the fraternal justice that upholds moral law, belying its purity and objectivity with a constituency that excludes those on the margins (or those functioning on the outskirts of the chase).

Moral law justifies the Hensman boys in their fraternal opposition to domestic and civil law, though it is clear that their adventure is only valid if they are able to accept that their status as outlaws is temporary. It is here that *Brendon Chase* implies a resistance to the paternally inherited ethical code that their fraternity appears to accept and refine. On first arriving in Brendon Chase, Robin states, ' "I vote we never go back" ' (p. 46), and frequently the boys express the desire to stay in 'the wilds' forever. Regardless, their desire to remain always in Brendon Chase is increasingly expressed in the knowledge that this is not possible:

> They knew this idyllic existence could not last for ever. It was all very well to lie on one's back and watch the firelight leaping like red and orange antlers, and say, 'we'll live here always, we won't go back to the old life.' Alas! They knew that in England at any rate, such an ambition was utterly impossible. A 'civilised' people in a highly cultivated island had advanced beyond that stage. One had to work and work and not lead a selfish existence such as theirs. They knew that in the New Year their people were coming back, and then it was 'good-bye', perhaps for ever, to this free forest life. (pp. 271–2)

Irony saturates this passage, pointing to ambiguities and conflicts of duty that expose divergent ethical concerns. Inverted commas disparage civilization, as supported by a recurrent comparative technique, 'Those folks with town minds would have been acutely unhappy in the Chase, just as the outlaws would have almost expired if had they found themselves transported to the middle of a great city, with brilliant shops all about them' (p. 270). The conceit of 'town minds' presents the progress of civilization as a state of consciousness in conflict with the boys' imaginative appreciation of the chase, as suggested by the dismissive use of pronoun to distinguish 'those folks' from the familiarized outlaws. That the town mind is the result of cultural evolution and not essential to human being is confirmed by the narrator's speculation, 'Perhaps [the boys] were "throwbacks" to the time when every man and woman lived as they were living, hunting for food and dwelling in caves and holes in trees' (p. 272). This aligns the boys with the primitive and anachronistic Charcoal Burner Smokoe Joe, who symbolizes a past way of living refused to the Hensman boys, ' "we can't stay here for ever, not like you" ' (p. 297). All this has the makings of an environmentalist perspective that opposes the city's 'din of wheels' (p. 270) and the bleak vision of the boys' future is distinctly Foucauldian, imbued with a sense of inevitability, constraint, and loss and in which they vanish bodily and materially from the chase they love.

The boys cannot stay in the forest because they are committed to a dominant model of masculinity that enforces a dualistic system of values, diminishing all that is female, primitive, and natural in favour of the male, civilized, and reasoned. Although the boys' sojourn in the forest might seem to break down these binaries as they commune with the natural world and yearn for a more primitive existence, they are unable to relinquish the allegiance to masculinity that shapes their response. As Val Plumwood observes, 'The set of interrelated and mutually reinforcing dualisms which permeate western culture forms a fault-line which runs through its entire conceptual system' (1993, p. 42). Hence, the comparative structure employed by B.B. to champion the winter beauty of the chase over the 'great city', encouraging the implied reader to reflect on the values attached to each, invests in a dualism that advocates man and reason over all else. The boys might find their duty repugnant, but it is irresistible because it favours and upholds them as white, upper-middle-class males. Although the boys yearn for and respect Smokoe's lifestyle, they save his life in the tradition of empire fiction, as primitive man submits to his civilized master; indeed Smokoe addresses them as 'masters' from the outset. This mastery also extends to some of the boys' dealings with the forest, so that although Robin is 'enthralled – bewitched!' (p. 104) by the blind pool, which is 'surely far more lovely than Thoreau's pond' (p. 106), his first action on discovering the pool is to shoot a moorhen, 'The bird rolled over, flapped a wing once, twice, and lay still' (p. 105). The debt and kinship to *Walden* or *Life in the Woods* (1854) is made explicit, although less obvious is the guiding force of the rational in Kantian ethics, which as Plumwood points out is 'taken to distinguish the civilised from the primitive and the higher from the lower classes' (1993, p. 24).

In recognizing and rationalizing their duty as boys-becoming-men to the conditions of civilization, the Hensman brothers succumb to Kant's moral law and embrace the supremacy of rational being. When Kant disassociates the a priori conditions of moral laws from empirical experience, he implies a civilized structure which moral autonomy pre-empts and reaches beyond, but where the Kantian model of pure philosophy refuses clear examples of how moral law relates to social structures and conditions, the Hegelian model of duty to self, family, and society helps to show how this works in actuality. Hegel explains that the '*particular person* is his own end' and 'one principle of civil society. But the particular person is essentially so related to other particular persons that each asserts himself and finds satisfaction by means of the others, and at the same time simply by means of the form of *universality*' (2008/1821, pp. 180–1). Furthermore, the particular and universal are 'reciprocally bound together and conditioned', and Hegel offers the example of tax payment which might seem to be injurious to the particular in favour of the universal, but that 'particular ends cannot be attained without the help of the universal' and thus the payment of taxes does not necessarily indicate an unjust society (p. 182). Hegel's conjoining through 'rightness' of the particular and universal can be seen reflected in Robin's recognition that 'a selfish existence' is incompatible with moral agency and manliness. Consequently, the boys' moral strength and muscular masculinity lies as much in their ability to survive alone in the natural world, as in having done so being able to return to the 'bricks and mortar' (p. 155) of civilization. Greenwood empiricism evidently has raised the boys to the point at which their good will comes to fruition and they are able to recognize the moral concepts that will shape their manhood – benevolence and industry can be identified as driving forces in the Epilogue's projected future for the boys.

The depth and ubiquity of negative response towards civilized manhood in *Brendon Chase* sends shockwaves nonetheless to the centre of a dominant masculine model that relies so heavily on fraternal bonds. The novel's ambivalent closure is shaped by the yearning glimpse of an ethical model that reimagines the future, and the key to this alternative destiny lies in Robin, the 'strange boy' (p. 257) who breaks away from the fraternal group repeatedly, 'Robin preferred to wander alone about the Chase' (p. 258) in order to come closer to the natural world. Robin's communion with nature has the potential to succeed fraternity, for Robin's response to the forest environment is akin to an ethical vision that recognizes biotic community: 'Robin's sight was . . . sensitive to colour and colour harmonies. A mass of autumn leaves beneath his feet would pull him up short, and those soft blending colours would hold him absolutely spellbound' (p. 261). The harmony and blending draws on Robin's senses, stimulating a thoughtful appreciation of his surroundings that are the prerequisites for the

'Outlook' offered by Leopold, which locates 'the evolution of a land ethic [as] an intellectual as well as emotional process' (1949/1968, p. 225). These outlooks (Robin and Leopold's both) require a fundamentally different ethical approach from the fraternal doctrines of Locke and Kant and a political approach that might challenge the dominion of capitalism. As Arne Naess argues, 'the large-scale realization of ecoeducation requires a new politics, green politics, a politics that does not systematically favor people who concentrate mainly on getting more of what there is not enough of' (2008, p. 63). *Brendon Chase* does not develop this political or ethical agenda, yet it does imply that a basic value change is desirable and necessary. The implied reader is left either to reconcile this sighting of an other way with an Epilogue that transforms outlaws into men, or in catching sight of it to find a way of releasing boys from the human bonds of masculinity, civilization, and reason.

Redeeming care

Where *Brendon Chase* searches for an alternative moral system through which to liberate its boys, *Ask Me No Questions* by Ann Schlee shapes its historical narrative through a feminist reassessment of a deontology that dominates and excludes. In Schlee's novel, Laura and her younger brother Barty have been sent to stay with their Aunt and Uncle Bolinger during the cholera outbreak of the late 1840s, while their father (an Evangelist minister) fights 'against that great injustice that caused the poor people to die before they understood that God loved them too and wanted them to be good' (2007/1976, p. 8). Encapsulated here is the Evangelist doctrine of Christian duty that is bound to relay a message of salvation to all people, regardless of class, race, or creed. The possibility of redemption hangs on a notion of goodness that becomes increasingly problematic as the book progresses though and Laura furtively attempts to feed starving children in a neighbouring asylum. Laura becomes entangled in a destructive conflict of duty and consequently it is the deontological conditions of goodness which are central to *Ask Me No Questions*, rather than specific Evangelist precepts that contribute peripherally to the historical conditions of the text. Laura's struggles can be identified more generally with the rule of moral law; elements of moral law can be located in the Judeo-Christian tradition, which are fully developed into a deontological system of pure philosophy at work in Kantian ethics, wherein a priori moral law is unbending to circumstance.

The children's Aunt Bolinger and most of the local community collude in ignoring the existence of Drouet's asylum, because the workhouse children it houses ' "are nothing to do with this village. They are all from other parishes. Slum parishes in London" ' (p. 59), and the villagers refuse to ask questions about their living conditions. The 'ask me no questions' of the title refers to an endemic refusal of responsibility and hypocrisy – several of the book's central scenes involve meetings of the 'Ladies' Committee', assembled to sew for *local* charitable concerns – that the book confronts directly. As Laura is caught up in the moral dilemma that challenges her commitment to duty and goodness, she adopts an inquisitive stance – framing related questions repeatedly, ' "But why are there so many poor people in this village?" ' (p. 47) and asking them of a range of characters, representing different ways of seeing the problem – in the hope of reaching resolution or understanding. The interrogative persistence of the philosopher is presented as a way of tackling and exploring moral issues that seem overwhelming, threatening, or even insurmountable. So the negative imperative 'ask me no questions' also reflects the book's philosophical agenda and contains the imperative 'questions must be asked'. The only characters in the book really willing to ask questions are Laura and Miss Roylance, an orphaned young teacher taken in by the vicar from outside the community to run the local school, but each is silenced by a deontological model that has no room for compassion or care and which shapes authority according to sex and wealth.

Laura and Barty soon discover that the workhouse children they catch eating pigswill from the trough in Uncle Bolinger's barn are being mistreated and significantly their reactions are differentiated and gendered. Barty treats the children dispassionately, ' "They're not the sort you like or dislike", said Barty. "They were nothing but beggar children" ' (p. 29) and his interest in them is surpassed by the death of a calf he hopes to observe out of scientific interest. When Barty does attend to the children it is to assert masculine authority, though they appear beneath the interest of a boy who aligns paupers with animals in common with the fraternal network that sees him colluding for reasons of intellectual interest with his Cousin Henry, Uncle Bolinger, and especially Mr Armitage (who schools Barty in the vague science of avian anatomy, while Laura stays home for domestic training by her Aunt). Evidently, Barty's masculine pursuits shield him from concerns beneath his immature and quasi-intellectual ambitions. Conversely Laura's reaction to the children shows her caught between the demands of patriarchal authority (enforced by Laura's love and respect for her father and with exacting stringency by Aunt Bolinger) and feelings of pity, compassion, and empathy that she acts on with increasing levels of guilt and self-loathing. Laura's urgent drive to sustain the children derives from a mix of Christian and sociocultural indoctrination (which champions charity) and a more elusive internal impulse to sympathize and nurture, thus *Ask Me No Questions* could be said to essentialize feminine characteristics that have come to justify dismissive attitudes to women in an ethical system of rational dominance. However, when considered in relation to questions of duty permeating Schlee's novel, the gendered positioning of characters apparently functions as part of a moral web in which sexual politics are deeply entwined – though it is also evident that Laura's resistance to masculine codes is an important aspect of her female being and nature, which the novel implies should not be dismissed on the grounds of gendered reduction.

So, when Laura steals food from her aunt's table to feed the Drouet children, she is trapped in a conflict of deontological duty, as articulated in passages that outline the rules to which she has been obedient until now:

> Once a week her mother made soup in the kitchen and weighed it out: so many carrots, so much barley, so much bones, so much meat. The whole house smelt of it, but they never ate it. It went to the poor. *Feed the poor.* It was an order. Week by week they obeyed it. (p. 102 – my emphasis)

> The blurred image she had of God was adult, and adult love, even Papa's, could wear a stern and dictatorial face in matters like this. He had said, *'Though shalt not steal.'* (p. 155 – my emphasis)

Laura attempts to reconcile the conflict between the imperatives that arise from her situation, but she is unsuccessful due to the deontological refusal of the material and relative; nor is there an alternative ethical system available to Laura (though the books's conclusion suggests that this is possible and necessary). Dealing first with the command to feed the poor, since Laura's theft arises from the paupers' lack of food, it becomes clear to Laura (though remains incomprehensible) that 'charitable' notions of poverty are relative and that 'the poor' qualified by her parents' obedience to moral law does not translate to the Bolinger household and environs. According to Aunt Bolinger, poverty does not in itself qualify for charity; it must be morally deserving and she denies the Drouet children because, unknown by the villagers, they cannot be judged by them: ' "For who is to say if a man is deserving of charity or undeserving if they have not grown up with him in the same village?" ' (p. 64). Already then, the notion of a pure moral

law is unravelling and Laura is torn by conflicting notions of rightness in regard
to poverty before ever she thinks of stealing; simply to acknowledge and visit
these unknown children is wrong according to Aunt Bolinger (though Kantian
ethics would also exclude Aunt Bolinger's acts of charity because they are driven
by ends, rather than being the product of a will that is good for its own sake).
Furthermore, Laura's response to the children is outside the remit of Kantian
rational thinking, so that she arrives at the moment of theft due to an emotional
concern with ends that denies the a priori conditions of moral duty. When Laura
and Barty discover the children in the barn, Laura responds with a sequence
of emotions that she is unable to understand or control, 'To her surprise she
began to cry' (p. 29). Laura is at first incredulous and disgusted that Lizzie, Will,
and Jamie are eating pig food, 'They ate like that because they were horrid', and
then 'She tore at the thought and tried to throw it away' (p. 29). Rarely does the
narrator venture an explicit opinion on narrative events, but here the implied
reader is prompted to recognize that Laura's reaction should be valued (and I
would add that it marks the beginning of moral awareness and agency in Laura
denied and unsupported by Kantian ethics): 'She knew quite well that they ate
that way because they were hungry, and that, to do her credit, was at least in part
why she wept' (p. 29).

Laura's moral dilemma begins with emotion and while eschewed by Kantian
moral law, it can be seen as a challenge to the 'ethical mistakes' described by
Irigaray as she finds a place for female sexuality in the ethical traditions from
which it has been excluded and in which 'pure obligation disassociates [the
sister] from her affect'; hence Irigaray observes, 'This duty, abstract and empty
of all feeling, is supposedly at the root of woman's identity' (2004/1984, p.100).
Acknowledging the role of emotion in moral agency and change, Midgley points
out: 'Spontaneous feeling is an essential raw material for advances in morality,
but it can't constitute them. Merely expressing it can't be the creation of values.
Nor can merely acting in a new and unexpected way' (2003/1981, p. 65). Like
Irigaray, Midgley is interested in how moral systems might be opposed, altered,
developed, and forged. While Laura is assigned no conscious role in any such
process, her discomfort, anxiety, and actions accumulate to suggest that change
is required; that something must be inherently wrong with a moral system which
allows children to be starved, abused, and left to die, silencing or disabling those
who might act to prevent these evils. An emotional response to starving children
is not enough to derail Laura's commitment to the moral law by which she has
lived for so long, though when she follows Barty into the barn for a second
visit – disobeying her Aunt's unspoken instruction that they should not associate

with the Drouet children – Laura is conscious of a shift away from sentiment, to something no less daunting:

> The misery, which surely had been a good thing, began to weaken and fade, and with its fading came a strange feeling of release as if by disobeying she had stepped outside herself and left the meek governed child behind her, while she – if it were she – ran unrestrained through the tangled trees with the wet grass soaking and weighting her skirts. (p. 93)

This is rare moment of 'unrestrained' optimism in the book for the possibility of a successful break from moral government, yet the tentative 'if it were she' points to the self-doubt and hatred to come as Laura fails to reconcile charity (if this is what it is) and theft (if this is what it is). From emotion then, Laura proceeds to action and the most important of the acts she engages in is that of truly seeing the children, for in seeing them she cannot deny them. When Laura observes Jamie, the youngest and weakest of the children, closely, she witnesses 'a concentrated love' for his older brother Will, 'that took Laura's heart from her' (p. 99). Schlee's usage of 'heart' here accords with Midgley's discussion of an understanding of the heart at work in *Macbeth* that alludes to 'the *core* or centre of someone's being, the essential person, himself as he is in himself and (primarily) to himself' (2003/1981, p. 2). Accordingly Laura's investment in the children is of herself, serving her own ends as well as theirs and exceeds notions of pity, charity, and compassion.

This opening of moral ground between self (Laura) and other (workhouse paupers) anticipates the mutuality described by Plumwood[4] in her formulation of a new of ethical selfhood. Laura's moral relationship with the Drouet children is prevented from fully embracing Plumwood's concept of mutuality though, since it rests in part on the Aristotelian notion of virtuous friendship and Laura is prohibited by social mores and exclusive moral law from claiming friendship, neighbourliness, or community with the children. When first Laura sees Lizzie skipping in the neighbouring yard, she observes her thoughtfully, 'But as she watched, as the possibility of a friendship formed in her mind, she noticed that the pinafore was neglected and dirty. She is a poor person's child, thought Laura sadly' (p. 13). There is an ambiguity in Laura's reflection that is not fully resolved for the reader and hence Laura's sadness embraces both her own sense of loss and pity for Lizzie's deprivation; this is offered as a positive response by a narrative framework that imagines and anticipates ethical developments that will come to challenge the moral outlook of its historical setting. Pity is not in itself a virtue, but caring and benevolent actions ensuing from pity enter the moral sphere of virtue ethics, an augmentation of which by Raja Halwani (2003) brings together Aristotelian virtue with Nel Noddings's care ethics as set out in *Caring* (1984). Halwani points out that care is not listed as a 'mean virtue'[5] by Aristotle, and that by incorporating care into a more comprehensive moral framework than Noddings allows, valuable elements of care can be preserved, such as 'its application to specific individuals in the agent's life, its emotive component, and its relevance to areas in moral life that have been neglected by some traditional moral theories' (Halwani, 2003, p. 162). Yet ethical strategies developed in the context of twentieth-century feminist and psychoanalytic reassessments of fraternal systems can only be considered by an implied reader embracing the novel's thrust toward moral change; Laura must act on her emotional response without any support from moral theories that might allow her to conceive of her actions as good.

Turning now to Laura's theft of food from the Bolinger household, it is clear that if Laura is to fulfil her promise to bring the children more food (given the villagers' negation and denial of them) then she must seek duplicitous means of doing so. From the first moment she takes scraps left for the cowman, Laura struggles with the nature of theft: 'It was not really stealing, she told herself. The children would have had it in the end in any case' (p. 102). Laura is unable to convince her dutiful conscience though and soon reflects:

> But it was stealing. Her aunt without a doubt would think it so. She had disobeyed. She had lied. Each morning she stared at the face in the blotched mirror and it started anxiously back again. But it was the same. The badness did not show. (p. 103)

Laura conceives of her badness as intrinsic to her and this knowledge chimes with the uneasy mantra with which she undermines herself repeatedly; '*If this be I, as it surely cannot be*' (p. 103). However, Laura's sense of internal and self-effacing badness is at odds with the narrative's ideological impetus. Frequent changes in focalization – allowing comparison with Laura's compassionate deeds and insights into the workhouse conditions – encourage the implied reader to consider that responsibility might be external to Laura. Furthermore, the question of whether stealing can ever be justified is posed so variously and frequently that the implied reader is simultaneously invited to reflect on the moral issues raised. An example of this interrogative approach – and a pivotal moment in the philosophical positioning of the book – comes when Laura addresses Miss Roylance who has previously challenged what she perceives as the villagers' collective denial, declaring: ' "we have a right, a duty, to know more of the conditions those children live under"' (p. 61). Laura trusts Miss Roylance as a result and seeks the teacher's moral approval for her own actions, asking: '"Is it always wrong to lie and steal?"' (p. 152). When Miss Roylance responds in the affirmative, Laura reflects:

> Surely she would not say so if she knew, thought Laura . . . She said again earnestly, as if offering a last chance, 'Always? Even if it is in order to do good?'
>
> Miss Roylance . . . stood looking steadily down at Laura. 'Yes, always. How can any good be done by evil means?' (p. 152)

Laura is seeking approval for her actions and for an ethical position that she cannot articulate since it is not recognized by the moral law to which Miss Roylance conforms so unbendingly. Laura is drawn to Miss Roylance as a woman who appears to care about the children as she does, but Miss Roylance believes that care is not within the remit of ethical concern. Aligning the maternal voice with care, Nel Noddings argues (like Irigaray) that the ethical bias towards moral reasoning has excluded feminine approaches, 'One might say that ethics has been discussed largely in the language of the father: in principles and propositions, in terms of justification, fairness and justice. The mother's voice has been silent' (2003/1984, p. 1). Laura looks fruitlessly to Miss Roylance for maternal guidance for the teacher is silenced on the grounds of her orphaned and impoverished status. When she contradicts the authority of Mrs Rees-Goring, chairwoman of the Ladies' Committee, Miss Roylance is persuaded of the relativity of moral action: '"Of course if at any time you cease to be the schoolmistress then you would truly be a private person and might act as you wish"' (p. 63). In the light of the fatal cholera outbreak at Drouet's asylum, readers are left to consider whether Miss Roylance lacks moral agency or courage in choosing to remain in her post (although she loses it eventually) and delaying her investigations into the children's welfare.

Lack of moral courage might be attributed to a range of characters in *Ask Me No Questions* – Cousin Henry and Uncle Bolinger, for example – though perhaps the most significant point of moral deficiency allows for a final rejection of the deontological position. When Laura is reunited with her beloved father, he reflects on her actions: 'She had of course in a way been right to lie and steal. She alone apparently had felt for those wretched children what he would have a child of his feel, but would he in his position be wise to tell her that?' (p. 225). Although clearly approving her behaviour (approval that echoes narrative position throughout), his ambivalence about telling Laura of this approbation is revealing. It implies that he will not have the courage to challenge the deontological foundations of his faith and ministry, and his question also seems to be directed to the reader for it is never answered. The challenge to the reader at this point is important because it means that no solution is provided by the narrator and consequently the reader is invited once again into an interrogative discourse of philosophical thinking.

Brendon Chase tests deontology from within (without) the leafy hollows of a verdant gentleman's club, while Ann Schlee's protagonist is hemmed in by the silent stitches of a ladies' committee worked by the thread of fraternal mastery. Each demonstrates that the gendered conditions of Kant's moral law are restrictive and in need of a challenge that rests outside their pages and while the future *might* be bleak for Robin and Laura, potential rests with the glimpse of alternative moral systems. *Brendon Chase* and *Ask Me No Questions* leave this potential in the mind of the implied reader, alternatively a number of books for young people move beyond the limitations of deontology and imagine an alternative moral framework through their narrative conjectures. *The Monster Garden,* for example, renders fraternity though the lens of feminist protest and offers an alternative ethical vision that breaks down the walls of the club from which petticoats are excluded.

Flourishing futures

Vivien Alcock's protagonist knowingly describes her father as 'a high-up scientist and a low-down male chauvinist pig' and because she 'wanted him to notice me' (1999/1988, p. 5), she decides to force entry into the club – in this case her father/brother's laboratory – not anticipating what she will find once inside. Conducting a scientific experiment on live cells, which produces Monnie (a living, growing, and needy 'monster'), Frankie opens a pathway to moral agency stretching back to Mary Shelley's *Frankenstein* (1818) and finds its own direction in an ethical model that draws together related concerns of feminism and environmentalism in a refusal of the fraternity of ethical reason. *The Monster Garden* draws from *Frankenstein* a suspicion towards scientific endeavour, though Marilyn Butler[6] traces a range of scientific debates at work in *Frankenstein,* challenging 'the widely held view that the novel is anti-scientific, even anti-intellectual' (Shelley, 1998/1818, pp. xxix–xxx). Butler confirms that Shelley invokes a populist knowledge of experimentation (p. xxx), and it is on the suspicious and sensationalist aspects of this response to science that

Alcock draws in order to heighten Frankie's paranoia about and exclusion from a world denied to her. *The Monster Garden* engages tangentially with the ethical implications of genetic research, disregarding its science and overlaying the Shelleyan pursuit of 'nature to her hiding places' (1998/1818, p. 36) with parochial anxiety about genetic engineering that amounts to local gossip: 'They call my father's laboratory a monster factory, and Debbie Scott says he tortures animals in it, which is not true' (1999/1988, p. 7). Frankie cannot entirely refute or resist these allegations because her sex excludes her from the laboratory; her brother David is shown round the laboratories by their father, and Frankie declares that she is refused the trip because 'I was only a girl and ought to be sitting at home and darning his socks' (p. 6). Science and sexual politics are thus mixed as Frankie partakes of a tradition of which she is self-consciously aware, musing, 'You can't really blame me for making a monster. What did they expect me to do with a name like that?' (p. 5), and in this interrogative defence of her actions, Frankie's moral agency is confronted, *The Monster Garden*'s central engagement with ethics is established, and the overtly addressed reader is drawn into a tale of ethical complexity.

The ethical structure of *The Monster Garden* is tripartite and the implied reader is guided through the different philosophical positions taken in the book through Frankie's *autodiegetic* narration; as her moral awareness grows and her position changes, so the implied reader is alerted to the ethical framework through which the narrative evolves. In identifying these phases, I have drawn on Plumwood's discussion of 'ethics and the instrumentalising self' in *Feminism and the Mastery of Nature* (1993), since Plumwood develops an ethical model that corresponds with the ethical issues played out in *The Monster Garden*. Plumwood argues that a satisfactory model of ethical environmentalism takes on board feminist concerns that have questioned the authoritative instrumentalism endemic in Western philosophy, which reduces 'the other to an instrument for use' (1993, p. 142), and she reaches for a notion of mutuality that draws on and reworks various ethical theories, from Aristotelian ethics to the self-eliding concerns of deep ecology. Returning to the structural workings of *The Monster Garden* then, the first ethical phase can be termed *instrumental*, confirming Frankie's collusion in and exclusion from rational dominance; the second ethical phase is related to *care*, as Frankie finds new ways of relating to Monnie; the third ethical phase is rooted in *mutuality* as Frankie and Monnie forge a reciprocal relationship of concern for the other.

As in *Brendon Chase*, a shift from patriarchal to fraternal dominance occurs early on and it is Frankie's duel with her 'spotted snake' (p. 7) of a brother that leads her to bribe David into giving him some of the live cells he has stolen:

> I was in a strong position. What David had done was pretty terrible, when you thought about it. I'd never have done it myself. I wouldn't have dared. Nicking something from a laboratory is a serious crime. Possibly a deadly one . . . If David was found out, he'd be in real trouble.
>
> I felt sorry for him now. Poor David. Trying to be as clever as Ben and Mike had driven him to dangerous lengths. (p. 9)

Frankie is unconcerned with the moral implications of David's theft, focusing instead on consequence; her empathetic response is important though since it underlies her moral agency subsequently. The damaging potential of fraternal competition impacts on David and Frankie, though while Frankie competes with David for her father's attention, David is driven to emulate the academic glory of his older brothers. Believing that self-validation and maturity requires patriarchal acceptance and entry into the fraternal order, each looks to scientific achievement as a means of self-empowerment and of fulfilling filial duties. Frankie and David are the children of science and reason and duly they approach growing up as a movement towards Cartesian objectivity, yet each is forced into a reconsideration of this position based on the outcome of their experiments.

The results of David's experiment are expressed in terms of failure, ' "I told you. It's dead", he said impatiently' (p. 23), sounding a requiem for Cartesian approaches that justify the dissection of 'non-sentient' animals: 'I looked at the tiny fragments in horror, feeling sick. / "Are you sure that it was really dead before you cut it up?" ' (p. 24). David's failed experiment suggests that he too must search for an alternative to fraternal dualism that only values one half of the equation (for he is in danger of failing as son *and* scientist if the logic of fraternal reasoning is followed). However, it is the triumph of Frankie's experiment that matters in terms of *The Monster Garden*'s challenge to reason based ethics, for if the shaping of an ethical alternative that validates otherness – figured throughout the book in terms of monster, female, and nature – can be deemed successful, then Frankie's experiment is a success in spite of her initial response:

> A growth came out of its side, like a short fat tentacle, and pounced. The tentacle drew back into the body. I saw the seed pod twist and wriggle as the grey, half-transparent flesh simmered around it like thick stew. Then it was gone.
>
> I bit my lip hard. Interesting, I told myself. Fascinating. Instructive.

> I *hated* it. I wished it were dead. I wanted to scrape it into a tin, tip it down the loo and pull the handle. (p. 13)

Linguistically reminiscent of an abortion fantasy in its juxtaposition of nebulous, squirming tissue with the metallic scrape of medical procedure, Frankie's reaction to her Promethean creation aligns her with the cold, procedural aspect of science that she comes to reject. In this moment, both creature and Frankie are products of the scientist's petrie dish and Frankie refuses responsibility, for the 'monster' was spawned in an unknown laboratory and she is refused identity as a scientist. Frankie attempts the language of dispassionate objectivity – 'Fascinating. Instructive' – but the swift transition to emotive subjectivity – 'I hated it' – hints at her eventual rejection of the masculinity she strives to perform. Such ambivalence can also be detected in Frankie's motivation for conducting the experiment, for she takes the cells from David with a view to forging fraternal allegiance: 'Just for once [I] didn't want to be left out of things . . . Perhaps I hoped David and I might work together on some scientific project', and furthermore, 'If I could keep my bit of goo alive as long as he did his, he might be impressed' (p. 10). Evidently, the experiment is a means to an end in self-gain, suggesting a lack of Promethean ambition or any commitment to scientific endeavour. Nevertheless, evidence of a creative will foreshadowing Frankie's moral agency is revealed on the back of her statement of fraternal ambition – 'However, I admit I said the words – "I want to grow a monster of my own"' (p. 10). Admission is the language of moral responsibility and Frankie retrospectively accepts culpability for the monster's existence. Also, Frankie's approach to the task of propagating a monster is subtly different from David's, who has been furnished with laboratory equipment. Frankie substitutes a petrie dish and blood algae with a white saucer used for her African violets (linked to the natural and domestic) and drops of her own blood (establishing a genetic and maternal bond), anticipating the ethics of caring friendship as conceived by Aristotle in *The Nicomachean Ethics*[7] and reworked as mutuality by Plumwood.

Ethical awareness and responsibility in *The Monster Garden* evolve gradually and the reader is invited to engage with moral developments through comparative statements and observations through which Frankie distances herself from the moral position of those around her. The most obvious challenge comes to the rationalist stance in which the experimental subject is deemed other, alien, and expendable: 'David says that if you want to be a scientist . . . You have to train yourself to think of the good of mankind, and forget that some small, shivering creature may enjoy the sunlight as much as you do' (p. 14). David's notion of science and selfhood can be recognized in Plumwood's definition of instrumentalism wherein, 'The structures of self involved in human domination and colonisation are reflected, repeated and confirmed in the reduction of non-human nature to an instrument' (p. 142). The instrumental model of self is tried on by Frankie and she attempts to flatten an ant in an effort to train herself, but she finds it as impossible to 'blot out its sun' as it is to flush her monster down the toilet, so instead she pricks her thumb 'in case it was thirsty' (p. 14), distancing herself from the fraternal and Cartesian stance. Frankie soon desists from feeding the creature her own blood, 'I didn't want it to develop a taste for it' (p. 14) and so self-preservation sits alongside her instinct to nurture the creature, hinting at the mutually balanced relationship forged by the end of the book.

Frankie's journey to moral agency is also made visible by the ideas about rational humanism expressed by Julia, the school friend she enlists to keep her monstrous secret; recruited because she seems sensible, capable, and experienced in keeping pets. Frankie discovers that Julia is as loyal as David to fraternal moral codes though, so Frankie is caught in a quandary whereby she must satisfy Julia's demands in order to prevent her from exposing the secret of Monnie's existence. Julia's initial response to the monster is distinctly Cartesian, rejecting Frankie's theory that the monster has a soul, '"It's not a proper animal. It's just something they made up in the lab – like nylon or polyester. I mean, it hasn't got a soul"' (p. 35), precisely the argument that led Descartes to describe animals as senseless automatons and inferior to humans. Julia also draws her moral arguments from Kantian deontology and modal formulations of responsibility to inferior, irrational beings. Initially Julia seeks to control the other she does not understand: '"you ought to make notes every day . . . You ought to have a record"' (p. 60), and finally she invokes the fraternal duty that betrays Monnie, Frankie, and the ethical model of care which Frankie has developed via her relationship with Monnie: 'She said we were stupid. She said Monnie was dangerous and she didn't want it hiding in her dad's yard. She said it was our duty to tell someone, and if we wouldn't, she would. She'd tell David' (p. 88). Frankie is betrayed not simply by individual characters, but by the moral values of fraternity that privilege authority and exclude the other from moral concern, and it is this that motivates Frankie to free Monnie to 'find a new world for itself, where no one would hate it because it was different' (p. 104).

Frankie's moral outlook begins to expand and shift as she comes to care for Monnie, who grows in size and intelligence, developing an empathy for those around it, extending from humans to the wider natural environment of waterways and wild creatures. Frankie cannot accept Julia's view that Monnie is 'a mistake' (p. 56), nor can Frankie sustain the instrumental idea of Monnie as a monster experiment, 'Cold words, I thought. Cold scientific words for a friendly little creature, jumping happily up and down in a sunlit garden, pretending to be a bird' (p. 60). In Monnie is figured a complex mix of the artificial and natural; it is the product of an unnatural scientific process and yet it has an affinity with the natural world and is a creature in its own right (*with* its own rights as Frankie comes to recognize). Monnie is thus symbolic of ethical systems that challenge and contradict each other, and the children's reactions to Monnie are aligned to positions polarized through philosophical discourse. When Julia and her brother react to Monnie with horrified revulsion, Frankie is overwhelmed by a 'wave of some new, strange feeling' (p. 30) that quickly shifts to protective empathy, 'I felt grief and bewilderment flooding out of it like an invisible current. It might have been any or every lost and frightened child' (p. 32). Midgley argues that such emotional responses are just as crucial to moral agency as reason and that ethical systems should not seek to divorce them: 'The heart is the centre of concern, the mind is the centre of purpose or attention, and these cannot be dissociated' (2003/1981, p. 3). This undercurrent of sensibility enhances Frankie's scientific knowledge and data gathering, so that the questions she asks herself before leaving home to free Monnie are charged with (not-yet-moral) responsibility that the implied reader is also invited to address:

> But Monnie was so young. How would it manage by itself, without me to bring it four meals a day, and hold its hand when it went to sleep? And I remembered the threatened whales I had given ten pence to save. Was there anywhere left on this planet where a baby would be safe from harm?
>
> 'What am I going to do, Monnie?' I said. (p. 84)

Frankie expresses maternal concern for Monnie in this passage, though without the framework of rational thinking and deontological purity, her questions are underscored with the anxiety of isolated responsibility. Frankie recognizes that culturally Monnie is located in a position of danger (as are whales) and surmises that relocation might reduce the ideological threat; thus the need for a renegotiation of idea and body is anticipated. Rudiments of a new ethical structure are evident in questions that indicate feminist and environmental thinking, yet they are in danger of reproducing 'the woman-nature equivalence that has served as legitimation for the domestication of women and their relegation to maternal and nurturing functions' (Soper, 1995, p. 123). Soper and Plumwood variously trace the sort of tensions raised by feminist critiques of a patriarchal hegemony that has aligned femininity with the natural as a means of justifying inequality and each agree that 'the ecological call for a re-thinking of our approach to the natural world has seemed not only to be consistent with, but in a sense to encompass, the feminist demand for an end to sexual hierarchy' (Soper, p. 122). Soper argues that a way of usefully reconciling feminist and environmental concerns is to reclaim the body and the natural from a constructivist position: 'If we are disallowed any appeal to natural needs, instincts, pleasures and pains, we remove the objective grounds for challenging the authority of custom and convention' (p. 138) and that it also necessary to 'discriminate between a number of different conceptions of "nature" or "naturality"'[8] (p. 141). Likewise, *The Monster Garden* seems to raise questions about the product and consequence of scientific research, suggesting that the natural might be endowed in the subject ensuing from experimentation, even if the process of creation is deemed unnatural. This shift from unnatural to natural brings with it the necessity to confer the needs of the *natural* to new/other/non-human species and, consequently, to consider their entitlements.

Plumwood's reconciliation of feminism and environmentalism looks back to systems that have done some of this groundwork, identifying 'the intrinsic value of the other' (Plumwood, 1993, p. 160) in Aristotle's notion of virtuous friendship and arguing that it offers a variation of the relational self, valuing the needs of others (Earth) as part of its own ends. Aristotle's expansive notion of friendship can be seen in a mother's selfless love for her child, which 'seems to consist more in giving than in receiving affection' (Aristotle, 2004, p. 213), and Aristotle reflects that 'in the case of a friend . . . one ought to wish him good for his own sake' (p. 203). Certainly, Frankie's emotional and thoughtful care for Monnie constitutes the sort of virtuous friendship described by Aristotle, comprising notions of care, respect, and equality. However, in order to conceive an ecological selfhood that breaks down the dualism of rational thought (avoiding the elision of self and otherness inherent in much deep ecology), Plumwood moves beyond Aristotle, arguing that 'the individual conceived in terms of mutuality is formed by, bound to and in interaction with others through a rich set of relationships which are essential to and not incidental to his or her projects' (1993, p. 156). This mutual concern for the other is pre-empted in Frankie's rhetorical question, ' "What am I going to do, Monnie?" ' for Frankie identifies Monnie's needs as her own, also inviting a reciprocal concern from the other that will recognize her own, potentially different, needs and entitlements.

Mutuality is then played out in the closing episodes of *The Monster Garden*, as Frankie delivers Monnie into a local river, and Monnie saves Frankie from drowning. Separated physically as Monnie disappears into its *natural* aquatic environment, child and creature allow each other to grow according to their own needs and in so doing they confirm their mutual love, respect, and concern. This is imagined for the reader when the fully grown Monnie returns a final time to visit the girl who saw in him a being worthy of attention, ' "Oh Monnie, you're so beautiful. Where have you been? Are you happy? Have you found any friends?" ' (p. 120). Frankie's questions shape for Monnie the sort of happiness associated with the Aristotelian concept of *eudaimonia*, translated variously as human flourishing, happiness, or fulfilment;[9] and as it happens, one of first adjectives Frankie applies to Monnie is 'flourishing' (p. 15). *Eudaimonia* is an important aspect of Aristotle's ethical system and describes someone who (through virtuous endeavour) has made 'a success of his life and actions, who realizes his aims and ambitions as a man, who fulfils himself'.[10] Aristotle's concept applies only to human experience, but with Plumwood's revisionary concept of mutuality, *eudaimonia* can be perceived as something wished for the other and can reach beyond humanity. Monnie's flourishing (potential for fulfilment and happiness) usefully captures that which Frankie values in the strange creature she is drawn to care for:

> We must have been an extraordinary sight, a thin girl and a great shining sea creature, chattering and whistling together, and neither really able to tell what the other was saying. But one thing we both understood without words. We loved one another. (pp. 120–1)

When Monnie dives into the water, Frankie wishes for Monnie 'a kinder, friendlier place than we have made on earth' (p. 121), yet this altruistic desire for the other is also self-facing and validated through a reconfigured relationship with Frankie's father and a re-evaluation and better understanding of the scientific process she once feared. When her father explains that he has been working on plants as a molecular biologist, he allays her fears about genetic engineering and so *The Monster Garden* introduces the reader to the possibilities and wonders of science as well as its limitations. In recognizing his daughter's anxieties and listening to her, her father shifts moral ground to a position of care that aligns him with Monnie, 'The funny thing was that he reminded me of Monnie' (p. 111), and Frankie's deceased mother, who looks out at Frankie from his desk (p. 113). Although Frankie tells her father 'many things I'd never dreamed I would be able to tell him', she 'did not tell him about Monnie' (p. 113), suggesting that the process of realigning political and ethical structures is gradual and for some place in Frankie's flourishing future, 'with life opening up before me' (p. 119).

The Monster Garden positively configures a moral agency that breaks down the barriers of fraternal exclusion, though while it implies that fraternity causes problems both for boys (David) and girls (Frankie), it focuses on the ways in which girlhood might be imagined in terms of moral awakening, lending moral weight to care and nurture. It encourages young readers to recognize and think through the possibilities of a flourishing life of mutual concern, extending beyond the self, out into the environment. In its environmental feminism, *The Monster Garden* gives moral validation to a future of biotic mutuality that *Brendon Chase* can only express in terms of hope, though we must look elsewhere to locate an alternative direction for B.B.'s masculine woodlanders trapped in the prospect of a dutiful manhood. Published 50 years after *Brendon Chase*, *The Real Plato Jones* evinces a masculinity in flux and resolves its central ethical dilemma by finding an alternative to dutiful adherence to masculine codes of honour. Bawden's 13-year-old protagonist is not able to take his masculinity for granted in the way that B.B.'s boys do and Plato's identity crisis is unravelled against a moral battle that pits deontology against consequentialism. In common with each of the books in this chapter universality is refused, for *The Real Plato Jones* engages readers in a thought experiment wherein morally good actions are revealed to be contingent upon what it means to be a good boy or man.

New consequences

Plato Jones is named for a dual nationality that is threaded through his struggle with selfhood – as formed via identification with his Welsh paternal grandfather, Constantine Llewellyn Jones (CLJ), and his Greek maternal grandfather, Nikos Petropoulos – that is precipitated by his parents' divorce. The novel deals with Plato's trip to a small mountain village in Greece for the funeral of Nikos Petropoulos, the reclusive Greek grandfather he knows little about. The hostility of local villagers to Plato, his mother, and sister intimates buried knowledge about Nikos and the untangling of this secret unleashes an ethical dilemma that disturbs Plato's masculine identity. *The Real Plato Jones* opens with an explanation of Plato's complicated family structure and it is evident that the celebrated heroism of his Welsh Grandfather, CLJ, plays a meaningful role in Plato's own boyhood: 'And CLJ is famous. He is a real hero, part of history like Julius Caesar or Robin Hood or George Washington' (1995/1994, p. 1). Echoing the Hensman boys in *Brendon Chase*, Plato uses Robin Hood as a marker for the sort of mythic masculinity and heroism that he responds and aspires to, but whereas this model of heroic and muscular masculinity remains stable in *Brendon Chase*, Plato is forced to reconsider his understanding of heroism and the extent to which it constitutes moral courage.

Like the Hensman brothers, Plato seeks to establish a sense of his own masculinity by looking to male role models within his family, though the Hensman brothers are able to justify their actions in terms of their father's 'model' boyhood. In contrast, Plato disapproves of his father's desertion of the marital home and refuses his father as a model of moral responsibility: 'My father used to swear and throw things. I try not to act like my father' (p. 9). In his father's absence, Plato adopts an awkwardly chivalrous attitude towards his mother, investing in a notion of masculine duty that sees women in need of protection: 'Did [my Welsh grandmother] really think I wanted to *talk* to my father, let alone live with him, after what he had done? . . . *someone* had to stay in England to look after my mother' (p. 4). Bawden's implied reader is invited to question Plato's perception of duty, since his tone of patriarchal pomposity points to pride bruised by paternal rejection. Furthermore, his mother's courageous actions when a fire consumes Molo (the Greek village they are visiting) force Plato to recognize that bravery is not the preserve of men and boys: 'Human nature is very peculiar. I was proud – as well as astonished – that my mother had turned out so brave' (p. 163). His mother's actions confirm that she is not in need of Plato's protection as he claims repeatedly, implying that his sense of duty is misplaced and the model of masculinity he invests in problematic. Plato struggles to satisfy the masculine ideal as confirmed by numerous references to his diminutive stature: 'I was bugged, haunted, obsessed, and *tormented* by the extra half-inch or so by which my little sister now over-topped me' (p. 29) and increasingly he finds it difficult to emulate the model of heroism he associates with CLJ. The paternal lineage he draws from their relationship is also unstable: 'I rather like to think of myself as Jones-the-Spy Junior./ Though of course only a quarter of me comes from CLJ' (p. 45), for Plato's awareness that he is not 'wholly' descended from CLJ undermines his ability to be properly male, let alone heroic. Plato describes himself as 'small for my age and boss-eyed and asthmatic' (p. 5) and (when seeking to protect his sister from intimidating village children) suggests that he has been bullied previously: 'I thought I had better take off my glasses. I knew from painful experience that if it came to a fight I would be bashed up if I kept them on' (pp. 36–7). Plato presents himself as the antithesis of the masculine hero and his efforts to overcome perceived antiheroic shortcomings invite the implied reader to question the premise on which his perceptions rest. Ultimately, it is the revelation of events involving CLJ and Nikos during the war that forces Plato to challenge the nature of heroism and to understand that moral courage is a question of choice and point of view irrespective of physical stature and robust masculinity.

Plato relates the tale of CLJ's wartime heroism early on, framing these events into a family mythology. As Plato explains, CLJ was decorated for bravery during the Second World War for his role in the Greek Resistance against the German occupation: 'CLJ lived [in a cave] with the Resistance for over a year [and t] he village below the cave was occupied by the Germans' (p. 2). The German army offered a reward for CLJ's capture and 'in the end one of the villagers told the German Commandant where he was hiding and he had to run for his life' (pp. 2–3). Plato also reveals that his grandfather is a reluctant hero: 'Even when it was over and CLJ got all his medals for bravery, he wasn't proud; he just shovelled them away in a drawer as if the idea of being picked out and decorated as a brave man was embarrassing to him' (p. 2). The reader is left to ponder CLJ's reaction, for Plato does not comment, deferring instead to his father's notion that this was just 'CLJ's way of telling him that war is a mug's game' (p. 2). Paternal authority in the book is quickly eroded though and Plato's father never appears in person, nor is he named. Eventually, it is revealed that Plato's father has misinterpreted CLJ's dismissal of his decorations. Significantly, in the absence of an authoritative explanation for CLJ's reaction to his war medals, there is room to doubt the value Plato attributes to them, and by association the model of heroism he has invested in.

Plato's sense of masculine identity is reliant upon his own place within a complex family structure, and although he is given advice and support from a number of female relations (his sister, mother, Welsh grandmother, and his Greek Great Aunt Elena), he invests in the male lineage bolstered by the heroic CLJ. Furthermore, Plato can only comfortably find a role for himself within this familial configuration if he can be sure of its moral foundations. If the framework is ethically unsound in his terms – and he is eventually forced to reconsider these terms – then *he* feels threatened. Plato's thoughtful disposition is established before his trip to Molo and he admits to sharing his Uncle's interest in philosophy, apparently concurring with Uncle Emlyn's view that 'human life is built around ideas' (p. 13). The ground is well prepared for Plato's extreme reaction to his discovery that Nikos was the man who betrayed CLJ to the German troops:

> Bad blood. Sins of the fathers.
>
> Obviously, I didn't take after CLJ, the sainted family Hero. So I must take after the family Villain. No wonder I was runty and skinny and half blind and asthmatic.

My Welsh grandmother had blamed the Greek in me and she had been right all the time!

Evil will out! My hideous physical appearance was the outward sign of my rotten inside; my treacherous character, my cowardly black heart. And admitting to something like that is like confessing that one of your immediate ancestors had a horrible and fatal disease like syphilis or Huntington's chorea. (pp. 87–8)

The revelation that Plato is descended from a traitor destabilizes Plato's selfhood and the faith he has placed in concepts such as goodness and heroism, which he attributes to CLJ and consequently himself. The full story of Nikos's betrayal of CLJ is more complex than Plato initially accepts though. Faced with the choice of allowing the Germans to shoot a church full of the village's women and children, or betraying members of the resistance, Nikos makes a decision that subjects him to torture by the Germans and to lifelong hatred from the villagers he saved. As Aunt Elena explains: '"the village never forgave him. Two of their young men had been shot. And in betraying CLJ, he had shamed them. They should have defended him with their lives. Nikos had betrayed their honour as Greeks"' (p. 79). Nikos's predicament amounts to another thought experiment and in placing this dilemma at the heart *The Real Plato Jones*, Bawden encourages the implied reader to consider the conflict between deontological and consequentialist ethics.

Nikos is ostracized from his village on the principles of deontological ethics that demand obedience to a priori absolutes regardless of consequence. From the villagers' point of view, Nikos's first duty is to the efforts of the Greek and British resistance to German occupation and nothing should keep him from this duty, yet Bawden offers another way of viewing Nikos's actions in ethical terms. Consequentialism, such as that advocated in the utilitarianism of Jeremy Bentham and John Stuart Mill, requires that the consequences of a given action be considered in measuring its moral substance, with emphasis on its potential to produce the most good or happiness. Especially significant in terms of understanding Nikos's actions, in 'Utilitarianism' (1861[11]), Mill proposes that

the happiness which forms the utilitarian standard of what is right in conduct, is not the agent's own happiness, but that of all concerned. As between his own happiness and that of others, utilitarianism requires him to be as strictly impartial as a disinterested and benevolent spectator. (Mill and Bentham,1987, p. 288)

Disregarding any concern for his own reputation or happiness, in deciding to save hundreds of lives (the women and children imprisoned in the church) in exchange for two members of the resistance, Nikos acts in accordance with the consequentialist position. It could be argued that in undermining the resistance, Nikos puts the whole war effort in danger and risks destroying the lives of thousands. However, Nikos's *intention* in confronting this dilemma is to save more lives and as Mill points out, 'The morality of the action depends entirely upon the intention – that is, upon what the agent *wills to do*' (Mill and Bentham, 1987, p. 290n). Plato does not recognize the consequentialist position unaided though, for his lifelong investment in masculine duty sways him towards the majority verdict against Nikos that 'Despis[es] him for a traitor' (p. 82). Moreover, having invested so much in his paternal heritage, Plato is forced to accept that if he is descended from the heroism of CLJ, then he must also carry treachery in his blood: 'The Coward and the Hero . . . "It's like having two people inside me who don't get on with each other. I mean, they might start a war any minute!"' (p. 118). It seems impossible for Plato to attain his goal of heroic manliness, until a pivotal conversation with CLJ persuades Plato that there might be other ways of conceiving morality and manhood.

Although Great Aunt Elena initially tells Nikos's story and seeks to show Plato that his choice was one of moral conviction (even heroism), it is CLJ who convinces Plato that there might be something to admire in Nikos's deeds. In CLJ's view of his own actions, he was not brave because there was no conscious decision to be made: '"I was too busy trying to stay alive to think about moral issues"' (p. 111). Conversely Nikos had to deal with an ethical dilemma: '"My friend Nikos was a brave man," CLJ said firmly. "He had an impossible decision to make. Between honour and death and dishonour and life"' (p. 111). CLJ's expression of friendship with Nikos is pointed and here the narrative opts for the consequentialist position and although (along with Plato) the implied reader is encouraged to consider both positions, it is difficult to read against CLJ's authority. Plato explains following his conversation with CLJ that the old man 'was going to leave me to "work it out" for myself' (p. 114), and this thoughtfulness preoccupies Plato, marking his movement towards a new-found acceptance of himself as boy and man. Set alongside this period of mental application is an interval of physical change for Plato; he becomes incessantly hungry and his mother observes, '"You've grown so much, nothing fits you"' (p. 123). As Plato's body grows into itself, so Plato reaches an understanding of Nikos's choice and it seems that physical growth is matched by cognitive maturation. Plato comes to accept that moral courage is a form of bravery that does not require physical strength. His short-sightedness and asthma might leave him without the physical prowess of the Robin Hood model he established for himself early on, but Bawden suggests that he does not need to be a hero in order to be a man and that his thoughtful intelligence might be also be a positive attribute of masculinity, thereby reinforcing John Stephens's observation that 'remodeled subjectivities may be depicted by affirming that gender norms are unstable and mutable and hence agency may take other forms' (2002, p. xi). When the fire threatens Molo, Plato watches and considers the actions of Spiro, a villager who displays the sort of courageous virtue described by Aristotle: 'in the strict sense of the word the courageous man will be one who is fearless in the face of an honourable death, or of some sudden threat of death' (2004, p. 67). Plato is content to take orders from this hero (as he describes him), for Plato no longer desires or needs heroism for himself, reflecting simply that Spiro's actions 'made all of us on the road a bit braver, too' (p. 151).

The destabilization of deontological ethics in *The Real Plato Jones* is mirrored by a reassessment of the muscular masculinity invested so heavily in duty ethics. As Plato comes to accept consequentialism, so he comes to see that there are other ways of being a man that are more relevant to him and his life experience. Plato embraces his dual cultural heritage finally, because he is able to draw the actions of both grandfathers into a broader ethical sphere:

> When people ask me my name it is easy to answer them. I am Plato Constantine Jones: Plato because of Nikos Petropoulos and Constantine because of CLJ. Everyone has heard about CLJ, but sometimes I have to explain that Nikos Petropoulos was just as brave and that I am just as proud of him. I aim to be a World Citizen. In the meantime, both my grandfathers fit very comfortably inside my own skin. (p. 172)

Plato reaches a point of comfort as yet out of reach of the Hensman brothers and of Laura in *Ask Me No Questions*, since the opening of his moral outlook is liberating and self-affirming, offering new ways of negotiating the world. In the late twentieth century, Nina Bawden's novel demonstrates that the deontological model maintained by gender conventions and fraternal rule can and should be challenged; this is not to say that positive male relationships are not possible, instead that readers ought to consider and recognize that moral agency does not begin and end in a narrow view of masculinity.

The Real Plato Jones is not alone in its reassessment of gendered hegemony, nor in its challenge to deontological ethics, but the path to change is gradual throughout this period of British children's literature, moving from a position of relatively passive discomfort and anxiety about gendered morality – *Brendon Chase*, *Ask Me No Questions*, and also Robert Leeson's challenge to the duties of familial domesticity in *It's My Life* (1980) – to more assertive articulations of alternatives in *The Monster Garden* and a range of ethically assertive books such as: *Midnight Blue* (1990) by Pauline Fisk; *Dear Nobody* (1991) by Berlie Doherty; *The Sterkarm Handshake* (1998) by Susan Price; *Postcards from No Man's Land* (1999) by Aidan Chambers; *Lady: My Life as a Bitch* (2001) by Melvin Burgess; *The Shell House* by Linda Newbery (2002); *The Curious Incident of the Dog in the Night-Time* by Mark Haddon (2003); *Finding Violet Park* (2007) by Jenny Valentine; and *Boys Don't Cry* (2010) by Malorie Blackman.

Although the renegotiation of fraternal moral networks is different in these variously subversive texts, in each the reader is confronted with the particular and intimate circumstances of ethical life and the idea that challenging these conditions entails risk or loss. Wrongdoing in these books is a question of challenging the fraternal authority of duty and locating new ways of being and doing in a journey towards the right and just. In Blackman's *Boys Don't Cry*, Dante is forced to renegotiate his future along with his unexamined assumptions related to sex and sexuality when he is thrust unexpectedly into fatherhood and an early question formulated in panic resounds throughout the novel: 'What was I going to do?' (p. 37). Dante's acceptance of a paternal duty that confounds his notions of male youth and entitlement are articulated in a first-person narrative that runs alongside that of Adam, his openly homosexual brother. As the voices of Adam and Dante speak to and against each other, so Blackman shows that responsibility and moral validation can come from unexpected sources, and the dual narrative invites readers to compare issues raised by each narrative thread and perspective. Dante's and Adam's understanding of duty and responsibility alters throughout the course of a narrative that explores violence, fear, denial, and silence as modes of response to rigid social conventions and expectations. The brothers gradually loosen their hold on the future(s) they had envisioned and *Boys Don't Cry* finally vindicates a caring ethics that indicates new ways of being male and performing masculinity. Melanie's unwitting gift to Dante, Adam, and their father is not only a baby daughter, niece, and granddaughter, but the creation of new possibilities framed by care and love as well: 'Before Emma had arrived, we'd occupied the same house and that was about it. But not any more. There were no questions answered, no blinding revelations, nothing had really been resolved. But we were a family and we were together' (2011/2010, p. 302). Blackman leaves answers and resolutions to a reader primed to envisage futures unforeseen, and in this she begins to realize Irigaray's vision:

This creation would be our opportunity, from the humblest detail of everyday life to the 'grandest,' by means of the opening of a *sensible transcendental* that comes into being through us, of which *we would be* the mediators and bridges. Not only in mourning for the dead God of Nietzsche, not waiting passively for the god to come, but by conjuring him up among us, within us, as resurrection and transfiguration of blood, of flesh, through a language and an ethics that is ours. (Irigaray, 2004/1984, p. 109)

It is through invitations to moral creativity – such as those offered by Blackman – that Irigaray's call to creation is answered. Alcock, Schlee, Bawden, and Blackman beckon young readers into a mode of being that forges new ideas through a giving of self that claims new ways of acting and speaking in the moral sphere.

6

The Greatness of Apple Seeds: Ethical Relationships in Miniature Literature

The cleverer I am at miniaturizing the world, the better I possess it. But in doing this, it must be understood that values become condensed and enriched in miniature. Platonic dialectics of large and small do not suffice for us to become cognizant of the dynamic virtues of miniature thinking. One must go beyond logic in order to experience what is large in what is small.

Bachelard, 1994/1958, p. 150

The 'dynamic virtues of miniature thinking' take Gaston Bachelard into spheres of the psychological and phenomenological as he argues for the provocative value of miniature poetic images in *The Poetics of Space* (1958). Meditation on 'a fragment from Cyrano de Bergerac' reveals that Cyrano's apple contains a little sun of a seed, which cannot be seen yet is lived in the imagination that makes the seed, '*hotter* than the entire apple' and hence Bachelard reflects: 'The apple itself, the fruit, is no longer the principal thing, but the seed, which becomes the real dynamic value' (1994/1958, p. 151). Bachelard contends that Plato's dialectical process of pure thought does not reach far enough after establishing that sight, along with the other senses, cannot 'distinguish properly whether [fingers] are large or small' (Plato, 1987, p. 330).[1] For Bachelard, 'Large issues from small, not through the logical law of a dialectics of contraries, but thanks to liberation from all obligations of dimensions, a liberation that is a special characteristic of the activity of the imagination' (pp.154–5). Bachelard is concerned especially with psychological laws that empower the imagination to explore the greatness residing in miniature and argues that 'The man with the magnifying glass – quite simply – bars the every-day world' in order that objects can be seen afresh with 'the enlarging gaze of a child' (p. 155). Bachelard's notion of the childhood gaze is here aligned with first-timeness and his conviction that the miniature involves such a closeness of looking that the reader sees as if never before. The botanist who writes of 'wedded life in miniature, in a flower' (p. 154) holds a magnifying glass that 'situates us at a sensitive point of objectivity, at the moment when we have to accept unnoticed detail, and dominate it' (p. 155).

Here is the key point of crossing for my discussion with Bachelard's reverie, for in common with writers throughout the history of literature – Swift and Carroll share this understanding, to name but two navigators of miniature provinces – Bachelard recognizes that the miniature can reveal that which is overlooked, or unseen in human being and experience, and further that the revelation of unnoticed detail entails domination. Abutting Bachelard's 'dominated worlds' (p. 161) is the domain of ethical enquiry, though Bachelard does not investigate the ethical conditions of domination, pursuing instead the 'metaphysical freshness' (p. 161) of the miniature that allows for a restful world consciousness emanating from the reading subject's experience of domination. Bachelard focuses on the reader/viewer's imaginative domination of miniature worlds; equally important though is the play and exchange of dominance performed by literary characters and it is here that discussion unfolds in my exploration of the ethical conditions of miniature British children's literature since 1945. During this period a number of influential and intriguing miniature tales for children appeared, including: *Mistress Masham's Repose* (1947) by T. H. White; *The Borrowers* (1952–82) sequence by Mary Norton; *The Twelve and the Genii* (1962) by Pauline Clarke; *The Indian in the Cupboard* trilogy (1981–9) by Lynne Reid Banks; and *The Man* (1992) by Raymond Briggs. Each of these texts engages with dominance on some level, although emphasis differs in each so that, for example, Clarke's novel is concerned with the creative life of the miniature awakened into being through mastery of the imagination, while *The Borrowers* explores power trades in the context of material culture, generational difference, and social transformation. Considered from an ethical perspective, miniature children's literature of this period draws together many of the moral concerns explored in earlier chapters, magnifying the moral conditions and complexities of human relationships. Especially relevant to young readers in this regard is the focus on the ethical circumstances of the fantastic conceit whereby the human child is rendered gigantic in relation to diminutive life forms (that may, or may not be, considered human); a conceit in which the question of dominance becomes central.

In *The Child That Haunts Us* (2009), a Jungian engagement with the symbolic potential of the child figure in miniature literature, Susan Hancock points to the 'enduring and wide-ranging nature of the literary miniature' (2009, p. 21), which has 'a well established place in folklore' (p. 20) and to its 'multiple manifestations of expression' (p. 21) in an array of different forms including picture books, poetry, novels, animated film, and graphic novels. Hancock argues that 'the symbolic resonance of these tiny creatures . . . far exceeds the minute nature of their imaginal appearances and could be regarded as the heart of a culture's collective engagement with "otherness"' (p. 24). Hancock explores this otherness in terms of Jungian realms of consciousness, while its ethical aspect moves into territory explored, for instance, by Midgley in *Heart and Mind* (1981) wherein she grapples with disparate strands of combatant moral philosophy, endeavouring to show the interconnectedness of human being, in terms of selfhood, relationships with others, and sociocultural demands/obligations. Midgley argues for the unity of human being in our view of morals – opposing the divorce between emotion and thought in numerous philosophical systems from Kantian deontology to the Nietzschean dominance of will – making a point underscored by the focus on otherness and domination in miniature literature that 'We very often have a prejudice against strangers, a prejudice which does not melt quite on its own, but which we must break down by a conscious effort at fairness' (2003/1981, p. 113). In Midgley's formulation, reason and feeling work together in a moral vision that offers a holistic sense of human being and relationships; a vision that can be identified (to a greater or lesser extent) in the ethical terrain of most miniature literature that imagines human-miniature relationships.

Miniature masterpieces of naturalism that amplify the ecological agenda of B.B.'s writing, *The Little Grey Men* (1942) and *Down the Bright Stream*[2] (1948), serve as cultural markers to a natural world in a state of passing presence: 'Secrecy was of utmost importance, especially in these modern days when discovery would mean the end of everything' (2004/1942, p. 6). Charting the 'shifting quarters' (1979/1948, p. 40) of the last gnomes in Britain, the rueful tone of narration, 'The heron nodded wistfully' (1979/1948, p. 90), contributes to their role as transitional texts in the history of children's literature, casting back like *Brendon Chase* in an effort to counter morally and politically the direction of sociocultural development. Similarly *Mistress Masham's Repose* is poised at a moment of historical and cultural transformation, as confirmed by Hancock's view that its nostalgic glance 'turn[s] away from twentieth-century urban living' via a narrative stance, albeit ironic, that 'looks toward the restoration of ancient estates and of the rightful heir' (2009, p. 114). The liminal status of T. H. White's novel is figured in various ways, including the gulf generated by the dimensional contrast of its imagined beings and its intertextual play with

Swift's *Gulliver's Travels* (1726), and to a lesser extent texts such as John Bunyan's *The Pilgrim's Progress* (1678); *Alice's Adventures in Wonderland* (1865) by Lewis Carroll; Mark Twain's *The Adventures of Huckleberry Finn* (1884); and *A High Wind in Jamaica* (1929) by Richard Hughes.[3] However, it is the intrusive and dogmatic *heterodiegetic* narration of *Mistress Masham's Repose*, combined with the interrogative function of Maria's eccentric companion, 'an old professor who lived in a distant part of the grounds' (1972/1947, p. 11), that drives its ethical inquiries in a progressive direction, while engaging with values of the past.

Set in the Northamptonshire estates of the sprawling and dilapidated Palace of Malplaquet, *Mistress Masham's Repose* melds ironized gothic fantasy – a direction taken later by Joan Aiken's *The Wolves of Willoughby Chase* (1962) – with miniature satire directed at a profusion of targets, such as pedagogy, colonialism, and (obsessive) philosophical endeavour. White relates the tale of the orphaned Maria – the 10-year-old heir of Malplaquet left in the dubious care of her governess Miss Brown and her guardian, the local Vicar – who discovers that exiled Lilliputians are residing on the little island of Mistress Masham's Repose, 'a plastered temple in the shape of a cupola, or to give it its proper name, of a monopteron' (p. 12) presiding over the Quincunx, one of Malplaquet's many lakes. White's novel offers a tangental sequel to *Gulliver's Travels*, departing from the Swiftian citation: 'I took with me six Cows and two Bulls alive, with as many Yews and Rams, intending to carry them into my own Country and propagate the Breed . . . I would gladly have taken a Dozen of the Natives' (White, 1972/1947, epigraph). White imagines that Captain John Biddel of Deptford (the seaman who rescues Gulliver after his voyage to Lilliput), having been made a 'Present of a Cow and a Sheep big with Young' (Swift, 2005/1726, p. 71) by Gulliver, returns to Lilliput to procure 'Natives' for exploitation on British soil. Biddel then exhibits his 'Captives among the Fair Grounds of the Kingdom' (White, p. 51) until the Lilliputians escape their 'Master's Tyranny' and 'Debauchery' (p. 52).

This history of captivity and exile is related to Maria by the Lilliputian Schoolmaster, a rare voice of reliable authority in the book. The language used to recount this history is morally charged, drawing the implied reader's attention to the concept of liberty as an ethical principle that shapes moral agency. Rendering Biddel's treatment of the 'miserable Captives' as ruthless and avaricious (p. 51), the Schoolmaster's historical lecture (as it is presented) assumes a modern approach to liberty as established by John Rawls: 'one might want to maintain . . . that the so-called liberty of the moderns is of greater value than the liberty of the ancients' (1999/1971, pp. 176–7). Rawls goes on to observe as he confirms the priority of liberty in a just society that 'the precedence of liberty means that liberty can be restricted only for the sake of liberty itself' (p. 214). *Mistress Masham's Repose* plays out this position through its two generic (miniature and gothic) strands, inviting from the reader a sympathetic response to the Lilliputian history of captive exile (and the fantastic conceit on which the miniature status of the book rests) and to Maria and the Professor's eventual incarceration in the Malplaquet dungeons at the hands of governess and guardian. Villainy is located in the denial of liberty (personified by Captain Biddel, Miss Brown, and the Vicar), although as this ethically aware and exuberant narrative demonstrates, the maintenance of liberty is not straightforward (for any of its characters) and the route to wickedness too easily navigated. In this regard, Maria's function as an identifiable narratee of a history rendered formally and in language that she is not conversant with is significant, since her response to it foreshadows her tentative and difficult journey into moral agency as she attempts to forge a sustainable alliance with the Lilliputians:

> Maria could not help feeling relieved when the History was over. Her head was buzzing with capital letters, and she secretly thought that it was more fun to ask questions, instead of listening to lectures. She was also doubtful about being called, 'Ma'am Y'r Honour, Miss', knowing that her proper name was Maria, and she was determined to keep the proceedings on a less formal level. (p. 54)

Maria recognizes that relationships of import are being forged here (between child and adult, human and Lilliputian) and that something significant is being asked of her that overreaches her – hence her discomfort with the pompous mode of address – in terms of maturity and life experience and which seeks to redress the indignities suffered by the Lilliputians in the past. Here (and elsewhere in the lectures Maria endures from the Professor) Maria's response emphasizes a tension between the import of the message conveyed and the mode of its delivery and her role as audience and participant is meaningful. As child narratee there are two functional aspects to Maria's narrative position: she is a vehicle for moral inquisition and expositional deflation, as she prods at the message being conveyed; plus she is a template for normative response that the implied reader is invited by the narrator to judge. Thus Maria's path to moral agency proceeds partly through her role as narratee as she listens to and then applies practically, or refuses, the lessons conveyed in formalized lectures or educational advice. Her response is assessed shortly after this passage when Maria seeks to converse informally with the Schoolmaster and is beset with the problem of how they might 'walk' together when their steps are of incompatible magnitude: 'she did not like to suggest the idea of carrying him. There was something babyish about being carried, and she did not want to humiliate him; for she had a certain amount of good taste, in spite of being only ten' (p. 54). The narrator's commentary implies that Maria has understood the loss of dignity enshrined in Lilliputian history, and that in her 'good taste' she also has the capacity for sensitive, morally aware, consideration of others.

Maria's orientation within literary convention is relevant to the framing of her discovery of the Lilliputians when she finds a baby in a walnut shell lying close to the doors of the Repose. Boating close to the little island Maria 'began to feel piratical. Swouns and Slids, she said to herself, but you could stap her vitals if she did not careen there, and perhaps dig up some buried treasure while about it' (p. 13). Just as the realist operators of *Swallows and Amazons* (1930) are augmented by layers of fantasized imagining as the Walker children enrich their Lakeland adventures through engagement with literary materials that have shaped their values and imaginations, Maria drifts into fanciful spaces drawn from literary codes, blurring the boundary between fantasy and reality in a meaningful way. Maria's piracy allows a temporary evasion of the powerlessness defining her orphaned and neglected childhood – just as Cutty Sarking is a rehearsal of command for Roger, the (almost) youngest of five siblings,[4] as he 'made his way up the field in broad tacks' (Ransome, 1958/1930, p. 15) – and Maria's attitude at this moment of discovery is coloured by the piratical trope. This trope might be interpreted as one of subversive challenge to colonial power structures, yet it also feeds from them, investing in concepts such as domination, exchange of power, materialist acquisition – as revealed in the writing of Ballantyne, Marryat, Stevenson, Barrie, Hughes, and Ransome. 'Her spectacles twinkling fiercely in the sun' (p. 14), Maria is caught in a liminal space that distances her routine existence, leaving her poised to react to the walnut infant with a moral attitude of defensive authority, keen to take possession of something that has been exposed to her alone and to sustain the feeling of liberty and control which she has weaved for herself during her efforts to break through the island's dense wall of weeds. Maria also draws with her an implied reader versed in the cutlass brandishing and shore swarming (p. 14) demanded of literary piracy, preparing the way for the complex web of ethical positioning spun in *Mistress Masham's Repose*.

Maria's initial response to the island is an uncanny feeling prompted by the unexpected smoothness of its interior, 'But what was strange – and here Maria's heart went Pat, she knew not why – the strange thing was that everything was neat' (p. 15). This elicits in Maria a heightened sense of (psychological) awareness, such as that attributed to the miniature by Bachelard: 'Everything was so clean, so different from the wasteland which she had just come through – so square and round and geometrical, just as it had been when first erected – that her eye was drawn to details' (p. 16). Bachelard points out that the miniature has an affective impact on the reader/viewer and Maria's examination of the baby – reminiscent of the close attention to miniature detail delineated by Bachelard – seems emotionally drawn from engagement with the miniature:

> She held it tenderly in the palm of her hand, not breathing for fear of spoiling it, and examined its wonderful perfection as well as she could. Its eyes, which were as small as a shrimp's, seemed to have the proper marble-blue for babies; its skin was slightly mauve, so that it must have been a new one; it was not skinny, but beautifully plump, and she was just able to distinguish the creases round its fat wrists – creases which looked as if the thinnest hair had been tied round in a tight bracelet, or as if the hands had been fitted, on the ball-and-socket principle, by the most cunning of all the dollmakers there had ever been. (p. 17)

Maria's keen and magnified attention to the baby approaches Bachelard's notion of domination, for her scrutiny covers every detail of the precious ('for fear of spoiling') miniature object in an act of sensory possession. That the status of this tiny being perplexes Maria is suggested by its 'wonderful perfection', shifting it into realms of otherness that exclude it from humanity and through reference to a 'dollmaker', which gives unconscious permission to toy with a creature designed for play. Maria's attitude of emotional domination is further confirmed as the narrator describes her 'rapture with this windfall' (p. 17), rendering the baby as something intended for her care or consumption. Consequently, Maria's emotional response to the Lilliputian child – influenced also by piratical priming – is difficult for her to govern morally.

Maria is wrenched out of her miniature reverie by the angry attack of the baby's protective mother and the narrator provides a commentary to Maria's moral response once she realizes that the baby is not and cannot be her own: 'She guessed immediately that this was the mother of the baby, and, instead of feeling angry . . . she began to feel guilty about the baby. She began to have an awful suspicion that she would have to give it back' (p. 18). Maria's guilt primes her for moral agency and positions her as an agent willing to act in accordance with justice and who recognizes the rights of others. The rights of a mother (unless there are grounds to doubt her fitness for mothering) to care for and protect her child is a fairly uncontested area of moral law in contemporary ethics and Maria's immediate concession of maternal entitlement places these (as yet unknown) miniature beings within the sphere of moral concern. The narrator also withdraws Maria from the fictional realm that she has been inhabiting, so that the gravity of the moral situation before her is realized:

> Now in spite of homicides or other torts which she might have committed as a pirate, who was partial to the Plank, Maria was not the kind of person who bore malice for injuries, and she was certainly not the kind of kidnapper who habitually stole babies from their heartbroken mothers, for the mere cynical pleasure of hearing them scream.[5] (p. 18)

The narrator establishes that the groundwork for moral agency is laid in Maria's character and that essentially she is inclined to the good (unlike Biddel, Brown, and the Vicar); the point is made emphatically and with purpose. The narrative weight given to Maria's inclination to moral empathy and right underscores the strain of moral agency, making it clear that moral choice is tough: 'Yet the temptation to keep it was severe . . . Think to yourself, truly, whether you would have returned a live one-inch baby to its relatives, if caught fairly in the open field?' (p. 18). This sort of direct address and moral signposting is common throughout *Mistress Masham's Repose,* rendering the novel overtly philosophical and shaping the implied reader as thoughtful and responsive to moral attitudes. Consequent to this provocative address, the implied reader is embroiled in Maria's situation and overtly invited to think through her subsequent actions in the manner of a thought experiment. Having resolved to return the baby to its mother, Maria is enraged when her moral generosity (from her gargantuan perspective) is rejected and bundles mother and baby into her skirt. Evidently, Maria is at an early stage of moral development during which emotion outweighs thought and morality is not functioning organically in Midgley's terms:

> Morality, like every other aspect of human activity, has both its emotional and its intellectual side, and the connection between them can't be just an external one, like that between stones brought together for a building. It is an organic one, like that between the shape and size of an insect. (2003/1981, p. 6)

Mistress Masham's Repose does much work towards organically uniting emotion and intellect and caricatured aspects of White's creations (human and Lilliputian) point to an author well versed in the battleground of ethical debates such as those charted by Midgley. In part this drive to holistic morality is achieved through Maria's evident struggle with emotional responses to the Lilliputians, whose miniature presence seem to emphasize – as Bachelard anticipates – the difficulties of her situation as child (opposed to adult) and orphan (opposed to guardian). The Professor recognizes that in the Lilliputians Maria sees her own relative insignificance and that this governs her desire to dominate: ' "people must not tyrannize, nor try to be great because they are little. My dear, you are a great person yourself, in any case, and you do not need to lord it over others, in order to prove your greatness" ' (p. 28). This observation expresses concerns central to miniature children's literature, exposing the subjection of less powerful others as a response to insecure and relatively powerless selfhood. The Professor also advises Maria to free mother and child on the grounds of liberty and a Kantian notion of good will that requires us to act towards others as we would wish ourselves treated, ' "How would *you* like to be wrapped up in a handkerchief?" ' (p. 28). Although Maria evidently understands the principles of the Professor's argument in cognitive terms, her judgment is obscured by her heart and she concludes her part in the exchange, ' "I have nobody to love" ' (p. 29), though as the Professor observes later (echoing Kierkegaard who also warns about the dangers of false love), ' "the trouble about loving things is that one wants to possess them" ' (p. 77).

The Professor's role in *Mistress Masham's Repose* is to tease out ethical issues associated with embarking on a relationship marked by difference, in which a race/species is disadvantaged by the spatial environment of the country to which they are exiled. The Professor seeks to make Maria aware of the difference between caring support and overbearing dominion and eventually she begins to understand his advice: 'She suddenly realized why, whenever she brought the Lilliputians a present, they tried to give her one. It was because they did not want to be possessed' (p. 80). This might seem to champion adult authority and reason over the emotion associated with Maria's inexperienced childhood, 'although she was decent . . . she was still young' (p. 67), yet the Professor's exclusive commitment to thinking is as problematic as Maria's emotive desire to adore and frolic with the Lilliputians until she 'lost grip of herself' and 'proceeded on the road to ruin with the speed of a Rake's Progress' (p. 68). The Hogarth reference indicates the satiric edge to White's novel, which also targets the Professor and some of his less self-aware observations:

'I think that Dr Swift was silly to laugh about Laputa[.] I believe it is a mistake to make a mock of people, just because they think. There are ninety thousand people in this world who do not think, for every one who does, and these people hate the thinkers like poison. Even if some thinkers are fanciful, it is wrong to make fun of them for it. Better to think about cucumbers even, than not to think at all.' (p. 165)

Maria struggles to interject the reflexive satire with a 'But' here, for she sees in this speech the delusions of a friend who is starving and impoverished due to his obsessive devotion to thinking and academic pursuit. The Professor's authority in the book diminishes as Maria's relationship with the Lilliputians matures and 'they saw that their child mountain intended to do her best' (p. 79). Consequently, when Maria is in need of rescue from the Malplaquet dungeons the Professor is 'sitting at the end of his vegetable garden, under a marble monument to the Tragic Muse' (p. 126), and instead of responding to the cook's anxiety about Maria's disappearance, 'He forgot about Maria and began looking up "bloaters" in a dictionary, to see if they were derived from the Swedish word "blöt", which they were' (p. 133). Evidently a re-evaluation of the Professor's moral standing is called for here, since moral thinking is presented as futile without action; Maria might need to 'keep hold of [her] emotions' (p. 77), but at least she acts to save the Lilliputians from discovery – and with good intentions in the end. Furthermore, although the Professor steers Maria on a clear moral course underscored by egalitarian liberty, there is a hiatus between the advice he offers her and his own moral capacity. This is suggested by a protracted sequence of daydreaming in which the Professor imagines capturing a Brobdingnagian, 'Think of the glory and the excitement of catching somebody who was as high as a church spire!' (p. 141) and doubts about the Professor's equity are also raised by his refusal to visit the island of Repose: 'The very thought of going made him feel awkward. He felt, if you can follow the idea, that the fact of visiting them would be an inroad on their proper freedom, because he was so much bigger than they were' (p. 140). Hancock observes that this can be interpreted as a 'critique of the abuse of power' (2009, p. 118), and again it draws attention to the gulf between moral principle and action; moral responsibility is daunting and revealed as a weight that the Professor fears he cannot bear. The narrator's interjection, 'if you can follow the idea', is especially significant for the agency of implied readers here, for they are prompted to challenge the thinking of a character who has served previously as a locus of authority. In destabilizing the Professor's role as ethical touchstone, the narrative expressly invites consideration of the range of moral positions articulated through the course of the novel.

Mistress Masham's Repose is a milestone in miniature children's literature, due in part to its overt and witty engagement with philosophical discourse, and also owing to the positive statement it makes about moral agency in childhood and the extent to which young people are open to engaging with moral issues through empirical experience and teaching. Explicit observations are made about the difficult conditions of childhood in terms of powerlessness, 'Children are under dreadful disadvantages compared with their elders' (p. 89) and immaturity, 'she was inexperienced and had not thought'(p. 70), nonetheless the narrative thrust towards Maria's moral agency makes it clear that these obstacles can be overcome with a mixture of good will and thoughtful consideration followed by active response. The proof of Maria's successful acquisition of moral agency is the lasting friendship she achieves with the Lilliputians. That this friendship contains Aristotelian contours of virtue is suggested by the banner hung by the 'Beautiful People' on Maria's return to Malplaquet after the Vicar's trial: 'WELCOME HOME! A LOYAL GREETING FROM LILLIPUT TO THEIR MARIA! AND TO HER ERUDITE FRIEND!' (p. 198). Maria is valued for her friendship to the Lilliputians and for the capacity for friendship demonstrated in her companionship with the Professor (her erudite friend).The quality of ownership here (their Maria) is markedly different from Maria's early attempts to possess the Walnut baby, accentuating instead the shared values and loyalty of friendship that 'holds communities together' (Aristotle, 2004, p. 201). Moreover, children are implicated as narratee and implied reader at several levels of the narrative structure, emphasizing that the ethical concerns of the novel are directed at them. As already established, Maria functions as both protagonist and narratee addressed by the Professor and the Schoolmaster, while the *heterodiegetic* narrator addresses unknown imaginative, thoughtful child readers and specifically Amaryllis, the book's dedicatee, 'But go you down past the Quincunx, Amaryllis, as you wind your long way home, and you might see . . .' (p. 204).

As Bachelard would concur that which Amaryllis sees (or indeed any sensory experience that she might have) is meaningful psychologically and ontologically, though miniature literature also reinforces the idea that moral agency begins with perceiving others at a close and deep level, while recognizing that sensory experience in abundance can impede entry into ethical life. This ability to translate empirical experience into ethical consideration of the miniature other also features in works of miniature literature that follow *Mistress Masham's Repose*. *The Twelve and the Genii* is largely an ontological exploration of the creative force that (re) animates the Bronte's 'Twelve' when Max finds their wooden soldiers hidden in his attic, but Max's desire to protect the soldiers from avaricious collectors and his recognition that he must allow them independence reveals his burgeoning moral awareness. At the outset, Max hovers in a space of liminal anxiety, 'His heart felt big with such a thrilling secret inside it' (Clarke, 1970/1962, p. 12), longing to share the phenomenon with his older siblings, and simultaneously keen to dominate this secret knowledge and to control the situation. Hoping to catch the soldiers in their live state (they revert to wood when in danger of discovery), Max listens at the attic door, focusing on the magnitude of the sound the soldiers make: 'His rather large ears stuck out from his head as if they were the larger for listening' (p. 11). Max seems physically altered by and implicated in the intensity of his sensory engagement with the miniature and their concerns become his in the sort of moral exchange Plumwood describes as mutuality.[6] Max listens closely, shifting the status of what he hears from translatable noise, 'of course they would say it was rats . . . or birds on the roof' to the miniature's meaningful language, already resisting any impulse to translate the sounds he hears into the province of human experience: 'Pit pat tipper tapper scrabble stamp. Whee. Whish. Sizzle whizzle. That was the whispering./He supposed that, to them, that size, it was proper speaking' (p. 11). Max's listening involves him in the sort of anti-imperial translation that Arnold Krupat associates with a challenge to colonialism that 'attempt[s] to imagine living other forms of life' (2006/1996, p. 178). Max refuses to translate to the 'imperial centre' of adult authority and to explain away these sounds, rather he finds a way of recognizing them as language through taking a mutually empathetic view of the other.

Max's listening skills reveal a precocious moral agency that lends him a generous awareness of his miniature companions from the commencement of their relationship, placing him further up the scale of moral agency than those who take in the miniature through sight, for the protagonists who see the miniature at first approach tend to consume through their gaze. This is rendered symbolically in *The Borrowers* by the Clock family's dread of being 'seen' by humans, a fear magnified when the diminutive Arrietty first goes borrowing with her father Pod and is seen by the boy: 'It was an eye. Or it looked like an eye. Clear and bright like the colour of the sky. An eye like her own but enormous. A glaring eye' (Norton, 2003/1952, p. 92). In contrast to the gargantuan (human) viewer's consumptive aspect of the miniature, Arrietty's view of the boy overwhelms her and she cannot take in the whole of him, so that his eye alone is her firmament. The boy's first words are immediately commanding, ' "Don't move!" ' (p. 93), and he proceeds with an attempt to categorize Arrietty, ' "Can you fly?" ' (p. 97), though in spite of Arrietty's indignant resistance, the boy swamps Arrietty and the Clock household with a spiralling materialism that eventually destroys their home. Like Norton's boy, the human protagonist of *The Indian in the Cupboard* takes in Little Bull – a plastic figure magically transformed into a living being – through sight initially: 'Omri peered closer, and his breath fell on the tiny huddled figure' (Banks, 1993/1981, p. 11), causing a defensive reaction from the frightened Indian that confirms Omri as a dominant force. Mirroring

Maria's grasping attack in *Mistress Masham's Repose*, Omri's reflex is to reinforce sight with touch: 'His next thought was that he must somehow get the Indian in his hand. He didn't want to frighten him any further, but he *had* to touch him. He simply had to' (p. 12). Omri's impulse is proprietorial, seeking to own the experience (and hence Little Bull): 'it was certainly the most marvelous thing that had ever happened to Omri in his life and he wanted to keep it to himself' (p. 12). This echoes Max's desire to keep his secret from his siblings, however Omri's attitude is more grasping literally and the route from visual sensing to ownership is swift and difficult to unpick, as Omri discovers when – having moved into the realm of moral agency – he witnesses the same process at work in his best friend Patrick.

It is possible to judge Omri's reaction in terms of racist bigotry,[7] in which his middle-class, white masculinity claims entitlement over a Red Indian male and to argue that the ideological force of the narrative is blind to issues of colonial terminology and 'imperial translation' in Krupat's (p. 176) terms – Little Bull remains an 'Indian' in spite of specific revelations of Iroquois heritage and history, Boone continues to be a 'Cowboy' and their dialogue is formulaic in contrast to Omri's 'standard' English. Nevertheless, such a judgement disregards and misunderstands the conceit of toy-to-miniature-human transformation and the cultural codes of play set up in *The Indian in the Cupboard*. Just as Maria discerns *her* Lilliputians through the lens of literary piracy, so Omri perceives Little Bull and Boone (the plastic cowboy transformed as a companion for Little Bull) through the cultural platitudes and tropes that define the Western genre and the gaming rituals developed through them – hence 'It occurred to Omri for the first time that his idea of Red Indians, taken entirely from Western films, had been somehow false' (p. 33). In addition, Omri's initial sense of ownership, 'After all, you are my Indian' (p. 13), comes less from assumptions based on racial difference, than a sense of entitlement related to ownership of private goods. Omri has long collected plastic figures, so when Patrick gives him 'a secondhand plastic Red Indian which he himself had finished with' for his birthday, Omri 'was really very grateful – sort of' (p. 7). His tentative gratitude here reflects his struggle to recognize Little Bull's rights as a fellow human, who cannot be reduced to the notional attributes of a child's toy, while also foreshadowing moral tensions arising between Omri and Patrick. Conceptually, when Omri claims proprietorial rights, Little Bull remains a gift bestowed upon him and Omri has yet to take the ethical leap that accompanies the knowledge he attains on first sight of Little Bull that 'he was alive. /Omri knew that immediately' (p. 11).

Meticulous observation is not always a negative aspect of miniature morality though and as Murdoch argues, literature and painting can 'show us the peculiar sense in which the concept of virtue is tied on to the human condition' (2001/1970, p. 84). In line with Bachelard's positive gaze, she also points out that this can only be revealed by the viewer's close looking. In *The Indian in the Cupboard*, this idea is figuratively conveyed through the creative pursuits of Boone and Little Bull that require Omri to reconsider the people with whom he attempts (not entirely successfully) to build a reciprocal relationship. For example, Boone proves to be an artist – an occupation and talent that forces Omri to reassess the Cowboy he thought he understood and knew – and he sketches a detailed impression of the town in the 1890s America from which he has been transported in time and space:

> From Boone's point of view, he was drawing something quite large, making the best use of his vast piece of paper; but from Omri's, the drawing was minute, perfect in its detailing but smaller than any human hand could possibly have made it. (p. 116)

Careful examination of the image allows Omri to place Boone historically and geographically and it forces him to recognize that Boone's talents and potential are inescapably limited by his relocation into miniature being (relocation being more appropriate than transformation, since the fantastic conceit in *The Indian in the Cupboard* allows people, animals, and objects to be transported from various points in history by the magical properties of a key which warps proportional dimensions). Rendered miniature in the future landscape of Omri's bedroom, Boone and Little Bull have been placed in a position of dependence that makes it impossible, in spite of Omri's recognition that they must be taken seriously as '*people*' (p. 107), for them to live independently. Although Omri reaches a stage of moral responsibility in which he 'would take on almost anything' in order that 'Little Bull should be happy' (p. 130), the disproportionate responsibility (reflected metaphorically in Boone's drawing) Omri undertakes for these tiny people diminishes his selfhood, just as it erodes theirs. The modal inflection entailed in 'should be happy' signals an is to ought formulation that necessitates the return of Little Bull and Boone to their proper state on moral grounds.

Sensory encounters are a convention of miniature literature that allow for a deep involvement with philosophical discourse, engaging with metaphysical and ethical spheres that explore the intimate and minutely significant conditions of humanity. The young implied reader is provided with figurative models of complex moral relationships that begin with an intense surge of the neurons, gradually moving towards a fusion of corporeal feeling and cognitive thinking. As Midgley points out, the relationship between these two aspects of human experience is complicated and 'Disentangling the intellectual from the emotional aspects of this whole is performing a piece of abstraction, one which needs enormously more care than theorizers usually give it' (2003/1981, p. 5). Miniature literature performs just this task of abstraction and frequently works it through in relation to the power structures of childhood. The symbolic relationships of miniature literature shape childhood in terms of a disempowered yearning for power and demonstrate that Bachelard's (minutely detailed) seed is so powerfully intense that it can burn on handling; thus Boone is almost killed by Little Bull's arrow (p. 132) and Maria nearly kills her 'beautiful but silly young fisherman' (p. 68). Sensory experiences conveyed through miniature literature frequently entail an amplified and ethically problematic appreciation of the beautifully strange, exotic, and other in which moral agency and equity can only be achieved via a working through of desire. Whereas Maria must come to terms with and expunge the desperate craving that unsettles selfhood and precludes balanced relationships – preventing progress of the spirit into ethical life in Hegelian terms – her counterpart in *The Man* by Raymond Briggs must overcome feelings of revulsion for the other, John's encounter with the miniature serving as a reminder that the senses reveal ugliness in addition to beauty and that the ethical dilemmas ensuing from this revelation are no less challenging or vital for the moral agent.

The Man refuses conscious sensory awareness to John at the outset, for he sleeps in ignorance of the man's presence visually signalled to the reader by cough sweets targeted at his dormant head. This reverses the direction of perception and balance of dominance typical of miniature literature in favour of the miniature character,[8] so that it is the man who observes, demands – ' "Can't you find me some clothes?" ' (1994/1992, p. 4)[9] – and acts during the opening sequence. This scene of forceful awakening establishes the tone for a graphic text that confronts a range of moral and social issues via a candid and inquisitive combination of combative dialogue and abrasive illustration that offers few solutions (as implied by the wordless opening frames leading into the narrative) to the problem of social exclusion. This is not to say that the man is presented as an empowered individual, but his assertive stance is established as a condition of his survival in a society that renders him invisible and inadequate and it is an aspect of his function as a figure of protest and resistance to social inequality.

The Man tells of the four-day relationship (the man leaves on the fifth day) that builds between John and an aggressively demanding unattractive little man who appears in his bedroom without explanation. The man lives an itinerant and scrounging existence, relying on the care of human strangers to sustain him. He selects relatively safe, sympathetic households to keep him, ' "I marked this one down as a good billet weeks ago" ' (p. 38), leaving once the pressure of intense dependency becomes dangerous; as the man eventually threatens John, ' "I've only got to pick up a MATCH!" ' (p. 58). The man's dynamic vocal presence is matched illustratively by the physical solidity of his naked frame, making it impossible for John and the reader to ignore him as he shivers into unloveliness on the first page. Echoing the narrative focus on the plight of a miniature man, Briggs's chosen hybrid form allows for an intense and magnified consideration of discrimination, dependence, and the boundaries of moral responsibility. Briggs visually expresses the man's vulnerability, as in an elongated frame he hangs from a worktop over a lethal mass of glass shards and the verbal anguish of his accompanying cry, ' "Boy! Boy! Boy! Help! Help! Help! HELP ME!" ' (p. 53) leaves John and the implied reader to wonder where responsibility lies for this perplexing and unfathomable being.

The man voices angrily the discontent of the marginalized and disturbs the comfortable complacency of liberal middle-class materialism by asking where the boundaries of familial and social care lie and what happens to those outside it, ' "You see, we can't lead a normal life. Can't go to work" ' (p. 45). Briggs's text makes it clear that this 'normal life' is relative, excluding those who cannot contribute wealth or labour to the economy and when he says that his size prohibits him from work, the man recognizes that he is excluded from the labour exchange that would render him valuable within capitalism. As Marx explains in his discussion of the buying and selling of labour-power:

> Nature does not produce on the one side owners of money or commodities, and on the other men possessing nothing but their own labour – power. This relation has no natural basis, neither is its social basis one that is common to all historical periods. It is clearly the result of a past historical development, the product of many economic revolutions, of the extinction of a whole series of older forms of social production. (1999/1867, pp. 109–10)

One of the moral questions framed in *The Man* asks whether the unnatural, social basis of human existence in capitalist society is ethically sound. Published in the early 1990s, *The Man* expresses a particular moment in British history, in the aftermath of a decade that celebrated individual wealth and in which social reform lost its sting under Margaret Thatcher's conservative government.

The Man's social conscience – and its edge is one of moral concern, rather than political direction – suggests that the historical aspect of social exclusion identified by Marx could be changed and challenged in a future imagined by the man as he gazes into a moon-washed cloudy night (rendered impenetrable by Briggs's bleeding watercolour) from John's rooftop. Indeed, the Socratic altercations between the man and John have moral purpose and the moral urgency of the man's plight is conveyed through the constraints of literary form in a graphic narrative comprised of illustrated frames interrupted and spliced by fast-paced exchanges of dialogue. In common with the other works of miniature literature discussed in this chapter, the matter of the miniature's humanity elicits ontological debate and frames questions about the miniature's place in the moral sphere.

When John does wake, he finds it difficult to accept that the man before him is real and he distrusts his own perceptive faculties: 'This is a dream . . . yes . . . I know I am dreaming' (p. 4). This is the first of many reasons John suggests for the man's presence – he wonders whether he is a Borrower, an extra terrestrial, a fairy, a gnome, an animal, or an undiscovered species – though no explanation is ever supplied, leaving the implied reader to speculate about the man's origin and actuality. When not distracted by the man's relentless demands for clothes, food, and entertainment, John thinks rather than feels and in the early stages of their relationship most of his reasoning is focused on rationalizing the man's presence and the situation in which he finds himself, though he is not offered the opportunity for a reflective consideration of the sort of ethical issues raised by the Professor in *Mistress Masham's Repose*. The Professor's wrangles with the 'legal definition of a human being' (1972/1947, p. 88) divert him from the moral question of whether the Lilliputians should be saved from a life in slavery and, likewise, John's obsessive desire to identify and categorize the man distracts him from ethical considerations of benevolent care and flags prejudice as a central theme, pushing the man to exclaim: ' "Intolerant, that's what you are. No freedom of speech in this house! No Human Rights here! Persecuted for my beliefs! Now I am to be exiled!" ' (p. 47). The man accuses John of caring for and about him only because he is small – ' "Suppose you'd been woken up by a naked starving man six foot tall? . . . You wouldn't have hid him and fed him?" ' (p. 42) – pointing out that John cannot see beyond his size and has no regard for him as an individual. These antagonistic exchanges between boy and man point to an uncomfortable truth about the limitations of moral concern in contemporary British society that neither of them are able to solve and that the reader is left to contemplate. In

a comparable discussion of 'Insiders and Outsiders' Singer discusses the national
boundaries of moral responsibility that dictate the treatment of refugees:

> All developed nations safeguard the welfare of their residents . . . protecting their
> legal rights, educating their children, and providing social security payments and
> access to medical care, either universally or for those who fall below a defined
> level of poverty. Refugees receive none of these benefits unless they are accepted
> into the country. Since the overwhelming majority of them are not accepted,
> the overwhelming majority will not receive these benefits. But is this distinction
> in the way in which we treat residents and nonresidents ethically defensible?
> (1993/1979, p. 252)

John actually suggests that the man might be a refugee, '"You're escaping
from oppression, tyranny and whatnot"' (Briggs, p. 46) and although the
man rejects this explanation as to his presence, he is similarly displaced, '"I
haven't got a place of my own. We have to move about . . . Have to keep on
the move. We can't live on our own, see?"' (p. 11), and so *The Man* poses a
question related to Singer's. Singer argues that distinctions between resident
and non-resident are not sustainable, for they are located in a position of
racial and social discrimination that cannot be supported ethically. Citing
Michael Walzer's *Spheres of Justice* (1983), Singer demonstrates that prejudices
embodied in national policies excluding benefits to refugees can be seen more
clearly when considered in terms of family or social structures: 'To take a
stranger into one's family is something that we might consider goes beyond the
requirement of mutual aid; but to take a stranger, or even many strangers, into
the community is far less burdensome' (p. 254). Singer goes on to contest this
position, implying that we should reconsider the family as a site for mutual aid;
similarly *The Man* shows that the familial context usefully emphasizes social
policies that exclude outsiders. When *The Man* places a stranger in the familial
home, the ensuing oscillations from concern to conflict between man and boy
suggest that the structure of modern family life (in conjunction with the wider
society that shapes it) is not designed to maintain care for those who are unable
to contribute to its functioning life; hence, the epigraphical Chinese Proverb,
'After three days, fish and visitors begin to stink' (p. 2). The focus on family as
a social structure with a limited capacity for ethical concern leads to moral
questions about Britain's commitment to a welfare state, asking where those
dependent on care – 'the borderline people in our society, the very old, the
mentally ill or handicapped'[10] – should go if they cannot look to family life or
wider social networks for support. Moreover, through its intimate illustrations

of domestic life (such as close-ups of kettles and bathtubs) *The Man* implies that the exclusive conditions of family life might not be ethically valid.

Just as the Marxist theories of Althusser show that the family is an ISA that shapes the child (and other family members) in terms of the dominant values of capitalism,[11] so *The Man* demonstrates that John is hemmed in and limited in his response to the man by the familial structures and material conditions that surround him. This idea is conveyed formally to the reader by the framing device of 'offstage' parental dialogue that comments on and puzzles over John's apparently subversive behaviour: ' "I'm so worried about Johnny . . . he's taken to buying his own expensive marmalade" ' (p. 48). These ironic asides on suburban anxieties reveal that John's parents are especially concerned with the financial outlay incurred in caring for the man – whom they know nothing about – and with John's negligent destruction of material goods, such as his father's antique glass and his stylus brush. This light-hearted approach to interrogating middle-class values is offset by the increasingly sombre mood of the illustrations though, as boy and man come to care about each other, ' "I'm growing quite fond of you, boy" ' (p. 40), while recognizing that their relationship can only ever be temporary, rendered impossible by the demands and boundaries of social structures. The contrasting position of man and boy in relation to state authorities lends *The Man* political potential, revealing that the capacity of state apparatus to support or punish is relative to the individual's social status. The man lives in fear of being discovered by 'the Authorities . . . School, Town Council, DHSS, Police' and by 'busybodies . . . Yes. Prodnoses, nosy parkers, tripe merchants – mucky newspapers, tatty magazines, soppy book publishers, twerp television, jabbering local radio – manufacturers and distributers of tripe by the ton' (p. 14), and when John eventually reveals that he is 'thinking of handing' the man over 'to the Local Authority' (p. 57), it is clear that their relationship must end. While *The Man* apparently blames political policy and social bureaucracy for the mistreatment of the dispossessed and marginalized, it also suggests that the individual should work harder to act morally (perhaps challenging ISAs ethically rather than politically), confirming that the potential for social change lies within the domain of ethical concern.

We have seen that for Hegel,[12] 'Education is the art of making people ethical' (2008/1821, p. 159), but Briggs asks what this means for people who are denied education. As the man advises John, ' "You stick to your education, boy! There's nothing worse than being uneducated . . . It's like being only half alive" ' (p. 19). Here *The Man* implies that the uneducated are outside the remit of ethical concern, for it seems that entry into ethical life requires reciprocity

Figure 6.1 The embrace of moral agency (p. 53).

Source: Image taken from *The Man* by Raymond Briggs, published by Red Fox. Used by permission of Raymond Briggs and The Random House Limited.

(labour exchange and material contribution). The miniature thus functions as a symbol of exclusion and this is echoed by its repellent manifestation in *The Man*. John finally admits, '"You <u>STINK</u>!"' (p. 56) and his reasoning approach to the man yields to sensory reactions that lead into the book's emotional territory. The affective dimensions of *The Man* are conveyed primarily through illustration and where John expresses his rational enquiries about the man through dialogue, their complex and ambivalent feelings towards each other are established mostly through posture, facial expression, changes in frame size, and tonal shifts of colour in Briggs's illustrations that leave behind the bright optimism and vigour of their early relationship for the blues, greens, and greys of inevitable parting and anguish. John's tentative movement into moral agency is figured in his increasingly emotional response to the man, flashing from angry outbursts to expressions of love, and moving from care based on the man's demands to a (good) willing sense of responsibility that values the man's life and recognizes his needs on an emotional level (Figure 6.1). It seems that the man's miniature presence has contributed to John's moral education and an aspect of this education is the provocation of feeling. In exposing John's values as relative – '"So are <u>you</u> the normal by which everyone is to be judged?"' (p. 26) – and forcing him to reflect on the exclusive conditions of his comfortable existence – '"Why is it other people get all the gravy?"' (p. 27) – the man makes him feel uncomfortable and angry, both emotions that lead into moral consideration, confirming that the getting of wisdom has an emotional aspect.

The Man draws on a cultural fascination with the miniature as confirmed by its allusion to *The Borrowers*, ' "I thought you were a Borrower, that's all. They're in a famous book. Borrowers are very good people. It's a great story" ' (p. 8). John's moral judgement of the Borrowers seems intended to placate the man who resists comparison to these fictional creatures, while drawing attention to the moral status of Briggs's protagonists. John and the man take their part in a literary tradition dealing in power relations and dominance that render moral integrity and goodness difficult to achieve given the social structures within (without) which they must develop and function. Indeed the thank you note left for John by the Man contains a malapropism that encapsulates the moral tensions magnified by miniature literature: 'YOU AR A GOD BLOKE' (p. 63) and also stresses the immensity of a personal and social responsibility that John is not yet able to take on emotionally or practically. *The Man* suggests that care is in the province of the insider and the social structures which might seem to support individuals are not universally applicable. The implied reader is then left to ponder whether love and moral agency can ever penetrate the boundaries of the social conditions into which we are born in order that outsiders such as those represented by the miniature are offered a way of crossing the threshold openly, freely, and legitimately. Singer argues that 'the status quo is the outcome of a system of national selfishness and political expediency, and not the result of a considered attempt to work out . . . moral obligations' (1993/1979, p. 262) and Briggs's haunting imagining of 'the status quo' figuratively charges the implied reader with the responsibility of 'working out moral obligations'. Depicting John grieving for the man, the final image of *The Man* (Figure 6.2) is expressive of a rupture in social conditions that impedes the individual's potential for goodness; evidently John feels this as a personal wound through which the forgotten and unconventional fall.

In common with each of the works of miniature literature considered in this chapter, *The Man* gives the child a central role in the dimensional play of the miniature, recognizing that the power relations it configures are symbolic of and relevant to power structures embedded in concepts and experiences of childhood. Issues of dominance, power, and control are worked out or puzzled over by Maria, Arrietty, Max, Omri, and John, and each in their own way is asked to deal with the Man's assertive statement of selfhood, ' "NO ONE, but NO ONE, <u>DOES ANYTHING</u> WITH ME! <u>I</u> DO IT!" ' (p. 33). Each feels the responsibility of this assertion and consequently Maria finds a healthy framework for care, forging a

Figure 6.2 Losing responsibility? (p. 64).

Source: Image taken from *The Man* by Raymond Briggs, published by Red Fox. Used by permission of Raymond Briggs and The Random House Limited.

successful relationship with the Lilliputians based on liberty; Arrietty chooses to act for herself against the wishes of her parents and confronts the dangers of the gargantuan outside world; Max facilitates the Twelves' march to Haworth, willingly relinquishing them and allowing them to forge their own quest; Omri recognizes that independence is a crucial condition of happiness and sends his miniatures back to a place and time in which they can act for themselves once more; and John is left to deal with the material remains of a man who must leave, but who forges his own rules for dealing with exclusion. Miniature literature for children also shapes a readership of thinking responsive minds, implying readers capable of thinking through the complex moral conditions of the miniature. This is achieved partly through the symbolic resonance of the miniature in which 'the minuscule, a narrow gate, opens up an entire new world' (Bachelard, 1994/1958, p. 155) and a range of literary strategies, such as direct address, Socratic dialogue, and the magnifying capabilities of graphic representation. Essentially these writers trust that their readers can and will engage with the issues raised by miniature life, because they recognize the potential for moral agency and growth in young people. As Briggs's man observes, in comparison to adults, ' "Children are more reliable, unless they are crawlers" ' (p. 9), for they know what it is to suffer the gaze of the magnifying glass and are not yet fully insiders.

Conclusion: Through the Library . . . Towards a Life Examined

. . . men are naturally inclined to hate and envy.

Education itself adds to natural inclination. For parents generally spur their children on to virtue only by the incentive of honor and envy.

Spinoza, 1996/1677, p. 99

Spinoza's ironic dig at the iniquitous motives of pedagogic ambition in *Ethics* (1677) reveals a suspicion of spurious virtue that has travelled the centuries as confirmed by Mary Midgley in *Heart and Mind* (1981). Midgley points to a malaise overhanging the terms of morality, observing: 'Anyone who uses *moral* in anything beyond the *Daily Mirror* sense is no longer a quite plain man anyway, and we had better follow careful writers than casual ones' (2003/1981, p. 119). She further remarks, 'In England *moral* etc. have had a depressing history of surfeit in the late eighteenth century, followed by nausea and nemesis in the nineteenth' (pp. 123–5), a state which Sayers playfully parodies in *Even the Parrot* (1944). Matilda asks of her eating routines, ' "Why must we always be told that it is good for us?" ' and her Uncle responds that ' "we do not like to admit that we do anything that has not a flavour of *morality* about it" ' (1944, p. 40). Sayers leaves the joke hanging, while Midgley goes on to rescue morality from a narrowness that has placed 'the word *moral* and its derivatives' under strain (2003/1981, p. 119) by demonstrating the misunderstandings and abuses of morality in philosophy and literature. She argues that to throw out morality as Nietzsche suggests (and Spinoza implies of moral education) 'would be wasteful' (p. 119) for its job is essential in marking 'a certain sort of seriousness' that belongs 'to a man's character, to his central system of purpose' (p. 144).

Midgley draws on a long history of philosophical development to support her validation of *moral* as a term and concept, though she also refers to a range of literary sources – including Shakespeare, Oscar Wilde, and Isak Dinesen –

suggesting an investment in those 'careful writers' and in the propensity for literature to stimulate the *serious* business of dealing with moral problems. Over a hundred years earlier, Schopenhauer deals with related concerns when he distinguishes between different types of writers, 'Only he who writes entirely for the sake of what he has to say writes anything worth writing' (2004/1851, p. 199), and he goes on to perceive in thoughtful writing a truth that can be gleaned from the works of children's literature exemplified in this book:

> A book can never be more that a reproduction of the thoughts of its author. The value of these thoughts lies either in the *material*, that is in what he has thought *upon*, or in the *form*, i.e. the way in which the material is treated, that is in *what* he has thought upon it. (p. 200)

I would add to this a conviction that writers for young people such as Richard Adams, B.B., Nina Bawden, Anne Fine, David Almond, Lynne Reid Banks, Peter Dickinson, Jan Mark, Melvin Burgess, Jacqueline Wilson, Janni Howker, Oliver Jeffers, Geraldine McCaughrean, Pauline Clarke, T. H. White, Gillian Cross, Vivien Alcock, Malorie Blackman, Susan Price, Ann Schlee, Raymond Briggs, and John Agard trust in the thoughtful response of their readers; trust that the matter and form of thought will indeed be thought upon. If Midgley is concerned for the longevity of morality as an intelligent and serious mark of purpose then she might look to the ethically aware books available to young readers of contemporary Britain. Bertrand Russell certainly takes seriously the role of story in the moral education of children and in unison with Spinoza and Midgley he insists that morality results from a freedom to shape ideas: 'In all cases it should be quite unnecessary to point the moral; the right telling of the story should be sufficient. Do not moralise, but let the facts produce their own moral in the child's mind' (2010/1926, p. 130). The vista of ethical landscapes in children's literature has (un)recognizably changed since 1945 – morphing from pastoral chalk-pits to urban rubbish-tips, via the 'make do and mend' ethic of 'Stiggish' (re)invention in Clive King's *Stig of the Dump* (1963) and the challenge to indifference through loving goodness of Melvin Burgess's *The Baby and Fly Pie* (1993) – still while the matter changes according to political, cultural, and social change, the ethical impetus remains. The sustained power of story to stimulate moral reflection is demonstrated in the range of literature for children and young adults discussed in this book and, looking back over the publishing trends of the last decade, it is evident that literature for young people continues to invest in Russell's sense of 'the right telling of the story'. Numerous children's books over the past ten years have posed questions that seek to stimulate moral thought through their unsettling. When Raymond Briggs's *UG* (2001) closes with an interrogative, ' "Things WILL get better . . . wont [sic] they?" ' (final page), the relativism of 'better' is left for the reader to contemplate. When Daphne justifies murder through the use of 'good, honest . . . poison' (2009/2008, p. 281) in Terry Pratchett's *Nation* (2008), the conditions of moral responsibility begin to unravel and twist through an ironic and philosophically provocative novel. When Mina's ethical sensibility is expressed through ruminative diary entries in Almond's *My Name is Mina* (2010), the reader is offered a model of moral imagining: 'Imagine the stupid boring people who trap birds, who put them in cages! How boring they must be! How stupid they must be! . . . What's a gang of bird trappers called?' (2010, p. 180).

The importance of such Mina-like imagining is expressed by Peter Hollindale in his essays published two decades apart, 'The Darkening Green' (1990) and 'Hope against Hope' (2011),[1] reflecting on children's fiction and its engagement with environmental issues and in which Hollindale explores rifts and shifts between thinking and imagining, hope and pessimism that shape the exchange between political discourse and fictional representation over the last 20 years. Stimulated by his own ethical stance, there is an urgency to Hollindale's reading of texts such as Peter Dickinson's *Eva* (1988) and in his validation of a pessimism that emphasizes 'the contrast between collective humanity and individuals' (2011, p. 107). Hollindale is interested primarily in the concerns of environmental ethics, although his validation of recent children's literature as questioning and intelligent has wider application, for finally he observes that 'stories are very important. They take us across the bridge from the thinkable, where we are, to the imaginable, where we need to be' (p. 110). My own conviction is that children's literature has the propensity to help young people decide where they need to be *and* to consider where others need to be – for this is the negotiation at the heart of ethics that negates indifference. Undoubtedly my particular moral interests are revealed during my close discussion of ethically aware children's literature in this book, but my point is not that children's literature should deal with certain ethical issues over others, rather that through a range of writerly tools it is able to stimulate moral agency and to negotiate the road from life unexamined to life examined.

Murdoch might not envisage the unexamined life as a state of being that is likely to change, for she claims on its behalf love and virtue. In the presentness of childhood wonder is virtue to be valued, yet Murdoch also articulates a moral maturity that is grown into and developed and this implies the possibility of a shift from life unexamined (Agard's wonder) to examined (Agard's seeking).

Inevitably for a novelist who recognizes literature as philosophy and morality in process, she observes, 'the most essential and fundamental aspect of culture is the study of literature, since this is an education in how to picture and understand human situations' (2001/1970, p. 33). Murdoch's picturing is Hollindale's imagining is Russell's right telling and for each there is a virtuosity in words and the meaningful potential of literature. When these philosophers, critics, and pedagogues invest in the potential of literature to contribute meaning and to take seriously the exchange of human experience, they enter into the realm of hermeneutics as described by Gadamer: 'hermeneutics must be so determined as a whole that it does justice to the experience of art. Understanding must be conceived as a part of the event in which meaning occurs, the event in which the meaning of all statements – those of art and all other kinds of tradition – is formed and actualized' (2004/1960, p. 157). The work of art (or literature) contributes to a much wider realm of understanding than that allowed by aesthetics; hermeneutics concerns itself with the understanding of art, although this is just one aspect of an eventful process of meaning making. Relating this to children's literature in particular and the dynamic exchange of childness described by Hollindale (1997), it seems that inherent in writing for children is its nature as fulcrum between levels and shades of understanding or interpretation that contribute to meaning in the deepest and broadest sense. In children's literature can be located the fulcrumic exchange between unexamined and examined and here lies its ethical potential.

A recent literary expression of this sort of exchange can be found in Aidan Chambers's *Dying to Know You* (2012), a novel that playfully engages with the extent to which we can ever know an other. Interpretation and understanding are central to the relationships played out, and as the friendship between an aging writer and a young fisherman develops, they are forced to negotiate unanticipated (though inevitable) moral terrain. During a layered and dialogic narrative, the ethical fabric of human relationships is never directly alluded to, nevertheless the clue to the importance of their ethical dimension is delivered in an aphoristic observation that highlights the exchange and slippage of understanding between man and boy: 'I like rugby because it's physical. [. . .] It's violence used with moral intelligence, if that makes any sense' (pp. 23–4). Resulting from an interpretive exchange in which the writer mediates Karl's words, this statement belongs neither to adult nor teen (or conceivably to both), but in the struggle to forge, claim and, make meaning, the readerly seeker who would/should leave behind childhood wonder in a move to moral agency is conceived.

Notes

Introduction

1 John Agard dedicates *The Young Inferno*, 'For the seeker in all of us'.

2 Dante's *The Divine Comedy* was written c.1308 to c.1321. I use Mark Musa's translation of *Volume 1: The Inferno* (2003/1971).

3 *The Young Inferno* is not paginated – this reference appears on the second page of the introduction.

4 Though Hegel does not appear to identify children in particular here, he does establish the child's education as an important aspect of 'the family' (a crucial strand of Hegel's ethical life) and as a vehicle for *the spirit's* entry into ethical life. Further indication that 'people' is inclusive and even indicative of children in this context is offered by his reference to Rousseau's *Émile* (which is specifically about a child's education): 'The educational experiments, advocated by Rousseau in *Émile*, of withdrawing *people* from the common life of every day and bringing them up in the country, have turned out to be futile. . .' – (my emphasis, 2008/1821, p. 160).

5 See note 3.

6 The three essays in *The Sovereignty of Good* (2001/1970) were first published separately: 'The idea of perfection' (1964); 'The sovereignty of good over other concepts' (1967); and 'On "God" and "Good" ' (1969).

7 Though Murdoch does not entirely reject Socrates on this as will become evident.

8 Murdoch does not relegate 'selfish care' to childhood, but her concept of selfish behaviour lacking a moral focus on the consideration of others is comparable to Freud's notion of id in early childhood.

9 The implications and conditions of Murdoch's peasantry are also worth further reflection of course.

10 See Chapter 1, pp. 11–12, for reference to Aristotle's definition of ethics and goodness.

11 Murdoch is careful to separate 'good art' from what she calls 'fantasy art': 'A great deal of art, perhaps most art, actually is self-consoling fantasy, and even great art cannot guarantee the quality of its consumer's consciousness . . . Art, and by "art" from now on I mean good art, not fantasy art, affords us a pure delight in the independent existence of what is excellent' (Murdoch, 2001, p. 83).

12 'I think this is an abiding and not a regrettable characteristic of the discipline, that philosophy has in a sense to keep trying to return to the beginning . . .' (Murdoch, 2001, p. 1).

13 Hollindale cites Priestly's 1931 phrase here.

14 Acknowledgement is due to Kate Siroon Proops for bringing *Nation* to my
    attention during an MA seminar presentation.
15 Though Russell employs the male pronoun here, this seems influenced by frequent
    references to his son, rather than a keener interest in male (than female) education,
    for he surmises: 'I suppose it is unnecessary at this date to argue that boys and girls
    must be treated alike' (p. 137).
16 For example, J. R. R. Tolkien's *Tree and Leaf* (1964); Bruno Bettelheim's *The Uses of
    Enchantment* (1976); Ruth Bottighemier's *Grimms' Bad Girls and Bold Boys* (1987);
    Marina Warner's *From the Beast to the Blonde* (1994); Peter Hunt and Millicent
    Lenz's *Alternative Worlds in Fantasy Fiction* (2001).

Chapter 1

1 Citation (here and subsequently) from 'The Perils of Indifference' by Elie Wiesel.
   Originally given as a speech, 12 April 1999. Copyright © 1999 by Elie Wiesel.
   Reprinted by permission of Georges Borchardt, Inc., on behalf of Elie Wiesel.
2 Dates identified by Barnes in revised Penguin Classics edition (2004).
3 Agard's notion of childhood wonder is worth pause for it touches on a range
   of conflicting philosophical perspectives on the child's (im)moral status. It is
   possible to interpret this wonder in terms of childly amazement; a sort of response
   to the world that is blinded by awe to its true qualities and partly this is what
   Agard is getting at here, as his seeker experiences a conflicting moment of loss
   and gain, such as that entailed in the transitions from innocence to experience,
   or from ignorance to knowledge. 'My childhood wonder' might also be seen as
   a blissful state, although perhaps not a happy state as envisaged by Aristotle's
   notion of eudaimonia, which involves living well through adult life. This blissful
   state from which Agard's youth has been awakened abruptly is a state recognized
   in Hellenistic philosophy, yet it is not a state conducive to moral discovery or
   growth. Aristotle observes that 'in youth people are in a condition resembling
   intoxication, because they are growing, and youth is sweet' (2004, p. 198) and that
   'to obtain a right training for goodness from an early age is a hard thing' (p. 278),
   while Plato recognizes that childish awe renders accurate judgement impossible.
   In modern philosophers such as Hume, this childhood wonder becomes a sort
   of indiscriminate enthusiasm, as children display excessive sympathy to others
   and 'implicitly embrace every opinion propos'd to them' (1978/1739–40, p. 316),
   while for Schopenhauer the child is a deluded object of envy, 'In our early youth
   we sit before the life that lies ahead of us like children sitting before the curtain in
   a theatre, in happy and tense anticipation of whatever is going to appear. Luckily
   we do not know what really will appear. For to him who does know, children can
   sometimes seem like innocent delinquents, sentenced not to death but to life,

who have not yet discovered what their punishment will consist of' (2004/1851, p. 47). Indeed, there is a blind aspect to wonder that intoxicates and falsifies; that ultimately conceals good and evil from childhood and the young.

4 There is some debate as to the origin and accuracy of these lines; the Opies observe that the attribution to Longfellow is 'very uncertain' (1973, p. 372) and various online sources suggest that the penultimate line should read 'she was very good indeed' (e.g. http://rpo.library.utoronto.ca/poems/there-was-little-girl.html – accessed 15 June 2012).

5 Such arguments gained force after the publication of Erving Goffman's *Stigma* (1963), an influential work of social psychology exploring the social conditions of stigma and related notions of abnormality, normalcy, and deviance.

6 Etymologically 'mores' is related to 'morals', both rooted in the Latin mōs 'custom'; mores can be seen as a branch of morality, but mores generally apply to 'conventions and customs of a social group', while morals are more directly associated with character and conduct in the ethical sense (Onions, 1966, p. 589).

7 Virtue appears to indicate moral excellence; theological and cardinal virtues are embedded in the poem's ethical framework.

8 Naughtiness also has sexual connotations of course, and as Jacqueline Rose has argued in *The Case of Peter Pan* (1984, 1994), there is a linguistic-conceptual link to be made between sexuality and childhood, paving the way for a discussion (elsewhere) of the power relations implicit in the child castigated as naughty. I do not pursue this line of enquiry here because it diverts from my particular concern with the ethical potential of naughtiness in childhood. Rose has usefully been revisited by a range of children's literature specialists in an edition of *Children's Literature Association Quarterly* (vol. 35, no. 3, Fall 2010) dedicated to her seminal text 'Twenty-Five Years On'.

9 Ziolkowski's study focuses primarily on 'literary and pictorial images of disrespectful, bad, or "evil" *boys*' (p. 8), explaining his interchangeable use of the term 'boys' and the gender-neutral 'children' philologically. While pointing to the dualistic treatment of girls (sweet) and boys (naughty) in much contemporary literature, he also observes that such distinctions are not true of early literature in the Western Christian tradition (p. 9).

10 Traditional verse cited in Opies (1997, pp. 116–17).

11 Close observation suggests that the same child appears in both images, but this has not been ascertained irrefutably.

12 As opposed to temperament, which refers to more permanent aspects of personality.

13 See Potter (1907, p. 17).

14 From *The Trinity* (c.399–419), cited in Ziolkowski (2001, p. 34).

15 Foxe produced a Latin precursor in 1554, but the first English-language edition was published in 1563; it was revised repeatedly during Foxe's lifetime and new editions have appeared regularly since then.

16 An earlier version of *The Tale of Peter Rabbit* was self-published by Potter in 1901.

17 Serving as a literary model for Goffman's theory, Amelia Jane's persistent naughtiness does indeed suggest that she will never be accepted as a 'normal' toy. 'Normals' are non-stigmatized members of society: 'We and those who do not depart negatively from the particular expectations at issue I shall call the *normals*' (1968/1963, p. 15).

18 I refer only to the first book in the series here, *Horrid Henry* (1995/1994).

19 The Darton and Co. school edition of *Brotherly Love* I consulted is held at The British Library; the book is undated, but the BL catalogue lists it as 1851. An e-book edition on Project Gutenberg attributes Mrs Streeton (Sherwood's daughter) as a co-author of *Brotherly Love*.

20 *The Young Inferno* is not paginated – these references are taken from the second page of the Introduction.

21 I realize that 'younger readers' is rather vague as a category of implied readership, but I do not want to be too reductive or prescriptive about this. When I talk about books for younger readers, I mean those that would not be marketed to the adolescent 'YA' market in particular – though some of the books I mention for 'younger' readers are suitable for a wide range of readers (including teenagers and adults).

22 *The Elephant and the Bad Baby* is not paginated-numbering commences from and is inclusive of the title page.

23 Acknowledgement is due to Kay Waddilove for bringing *Six Bad Boys* to my attention in her MA dissertation, *The Open Path? Career Novels for Girls in the 1950's* (2008, unpublished, held in the Children's Literature Collection, University of Roehampton).

24 Lisa O'Kelly uses this phrase to describe Wilson's books in an interview for *The Observer*, Sunday, 17 October 2010: www.guardian.co.uk/books/2010/oct/17/jacqueline-wilson-happiness-blyton (accessed 20 March 2012).

25 Andy Mulligan's *Trash* (2011) explores a similar theme and is discussed in Chapter 4, pp. 129–30.

Chapter 2

1 See discussion of childhood wonder in Chapter 1, n.3.

2 A journey reminiscent of Wordsworth's cognitive return in 'Intimations of Immortality from Recollections of Early Childhood' (1804): 'We in thought will join your throng,/ Ye that pipe and ye that play,/ Ye that through your hearts to-day/ Feel the gladness of the May!'

3 In 'Upon Appleton House, to My Lord Fairfax' (1651), Andrew Marvell applies 'loophole' figuratively to refer to men who might wish to avoid the humility required of true pilgrimage and dupe their way into heaven: 'When larger-sizèd men did stoop/ To enter at a narrow loop;/ As practising, in doors so strait,/ To strain themselves through heaven's gate' (2005/1972, p. 76, lines 29–32). Onions (1966, p. 536) opines that 'the identity of later senses is not certain', but suggests that the sense of 'outlet, means of escape' could be influenced by the Dutch *loopgat*.

4 As does much of Stevenson's work – think of *Kidnapped* (1886) or *The Strange Case of Doctor Jekyll and Mr Hyde* (1886).

5 In his introduction to *Treasure Island* (Stevenson, 2011/1883, p.vii).

6 Of course, theology is an important strand of philosophical tradition, but children's books with strong theological positions tend to be authoritative in their moralizing, rather than to open philosophical enquiry. Examples include Sherwood's *The History of the Fairchild Family* or C. S. Lewis's *Narnia* sequence.

7 See note 5.

8 Jenks (2005) and Eagleton (2012) offer discussion of media response to the 1993 murders and discuss the climate of anxiety about childhood that ensued.

9 Copyright 2008 Youth Justice Board, http://labspace.open.ac.uk/file.php/5193/ YJ_k523_1/sco.htm# (accessed 29 April 2012).

10 Walsh cites Laws in her article, but his findings can also be accessed here: www.vanuatu.usp.ac.fj/courses/la205_criminal_law_and_procedure_1/cases/C_ (A_Minor)_v_DPP.html (accessed 4 May 2012).

11 The age of criminal responsibility in the United Kingdom is lower than in many European countries where it ranges from 14 to 16. Debate is ongoing in the United Kingdom as to whether 10 is too young to be considered criminally responsible – in 2010 Maggie Atkinson, England's children's commissioner, called for the age to be raised to 12, but her recommendations caused a backlash in the tabloid press and her recommendations were rejected by the government.

12 www.justice.gov.uk/courts/glossary-of-terms (accessed 4 May 2012).

13 www.nationalarchives.gov.uk/erorecords/ho/421/2/cpd/jou/tyc.htm (accessed 4 May 2012).

14 First given as a lecture in 1984.

15 The adoration to which Angela is subject is reminiscent of the 'cult of childhood' fashionable in the late nineteenth to early twentieth centuries; Frances Hodgson Burnett's *Little Lord Fauntleroy* (1886) and J. M. Barrie's *Peter and Wendy* (1911) can be linked to the sentimental and darker aspects respectively of what became an international obsession with idealized children.

16 See Chapter 1 for detailed discussion of terminology defining childhood naughtiness.

17 Class conventions and associations are parodied throughout. For example, the twins' parents are unable to find willing godparents for Diabola so they resort

to bribing a 'homeless and hungry' couple (p. 25), and conversely, middle-class relatives clamour for the chance to godparent Angela.

18 *The Guardian*, Thursday, 25 November 1993. www.guardian.co.uk/uk/1993/nov/25/ bulger2 (accessed 4 May 2012).

19 Public, media, and government controversy centred on the payments Sereny made to Bell for her contributions to the book, as discussed in Gerrard et al. (1998).

20 See Chapter 1 for discussion of Schopenhauer's interpretation of Schadenfreude, p. 32.

21 I do not claim that Fine's 'Little Visits' represent an intentional replication of details arising from the Mary Bell case, but there are links to be made between *The Tulip Touch* and Bell's visits, which were well documented in the press and described in Gita Sereny's *The Case of Mary Bell* (1972, rev. 1995).

Chapter 3

1 First published in 1820, but dated in 1821.

2 Another recent book that employs this convention is *Trash* (2010) by Andy Mulligan. Mulligan creates an imaginary city called Behala to serve for Manila in the Philippines to explore the issue of children working on 'trash mountains'.

3 Dorian Lynskey documents the mixed responses to Band Aid and Live Aid (2010, pp. 481–7).

4 *Little Soldier* (1999) by Bernard Ashley also explores the ethical context of child soldiering through its depiction of street gangs in London linked with African tribal warfare.

5 'Between the Wars' first released as an EP Single in February1985 by Go! Discs.

6 This quotation is from Hartman's essay, 'The Heroics of Realism', collected in G. Hartman and D. T. O'Hara (eds) (2004) *The Geoffrey Hartman Reader*.

7 Althusser's *On Ideology* (2008/1971) collects essays first published in French between 1964 and 1973. Translation information is not provided in the Verso edition.

8 It is worth noting that in *On Evil* (2010) Eagleton distinguishes wickedness from evil, whereas Midgley refers to evil and wickedness synonymously in *Wickedness* (2001/1984).

9 The moral conditions of poaching are considered during the discussion of *Brendon Chase* in Chapter 4 and again in Chapter 5.

Chapter 4

1 'Frost at Midnight' first appeared in a Joseph Johnson pamphlet in 1798 and was eventually published in Coleridge's collection, *Sibylline Leaves: A Collection of Poems* (1817). The edition I use here is Coleridge (1997, pp. 231–2).

2 This quotation is from Hartman's essay, 'Wordsworth's magic mountains', collected in G. Hartman and D. T. O'Hara (eds) (2004), *The Geoffrey Hartman Reader*.

3 There is no pagination-numbering commences from and is inclusive of the title page.

4 Further discussion of Hegelian communities can be found in Chapter 3.

5 Of course this affinity is rendered differently in each of the texts I mention, for the Romantic proximity of child and nature is complex and shifting across a range of texts.

6 Although Peter Singer notes that political action often gives way to financial concerns in charitable organizations: '. . . it is a condition of being registered as a charity, in both Great Britain and the United States, that the charitable organization does not engage in political activities' (Singer, 1991/1975, p. 218).

7 For a full discussion of the tensions embedded in various pastoral constructions of childhood, see *The Poetics of Childhood* (2003) by Roni Natov in which she 'addresses the persistent longing for childhood in adulthood and those states of mind we connect with childhood' (p. 6).

8 Singer seeks to combat speciesism and his 'implied reader' can be identified as the speciesist he wishes to convert; Singer argues that most humans are indeed speciesists and demonstrates why he believes this to be the case through a range of passionate arguments in *Animal Liberation*.

9 First published in 1991 as *How Green Are You?* The 2008 edition by Frances Lincoln is printed on pulp from a sustainable forest and recycled paper.

10 Singer identifies Leopold's land ethic as a forerunner to and an example of the deep ecology, which developed as a field of ethical enquiry from the 1970s (1993/1979, pp. 280–4).

11 There is no pagination-numbering commences from and is inclusive of first title page (there are two in this edition); pagination is inclusive of pullout pages.

12 In his essay, 'Faking Nature' [1982], Robert Elliot mounts an ethical response to the 'restoration thesis' – for my extended discussion of this, see pp. 124–5.

13 Callicott (1995/1980, p. 35) employs these terms to distinguish between philosophical schools that limit the ethical sphere to the interests of human, rational beings (ethical humanism) and those which argue for the rights of animals and for their entry into the moral sphere (humane moralism).

14 The date of publication is 1902 for the Frederick Warne version of *The Tale of Peter Rabbit*, but Potter self-published an earlier version in 1901. *The Tale of Peter Rabbit* is the first of the Peter Rabbit books. The last in the series has been recorded elsewhere as Cecily Parsley's *Nursery Rhymes* (1922), but I include *The Tale of Little Pig Robinson* (1930) as the last in the Peter Rabbit series.

15 High-level anthropomorphism is exemplified in Beatrix Potter's books, in which animals wear human clothes and live in furnished houses; the mid-level anthropomorphism of *Watership Down* and the *Jungle Books* allows animals to speak and reason, placing them in natural habitats and (mostly) describing

behaviour typical of the animal represented; low-level anthropomorphism is
evident in naturalistic renderings of creatures, such as that in *Tarka the Otter*,
which do not allow for human speech, but through narrative engagement invest
creatures with human emotion or response.

16   Genette's concept as formulated and described in *Narrative Discourse* (1980, p. 190).

17   The rabbits speak an invented language (Lapine) in *Watership Down* and 'elil' is
Lapine for 'predator'.

18   Adams acknowledges, 'I am indebted, for a knowledge of rabbits and their ways, to
Mr R. M. Lockley's remarkable book, *The Private Life of the Rabbit*' (1973/1972, p. 8).

19   Svendsen's point is also used to illuminate discussion of *The Tulip Touch* in
Chapter 2, p. 65.

20   The appearance of Doctor Adams echoes the appearance of Miss Potter at the end
of *The Tale of Samuel Whiskers* (1908/1926).

21   In developing their own philosophical positions, Singer (1991/1975; especially
Chapter 5 'Man's Dominion') and Midgley (1983) offer comprehensive overviews of
the philosophical development of attitudes towards animals and their relationship
to the moral sphere.

22   Mill's observation is taken from 'Utilitarianism' which first appeared as three
articles during 1861; this text comes from the 1871 edition and is collected in
Utilitarianism and Other Essays (Mill and Bentham, 1987).

23   Bentham's view is expressed in 'An Introduction to the Principles of Morals and
Legislation'; this text comes from the 1824 edition and is collected in *Utilitarianism
and Other Essays* (Mill and Bentham, 1987).

24   The symbolic shortening of distance allowed by the car must be stressed here, for
elsewhere in *Watership Down* roads and cars are presented as human, unnatural,
and dangerous to environmental well-being. Similarly, Leopold perceives roads and
transport networks as detrimental to a healthy biosphere and suggests that they
'split' the wilderness (1968/1949, p. 191).

25   This passage might be brief, but like 'Dea ex Machina' in *Watership Down*, it was
critical to my reading self in girlhood. This sequence leapt at me when I read *Tarka*
as a 9-year-old, hoping and imagining that I might be the girl that would keep such
creatures from harm. I have never forgotten it.

26   'The Howling of Wolves' from *The Thought Fox* (1995, p. 39).

27   There is ongoing debate as to when wolves became extinct in Britain, but consensus
suggests that English and Welsh wolves disappeared during the fifteenth and
sixteenth centuries, while wolves remained in Scotland until the late seventeenth
and in Ireland until the eighteenth century.

28   An unflinching narrative approach/tone marked a trend in British children's
literature in the late 1980s and the 1990s. Other examples of writing from this
period that bring the bleaker aspects of experience to young readers include: Janni

Howker's *The Nature of the Beast* (1985); Vivien Alcock's *The Trial of Anna Cotman* (1989); Robert Swindell's *Stone Cold* (1993); Anne Fine's *The Tulip Touch* (1996); Gillian Cross's *Pictures in the Dark* (1996); and Melvin Burgess's *Junk* (1996).

29 Red wolves were reintroduced into the North Carolina, United States, in 1986 and the EU Habitats and Species Directive of 1992 required the British government to consider proposals for the reintroduction of species, such as the Grey Wolf to the Scotland. In 2012, discussions are ongoing in relation to the release of wolves, but the European Beaver was reintroduced into the Scottish Highlands in 2009 (the first mammal to be reintroduced to the United Kingdom).

30 See Genette (1983/1972, p. 194) for discussion of alterations in narrative focalization.

31 For further discussion of the dominant and oppositional conceptions of childhood, see discussion in Chapter 2, pp. 45–8.

32 Fox hunting was banned in Scotland in 2002, but remains legal in Ireland.

33 Credit must go to Emilia Lamkin here for her observation (in her review of *Can We Save the Tiger?* as member of a Carnegie/Greenaway shadowing group) that White's illustration of the American Bison becomes fainter as it recedes into the background, making it seem that they are about to disappear into extinction.

34 No page number – author's notes adjacent to title page.

35 As printed in the publication information in *The Great Paper Caper*: 'FSC is a non-profit international organisation established to promote the responsible management of the world's forests.'

36 There is no pagination-numbering commences from and is inclusive of the title page.

37 In the context of his discussion, Stephens defines cathetic relationships as those 'grounded in the ideational and emotional investment one person has in another, which may range from pre-teen close friendships to young adult incipient romances' (2010, p. 207).

38 This essay was first published in *Signal Approaches to Children's Books* (January 1990) and is now collected in Hollindale (2011).

Chapter 5

1 The Opies offer an alternative version to this rhyme in the notes of *I Saw Esau*, with a different final couplet: 'Both put together/ Make a pretty face' (1992, p. 142).

2 John Passmore discusses this emphasis in his essay on 'Attitudes to Nature' (1995). For further discussion of this, see Chapter 4, p. 104.

3 I include *Bevis* in this tradition, since the boys' escape in *Brendon Chase* is clearly modelled on the 'shipwrecked' isolation of Mark and Bevis. Technically, however,

Bevis and Mark deceive their parents as to their whereabouts so as to avoid detection on their island paradise, rather than running away.

4   For further discussion of Plumwood's theory of mutuality, see my discussion of *The Monster Garden*, pp. 153–60.

5   As opposed to an excess of deficient virtues – the 'mean virtue' for Aristotle is the ethical ideal and involves acting as you should act.

6   In her introduction to the 1994 Oxford World's Classics edition of *Frankenstein*.

7   The precise date that *The Nicomachean Ethics* appeared is unknown, but Jonathan Barnes suggests c.335–23 BC in the 2004 revised Penguin Classics edition.

8   See Chapter 4, p. 115–16, for a discussion of Soper's 'nature' in relation to *Watership Down*.

9   Greetham (2006) refers to *eudaimonia* as human flourishing and Barnes (in Aristotle, 2004) refers to fulfilment and 'happiness' (though Barnes's use of inverted commas signals a far more complex notion of happiness than suggested by common English usage).

10   From Jonathan Barnes's introduction to *The Nicomachean Ethics* (2004, p. xxxii).

11   'Utilitarianism' first appeared as three articles during 1861; this text comes from the 1871 edition and is collected in *Utilitarianism and Other Essays* (Mill and Bentham, 1987).

Chapter 6

1   In his introduction to Plato's *The Republic* (1987), Desmond Lee observes, 'We cannot be certain of its exact date; but if we think of it as having been written round about 375 BC we shall not be far wrong' (1987, p. 19).

2   Title of first hardback edition by Eyre and Spottiswoode. Some subsequent paperback editions lengthened the title to *The Little Grey Men Go Down the Bright Stream*.

3   White's narrator opines that 'the immortal Richard Hughes . . . wrote the best book about children that was ever written'. Although a source is not provided, the citation that accompanies this view reveals that the allusion is to *A High Wind in Jamaica*, Hughes's book about children who descend into savagery and piracy: 'Parents. . . finding that they see through their child in so many places the child does not know of, seldom realize that, if there is some point the child really gives his mind to hiding, their chances are nil.' (White, 1972/1947, p. 110; or Hughes, 2002/1929, p. 86).

4   There are five Walker siblings, but baby Vicky remains outside of boating escapades in *Swallows and Amazons*, so in the context of the Wildcat adventure, Roger is the youngest sibling.

5 For a comparative piece of ethical positioning, see Sham and Fly's discovery of the baby in *The Baby and Fly Pie* (1993) by Melvin Burgess: 'The baby was horrible . . .' (1995/1993, pp. 16–17).

6 For a fuller discussion of Plumwood's mutuality, see Chapter 5, pp. 153–60.

7 Public reviews sourced on the internet suggest that the book has been perceived in this way by readers.

8 It also reverses the direction of miniature relations in Briggs's picture book *Jim and the Beanstalk* (1970), in which Jim plays miniature to a demanding giant; both books raise related ethical issues and are visually linked by notes left by the Giant and man at the end of each book.

9 Since there is no pagination in *The Man*, numbering proceeds from the title page.

10 Sourced from interview with Briggs cited in Briggs and Jones (2003, p. 192). During this interview, Briggs explains that he had such 'borderline' members of society in mind when he created the man.

11 For further discussion of ISAs, see Chapter 3, p. 94.

12 In the Introduction, p. 1.

Conclusion

1 Hollindale's essays are collected in *The Hidden Teacher* (2011).

References

Primary sources

Adams, R. (1973), *Watership Down*. London: Penguin. First published 1972.

Agard, J. (2008), *The Young Inferno* (illus. S. Kitamura). London: Frances Lincoln Children's Books.

Alcock, V. (1999), *The Monster Garden*. London: Mammoth. First published 1988.

Almond, D. (2009), *Jackdaw Summer*. London: Hodder Children's Books. First published 2008.

—. (2010), *My Name Is Mina*. London: Hodder Children's Books.

B.B. (1979), *The Little Grey Men Go Down the Bright Stream*. London: Magnet. First published 1948.

—. (2000), *Brendon Chase*. London: Jane Nissen Books. First published 1944.

—. (2004), *The Little Grey Men*. Oxford: Oxford University Press. First published 1942.

Banks, L. R. (1993), *The Indian Trilogy: The Indian in the Cupboard; Return of the Indian; The Secret of the Indian*. London: Collins. First published 1981; 1986; 1989.

—. (1997), *Angela and Diabola*. London: Collins.

Bawden, N. (1995), *The Real Plato Jones*. London: Puffin. First published 1994.

Blackman, M. (2004), *Pig-Heart Boy*. London: Corgi. First published 1997.

—. (2011), *Boys Don't Cry*. London: Corgi. First published 2010.

Blyton, E. (2001), *Naughty Amelia Jane*. London: Egmont. First published 1946.

Briggs, R. (1994), *The Man*. London: Red Fox. First published 1992.

—. (2001), *UG*. London: Jonathan Cape.

Burgess, M. (1995), *The Baby and Fly Pie*. London: Puffin. First published 1993.

—. (2011), *The Cry of the Wolf*. London: Andersen Press. First published 1990.

Carroll, L. (2009), *Alice's Adventures in Wonderland and through the Looking Glass* (ed. P. Hunt). Oxford: Oxford University Press. First published 1865 and 1871, dated 1872.

Cassidy, A. (2005), *Looking for JJ*. London: Scholastic. First published 2004.

Chambers, A. (2012), *Dying to Know You*. London: The Bodley Head.

Clarke, P. (1970), *The Twelve and the Genii*. London: Faber and Faber. First published 1962.

Coleridge, S. T. (1997), *The Complete Poems* (ed. W. Keach). London: Penguin.

Cooper, S. (1976), *The Dark Is Rising*. Harmondsworth: Puffin Books. First published 1973.

Cross, G. (1987), *On the Edge*. London: Puffin. First published 1984.

Dante, A. (2003), *The Divine Comedy – Vol. 1: The Inferno* (trans. M. Musa). London: Penguin. Translation first published 1971; first written c.1308–21.

Deacon, A. (2002), *Slow Loris*. London: Hutchinson.

Dickinson, P. (2001), *AK*. London: Macmillan. First published 1990.

Edwards, D. (2002), *My Naughty Little Sister*. London: Egmont. First published 1952.

Fine, A. (1997), *The Tulip Touch*. Harmondsworth: Puffin Books. First published 1996.

Foreman, M. (1974), *Dinosaurs and All That Rubbish*. London: Picture Puffins. First published 1972.

Foxe, J. (2009), *Foxe's Book of Martyrs: Select Narratives* (ed. J. N. King). Oxford: Oxford University Press. First published 1563, 1570, 1576, and 1583.

Grimm, M. M. (1977), *Fairy Tales: The Brothers Grimm, Vol. Two* (trans. E. Taylor). London: Scolar Press. Translation first published 1826; first published in German 1815.

Hines, B. (1969), *A Kestrel for a Knave*. Penguin: London. First published 1968.

Howker, J. (2003), *Isaac Campion*. London: Walker Books. First published 1986.

Hughes, R. (2002), *A High Wind in Jamaica*. London: Vintage. First published 1929.

Hughes, T. (1995), *The Thought-Fox, Collected Animal Poems: Volume 4*. London: Faber and Faber.

Hughes, T. (1989), *Tom Brown's Schooldays* (ed. A. Sanders). Oxford and New York: Oxford University Press. First published 1857.

Jefferies, R. (1989), *Bevis* (ed. P. Hunt). Oxford: Oxford University Press. First published 1882.

Jeffers, O. (2008), *The Great Paper Caper*. London: Harper Collins.

Jenkins, M. (2011), *Can We Save the Tiger?* (illus. V. White). Somerville: Candlewick.

Jones, D. W. (2002), *Wilkins' Tooth*. London: Collins Voyager. First published 1973.

McCaughrean, G. (2007), *Stop the Train*. Oxford: Oxford University Press. First published 2001.

Mark, J. (1979), *Divide and Rule*. Harmondsworth: Kestrel.

Marryat, Captain F. (1994), *The Children of the New Forest*. London: Puffin. First published 1847.

Marvell, A. (2005), *The Complete Poems*. London: Penguin. First published 1972.

Mulligan, A. (2011), *Trash*. Oxford: David Fickling Books. First published 2010.

Norton, M. (2003), *The Borrowers*. London: Puffin. First published 1952.

Opie, I. and Opie, P., eds. (1973), *The Oxford Book of Children's Verse*. Oxford: Oxford University Press.

—. (1992), *I Saw Esau: The Schoolchild's Pocket Book* (illus. M. Sendak). London: Walker Books.

—. (1997), *The Oxford Dictionary of Nursery Rhymes* (2nd edn). Oxford: Oxford University Press. First edition 1951.

Potter, B. (1907), *The Tale of Tom Kitten*. London: Warne & Co. Ltd.

Pratchett, T. (2009), *Nation*. London: Doubleday. First published 2008.

Price, S. (1991), *Twopence a Tub*. London: Faber and Faber. First published 1975.

Ransome, A. (1958), *Swallows and Amazons*. London: Jonathan Cape. First published 1930.

Sayers, D. L. (1944), *Even the Parrot: Exemplary Conversations for Enlightened Children*. London: Methuen.

Schlee, A. (2007), *Ask Me No Questions*. London: Jane Nissen Books. First published 1976.

Shelley, M. (1998), *Frankenstein or the Modern Prometheus* (ed. M. Butler). Oxford: Oxford University Press. First published 1818.

Sherwood, Mrs M. M. (1824), *The History of the Fairchild Family*. London: Hatchard and Son. First published 1818.

—. (undated), *Brotherly Love*. London: Darton and Co. (edition printed and bound for Cave House, Uxbridge). First published 1851.

Simon, F. (1995), *Horrid Henry*. London: Orion Children's Books. First published 1994.

Stevenson, R. L. (2011), *Treasure Island* (ed. P. Hunt). Oxford: Oxford University Press. First published 1883.

Swift, J. (2005), *Gulliver's Travels* (ed. C. Rawson). Oxford: Oxford University Press. First published 1726.

Valentine, J. (2011), *Broken Soup*. London: HarperCollins. First published 2008.

Vipont, E. (1971), *The Elephant and the Bad Baby* (illus. R. Briggs). London: Puffin. First published 1969.

Weddell, C. M. (1940), 'The horse that went to heaven'. *Riding*, 4(10), 282–3.

Westall, R. (1993), *Gulf*. London: Mammoth. First published 1992.

White, T. H. (1972), *Mistress Masham's Repose*. Harmondsworth: Puffin. First published 1947.

Williamson, H. (1963), *Tarka the Otter*. Harmondsworth: Puffin. First published 1927.

Wilson, J. (2006), *Bad Girls* (illus. N. Sharratt). London: Corgi Yearling. First published 1996.

Secondary sources

Althusser, L. (2008), *On Ideology*. London and New York: Verso. First published 1971.

Aquinas, T. (1998), *Selected Writings* (trans. and ed. R. McInerny). London: Penguin.

Aristotle (2004), *The Nicomachean Ethics* (trans. J. A. K. Thomson, ed. H. Tredennick, intro. J. Barnes). London: Penguin. Translation first published 1953; first written c.335–23 BC.

Augustine, St. (1961), *Confessions* (trans. R. S. Pine-Coffin). London: Penguin. First written c.397–8.

Bachelard, G. (1994), *The Poetics of Space* (trans. M. Jolas). Boston: Beacon Press. Translation first published 1964. First published in French 1958.

Baudrillard, J. (1987), *The Evil Demon of Images* (trans. P. Patton and P. Foss). Sydney: Power Institute of Fine Arts.

—. (1993), *The Transparency of Evil: Essays on Extreme Phenomena* (trans. J. Benedict). London and New York: Verso. First published in French 1990.

—. (2008), *Fatal Strategies* (trans. P. Beitchman and W. G. J. Niesluchowski). Los Angeles: Semiotext(e). First published in French 1983.

Briggs, R. and Jones, N. (2003), *Blooming Books*. London: Jonathan Cape.

Brooks, L. (2006), *The Story of Childhood: Growing Up in Modern Britain*. London: Bloomsbury.

Callicott, J. B. (1995), 'Animal liberation: a triangular affair', in R. Elliot (ed.), *Environmental Ethics*. Oxford: Oxford University Press, pp. 29–59. Article first published 1980.

Carr, D. (2009), 'Virtue, mixed emotions and moral ambivalence'. *Philosophy*, 84(01), 31–46.

Cassidy, A. (2005a), 'Why I wrote *Looking for J.J.*'. URL: www5.scholastic.co.uk/zone/ authors_a-cassidy_looking-jj.htm (accessed 9 May 2012).

DesJardins, J. R. (1997), *Environmental Ethics: An Introduction to Environmental Philosophy* (2nd edn). Belmont, CA: Wadsworth.

Eagleton, T. (2010), *On Evil*. New Haven and London: Yale University Press.

Elliot, R. (1995), 'Faking nature', in R. Elliot (ed.), *Environmental Ethics*. Oxford: Oxford University Press, pp. 76–88. Article first published 1982.

Foot, P. (2007), 'Morality as a system of hypothetical imperatives', in R. Shafer-Landau (ed.), *Ethical Theory: An Anthology*. Oxford: Blackwell, pp. 153–9. Article first published 1972.

Foucault, M. (1991), *Discipline and Punish: The Birth of the Prison* (trans. A. Sheridan). London: Penguin. Translation first published 1977; first published in French 1975.

Gadamer, H.-G. (2004), *Truth and Method* (trans. rev. J. Weinsheimer and D. G. Marshall). New York and London: Continuum. First published in German 1960.

Garrard, G. (2004), *Ecocriticism*. London and New York: Routledge.

Genette, G. (1983), *Narrative Discourse* (trans. J. E. Lewin). Oxford: Basil Blackwell. Translation first published 1980; first published in French 1972.

Gerrard, N., Brooks, R., Calvert, J., Johnston, L. and McSmith, A. (1998), 'The mob will move on, the pain never can'. *The Observer*, Sunday, 3 May. URL: http://observer. guardian.co.uk/comment/story/0,6903,688108,00.html (accessed 8 May 2012).

Goffman, E. (1968), *Stigma: Notes on the Management of Spoiled Identity*. Harmondsworth: Penguin. First published 1963.

Grant, O. (2011), 'Interview: John Craven on the 40th Anniversary of Newsround'. *The Telegraph*, 23 November. URL: www.telegraph.co.uk/culture/tvandradio/8907584/ Interview-John-Craven-on-the-40th-anniversary-of-Newsround.html (accessed 6 June 2012).

Greetham, B. (2006), *Philosophy*. Basingstoke: Palgrave Macmillan.

Grenby, M. O. (2008), *Children's Literature*. Edinburgh: Edinburgh University Press.

Halwani, R. (2003), 'Care ethics and virtue ethics'. *Hypatia*, 18(3), Fall, 161–92.

Hancock, S. (2009), *The Child That Haunts Us*. Hove and New York: Routledge.

Hartman, G. and O'Hara D. T., eds. (2004), *The Geoffrey Hartman Reader*. Edinburgh: Edinburgh University Press.

Hattenstone, S. (2000), 'They were punished enough by what they did'. *The Guardian*, 30 October. URL: www.guardian.co.uk/uk/2000/oct/30/bulger.simonhattenstone?INTCMP=ILCNETTXT3487 (accessed 4 May 2012).

Hegel, G. W. F. (2008), *Outlines of the Philosophy of Right* (ed. S. Houlgate, trans. T. M. Knox). Oxford: Oxford University Press. Translation first published 1952; first published in German 1821.

Hollindale, P. (1997), *Signs of Childness in Children's Books*. Stroud: Thimble Press.

—. (2011), *The Hidden Teacher*. Stroud: Thimble Press.

Hume, D. (1975), *Enquires: Concerning Human Understanding and Concerning the Principles of Morals* (3rd edn, ed. L. A. Selby-Bigge, notes P. H. Nidditch). Oxford: Clarendon Press. First published 1748 and 1751.

—. (1978), *A Treatise of Human Nature* (2nd edn, ed. L. A. Selby-Bigge, notes P. H. Nidditch). Oxford: Clarendon Press. First published 1739–40.

Irigaray, I. (2004), *An Ethics of Sexual Difference* (trans. C. Burke and G. C. Gill). London: Continuum. Translation first published 1993; first published in French 1984.

Jaggar, A. (2000), 'Feminism in ethics: moral justification', in M. Fricker and J. Hornsby (eds), *The Cambridge Companion to Feminism in Philosophy*. Cambridge: Cambridge University Press, pp. 225–44.

Jenks, C. (2005), *Childhood* (2nd edn). London and New York: Routledge. First published 1996.

Kant, I. (1998), *Groundwork of the Metaphysics of Morals* (trans. and ed. M. Gregor). Cambridge: Cambridge University Press. First published in German 1785.

—. (2007), *Critique of Pure Reason* (ed. and trans. M. Weigelt). London: Penguin. First published in German 1781, 1787.

Kierkegaard, S. (1998), *Works of Love* (ed. and trans. H. V. Hong and E. H. Hong). Princeton, NJ: Princeton University Press. Translation first published 1995; first published in Danish 1847.

Krupat, A. (2006), 'Postcolonialism, ideology, and native American literature', in B. Ashcroft, G. Griffiths, and H. Tiffin (eds), *The Post-Colonial Studies Reader* (2nd edn). London and New York: Routledge, pp.176–9. Extract taken from book first published 1996.

Kuhn, R. (1982), *Corruption in Paradise: The Child in Western Literature*. Hanover and London: University Press of New England.

Leopold, A. (1968), *A Sand County Almanac: And Sketches Here and There*. Oxford: Oxford University Press. First published 1949.

Locke, J. (2004), *An Essay Concerning Human Understanding* (ed. R. Woolhouse). London: Penguin. First published 1690.

Lynskey, D. (2010), *33 Revolutions Per Minute: A History of Protest Songs*. London: Faber and Faber.

McGinn, C. (1999), *Ethics, Evil, and Fiction*. Oxford: Oxford University Press. First published 1997.

McMahan, J. (2006), 'Child soldiers: the ethical perspective'. URL: www.sas.rutgers.edu/ cms/phil/dmdocuments/Child%20Soldiers.pdf (accessed 18 May 2012).

Marwick, A. (1996), *British Society Since 1945* (3rd edn). London: Penguin. First published 1982.

Marx, K. (1999), *Capital: An abridged edition* (ed. and trans. D. McLellan, trans. S. Moore, E. Aveling, Anon). Oxford: Oxford University Press. Abridged edition first published 1995; first published in German in three volumes 1867, 1885, 1894.

Marx, K. and Engels, F. (2002), *The Communist Manifesto* (ed. G. Stedman Jones, trans. S. Moore). London: Penguin. Translation first published 1888; first published in German 1848.

Midgley, M. (1983), *Animals and Why They Matter: A Journey around the Species Barrier*. Harmondsworth: Penguin.

—. (2001), *Wickedness*. London and New York: Routledge. First published 1984.

—. (2003), *Heart and Mind*. London and New York: Routledge. First published 1981.

Mill, J. S. and Bentham, J. (1987), *Utilitarianism and Other Essays* (ed. A. Ryan). London: Penguin.

Murdoch, I. (2001), *The Sovereignty of Good*. London and New York: Routledge. First published 1970.

Myers, M. (1989), 'Socializing Rosamund: educational ideology and fictional form'. *Children's Literature Association Quarterly*, 14(2), Summer, 52–8.

Naess, A. (2008), *The Ecology of Wisdom: Writings by Arne Naess*. Berkeley, CA: Counterpoint.

Natov, R. (2003), *The Poetics of Childhood*. London and New York: Routledge.

Newton, M. (2002), *Savage Girls and Wild Boys: a History of Feral Children*. London: Faber and Faber.

Nietzsche, F. (2003), *Beyond Good and Evil* (trans. R. J. Hollingdale). London: Penguin. First published 1886.

Noddings, N. (2003), *Caring: A Feminine Approach to Ethics and Moral Education* (2nd edn). Berkley, Los Angeles, and London: University of California Press. First published 1984.

Nodelman, P. (2002), 'Making boys appear: the masculinity of children's fiction', in J. Stephens (ed.), *Ways of Being Male: Representing Masculinities in Children's Literature and Film*. London: Routledge, pp. 1–14.

Onions, C. T., ed. (1966), *The Oxford Dictionary of English Etymology*. Oxford: Oxford University Press.

Passmore, J. (1995), 'Attitudes to nature', in R. Elliot (ed.), *Environmental Ethics*. Oxford: Oxford University Press, pp. 129–41. Article first published 1975.

Plato. (1987), *The Republic* (rev. edn, trans. D. Lee). London: Penguin. Translation first published 1955; first written c.375 BC.

—. (2010), *The Last Days of Socrates* (ed. and trans. C. Rowe). London: Penguin. First written c.390–80 BC.

Plumwood, V. (1993), *Feminism and the Mastery of Nature*. London: Routledge.

Rawlinson, M. C. (2006), 'Liminal agencies: literature as moral philosophy', in D. Rudrum (ed.), *Literature and Philosophy: A Guide to Contemporary Debates*, Basingstoke: Palgrave Macmillan, pp.129–41.

Rawls, J. (1999), *A Theory of Justice* (rev. edn). Oxford: Oxford University Press. First published 1971.

Reynolds, K. (2011), *Children's Literature: A Very Short Introduction*. Oxford: Oxford University Press.

Riddick, B. (2000), 'An examination of the relationship between labelling and stigmatisation with reference to dyslexia'. *Disability & Society*, 15(4), 653–67.

Rolston III, H. (1995), 'Duties to endangered species', in R. Elliot (ed.), *Environmental Ethics*. Oxford: Oxford University Press, pp. 60–75. Article first published 1985.

Rousseau, J. J. (1911), *Émile, or Education* (trans. B. Foxley). London and Toronto: J.M. Dent. First published in French 1762.

Routley, R. and Routley, V. (1995), 'Against the inevitability of human chauvinism', in R. Elliot (ed.), *Environmental Ethics*. Oxford: Oxford University Press, pp. 104–28. Article first published 1979.

Russell, B. (2010), *On Education*. London and New York: Routledge. First published 1926.

Schopenhauer, A. (1969), *The World as Will and Representation* (trans. E. F. J. Payne). New York: Dover. Translation first published 1958; first published in German 1819.

—. (2004), *Essays and Aphorisms* (ed. and trans. R. J. Hollingdale). London: Penguin. Translation first published 1970; first published in German 1851.

Singer, P. (1991), *Animal Liberation* (2nd edn). London: Thorsons. First published 1975 (1st edn), 1990 (2nd edn).

—. (1993), *Practical Ethics* (2nd edn). Cambridge: Cambridge University Press. First edition published 1979.

Soper, K. (1995), *What Is Nature?* Oxford, UK and Cambridge, US: Blackwell.

Spinoza, B. (1996), *Ethics* (ed. and trans. E. Curley). London: Penguin. First published 1677.

Stephens, J., ed. (2002), *Ways of Being Male: Representing Masculinities in Children's Literature and Film*. London: Routledge.

—. (2010), 'Impartiality and attachment: ethics and ecopoeisis in children's narrative texts'. *International Research in Children's Literature*, 3(2), 205–16.

Svendsen, L. (2010), *A Philosophy of Evil* (trans. K. A. Pierce). Champagne, IL and London: Dalkey Archive Press. First published in Norwegian 2001.

Voltaire. (1980), *Letters on England* (trans. L. Tancock). London and Harmondsworth: Penguin. First published in French 1734.

—. (2011), *A Pocket Philosophical Dictionary* (ed. N. Cronk, trans. J. Fletcher). Oxford: Oxford University Press. First published in French 1764.

Walsh, C. (1998), 'Irrational presumptions of rationality and comprehension'. *Web Journal of Current Legal Issues*. URL: http://webjcli.ncl.ac.uk/1998/issue3/walsh3.html. (accessed 10 May 2012).

Wiesel, E. (1999), 'The perils of indifference: lessons learned from a violent century'. Number Seven in the White House Millennium Lecture Series, 12 April 1999. Originally given as a speech.

—. (2008), *Night* (trans. M. Wiesel). London: Penguin. First published in French 1958.

Winnicott, D. W. (2005), *Playing and Reality*. London: Routledge. First published 1971.

Ziolkowski, E. (2001), *Evil Children in Religion, Literature, and Art*. Basingstoke and New York: Palgrave.

Index

Adams, Richard,
  Watership Down 105, 111–22, 127–9,
    131
Aesop's Fables 1, 42
Agard, John,
  Young Inferno, The 1–2, 4–5, 8, 11–13,
    26–7, 37–8, 41–2, 52
Agard's seeker (pilgrim) 1–2, 4–5, 8,
    11–13, 15, 19–20, 24, 26–7, 37, 40–2,
    52, 193–4, 195n. 1
Alcock, Vivien,
  Monster Garden, The 136–7, 152–60,
    166
Almond, David,
  Jackdaw Summer 70–2, 75, 82–3
  My Name is Mina 193
Althusser, Louis,
  Ideological State Apparatus (ISA) 88,
    94, 187
  (Repressive) State Apparatus (SA) 94
animal(s),
  and children 118–22, 126–9
  hunting 106–7, 121–9, 203n. 32
  philosophical perspectives 25, 105–12,
    115, 117–23, 127–9, 154, 156, 202n. 21
anthropomorphism 9, 112–15, 118–19,
    201n. 15
Aquinas, Thomas,
  dualistic notion of childhood 46
  evil 42–3
Aristotle,
  childhood 196
  courageous virtue 165
  eudaimonia 159, 196n. 3, 204n. 9
  goodness 3, 11–12
  mean virtues 150, 204n. 5
  virtuous friendship 149, 155, 158–9,
    179
Augustine, St.,
  infant lack 19
  original sin 53, 65
  theological concepts of good and evil 57

B. B.,
  Brendon Chase 5, 103, 106, 126, 138–45,
    152, 154, 160–1, 165, 171, 203n. 3
  Down the Bright Stream 171
  Little Grey Men, The 171
Bachelard, Gaston,
  affective impact of miniature 175–6
  intensity of miniature 183
  miniature and domination 170
  new worlds of the miniature 190
  on Plato's dialectics 169
  sensory experience of miniature 179,
    182–3
  virtues of miniature thinking 169–70
badness 13–15, 27–38, 54, 57, 150
Banks, Lynne Reid,
  Angela and Diabola 48, 50–8, 70
  Indian in the Cupboard, The 170, 180–3,
    189–90
Baudrillard, Jean,
  ecstatic 52, 54–6
  fractal culture 57–8
  images 51–2
Bawden, Nina,
  Carrie's War 75
  Real Plato Jones, The 137, 160–5, 167
Bentham, Jeremy *see also* Mill
  benevolence to animals 120, 122
  utilitarianism 163
Birche engravings 15–19, 23
Blackman, Malorie,
  Boys Don't Cry 166–7
  Pig-Heart Boy 111
Blyton, Enid,
  Naughty Amelia Jane 20–4, 27–8, 198n. 17
  Six Bad Boys 31, 34
Bragg, Billy,
  'Between the Wars' 84
  political power of music 84–5
Briggs, Raymond,
  Elephant and the Bad Baby, The 27–31,
    36–7

Man, The 170, 183–90, 205n. 8
  UG 193
Burgess, Melvin,
  Baby and Fly Pie, The 38–40
  Cry of the Wolf, The 105, 111–12, 122–9
  Junk 34

Callicott, J. Baird,
  humanist community 102
  unification of environmental
    positions 105–6, 111–12
capitalism 38, 82, 88, 90, 94, 97, 129, 145,
    184, 187
  see also Marx; Marxist theory
Carr, David,
  affective states in infants and animals 25
Carroll, Lewis,
  Alice's Adventures in Wonderland 13
Cartesian perspectives 119, 154–6
Cassidy, Anne,
  Looking for JJ 34, 59–61, 74
Chambers, Aidan,
  Dying to Know You 194
child soldiers 71, 75–83, 200n. 4
  see also McMahan
childhood,
  conceptions of 45–8, 50–2
  innocence 38, 45–7, 50, 53–5, 65–6,
    68–71, 78–9, 126–7, 196n. 3
  murder 34, 43, 45–50, 58–62, 67, 71,
    74, 193
  pastoral 104, 120, 136, 192, 201n. 7
  sin 7, 25, 31, 46–7, 50, 53, 65–6
  wonder 1, 13, 27, 41–2, 71–2, 193–4,
    196n. 3
Clarke, Pauline,
  Twelve and the Genii, The 170, 179–81,
    189–90
Coleridge, Samuel Taylor,
  'Frost at Midnight' 99–102, 104, 113,
    120, 126, 131
consequentialism *see* utilitarianism
Cooper, Susan,
  Dark is Rising, The 66
Crime and Disorder Act 48–9
Cross, Gillian,
  On the Edge 83, 85, 90–8

Dante, Alighieri,
  Divine Comedy, The 1, 27, 37, 42

Deacon, Alexis,
  Slow Loris 107–10, 131
deontology 93, 137, 139, 145–6, 151–2,
    157, 160, 163, 165
  see also Kant
Descartes, René *see also* animals/
    philosophical perspectives; Cartesian
    perspectives
  soulless state of animals 119, 156
Dickinson, Peter,
  AK 75–83
doli incapax 48–50, 60, 70
Duché, Thomas *see* Birche engravings
duty *see* deontology; Kant

Eagleton, Terry,
  child murder 46
  evil 27, 42, 50, 66, 69
  reason and freedom 34
  terrorism 93
Edgeworth, Maria 6
Edwards, Dorothy,
  My Naughty Little Sister 20–1, 24–5,
    27–8
Elliot, Robert,
  ethical value of natural
    phenomena 104–5
  restoration (faking nature) 110, 124–5
Engels, Friedrich *see* Marx
environmental ethics,
  biotic communities *see* Leopold
  and childhood culture 100–12
  conservation 104, 107, 110, 123–5,
    131
  land ethic *see* Leopold
  restoration 124–5, 128–9
  speciesism *see* Singer
  wilderness 127–8 *see also* Leopold
evangelism 13, 25–6, 53, 145
evil 2, 5, 7, 12–13, 15, 27, 34, 36–8, 40–72,
    82, 88–9, 93, 96, 104, 117–18, 124,
    126–9, 151

family and ethical life 50, 69, 73–97, 102,
    144, 186–7, 195n. 4
feminist ethics,
  care (as virtue) 136, 146, 149–51
  challenge to moral absolutes 135–6,
    145, 147–52, 166–7
  ecofeminism 111, 152–60

Fine, Anne,
  Tulip Touch, The 48, 50, 58–9, 61–70,
    81, 94, 200n. 21
Foreman, Michael,
  Dinosaurs and All That Rubbish 101
Foucault, Michel,
  bodily absence 143
  discipline 85
  prison and docile bodies 108–9
Foxe, John,
  Foxe's Book of Martyrs 19, 197n. 15
fraternity 136–7, 140–6, 150, 152, 154–6,
    160, 166
  see also Kant; Locke; Rawlinson

Gadamer, Hans-Georg,
  hermeneutics and art 194
Garrard, Greg,
  pollution 131
Genette, Gérard,
  autodiegetic narration 64, 84, 153
  diegesis 62, 86–7
  duration (narrative) 91–2
  heterodiegetic narration 63–4, 172, 179
Goffman, Erving,
  stigmatization 22, 54, 198n. 17
goodness 2–5, 12–18, 22–4, 28, 30–1,
    37–45, 48, 50, 52, 56–8, 66, 69–72, 79,
    82, 104–5, 128, 137–8, 145–6, 148–51,
    160, 163, 189
Grenby, Matthew,
  moral and instructive writing 7

Halwani, Raja,
  care as virtue 150
Hancock, Susan,
  miniature literature 170–1, 178
Hartman, Geoffrey,
  art and the dangers of familiarity 86–7
  poetry and imagination 100
Hegel, Georg Wilhelm Friedrich,
  community (social unity) 96–8, 102,
    112, 144
  education 1–2, 9, 187–8, 195n. 4
  ethical dissolution 81–2, 89–90, 92, 96
  ethical life 50, 73–8, 80–3, 86, 92–3,
    96–7, 166, 179, 183, 195n. 4
  family 73–4, 77–8, 82, 89, 92–3
  individual freedom 86, 97–8, 112
  just society 86–7, 89, 93

war 75, 80
Hines, Barry,
  Kestrel for a Knave, A 100, 104
Hollindale, Peter,
  childly 4, 19, 25, 29, 100, 120, 136,
    196n. 3
  childness 3–4, 38, 48, 61, 79, 194
  ecocriticism 121, 132–3, 193
  pessimism 40, 128, 193
Howker, Janni,
  Isaac Campion 84–5
Hughes, Richard,
  High Wind in Jamaica, A 47–8, 204n. 3
Hughes, Ted,
  'Howling of Wolves, The' 123, 128
Hughes, Thomas,
  Tom Brown's Schooldays 138–9, 174
Hume, David,
  animals 119, 121
  childhood 196n. 3
  evil 43–4

indifference 11–13, 15, 19, 26, 38–41, 68,
    72, 96, 192–3
Irigaray, Luce,
  revolution in ethics 135–6, 148, 151, 166–7
  see also feminist ethics

Jefferies, Richard,
  Bevis 5, 102, 106, 126, 138–40, 203n. 3
Jeffers, Oliver,
  Great Paper Caper, The 130–3
Jenkins, Martin,
  Can We Save the Tiger? 129, 203n. 33
Jenks, Chris,
  childhood murder 47–8, 199n. 8
  see also childhood
  concepts of childhood (evil and
    innocence) 46–8, 53
  see also childhood
John Craven's Newsround 83–4

Kant, Immanuel,
  deontology 137, 139, 145–8, 152, 156,
    160, 171
  education 136
  good will 177
  moral law 135–9, 141, 143–4, 148, 152
  moral optimism 50
  rationality 143, 148

Kierkegaard, Søren,
love 2, 37, 39, 41–2, 56, 177
Krupat, Arnold,
anti-imperial translation 180–1

Leopold, Aldo,
biotic communities 102, 111–14,
117–18, 120, 124, 130, 144, 160
land ethic 102–3, 105–7, 111–13,
117–22, 131, 139, 144–5, 201n. 10
'thinking like a mountain' 122–3, 127
wilderness 128, 138, 202n. 24
Locke, John,
evil 43
fraternity 145
learning through experience 138
love 3, 37–9, 41–2, 56, 72–3, 77, 81, 91,
158–9, 166, 177, 188–9, 193

McCaughrean, Geraldine,
Stop the Train 97–8
McGinn, Colin,
evil 66–7
McMahan, Jeff,
ethics of child soldiers 76
see also child soldiers
Mark, Jan,
Divide and Rule 97
Marryat, Captain Frederick,
Children of the New Forest, The 102,
106–7, 139, 174
Marx, Karl,
abolition of family (Marx and Engels) 92
economic relations 90, 184–5
reactionary socialism (Marx and
Engels) 95
Marxist theory 89, 93, 111
see also Althusser; Marx
masculinity 5, 135, 137–47, 152, 154–5,
160–2, 164–6, 181
Midgley, Mary,
animals 112, 119–20, 202n. 21
death wish 57
emotion (heart) 120, 148–9, 157
evil (wickedness) 18, 34–6, 43, 54, 58,
66, 69, 74, 104, 200n. 8
holistic ethics 171, 176, 183
moral malaise 191–2
Mill, John Stuart *see also* Bentham
utility 120, 163–4

miniature literature,
colonialism 172, 174, 180–1
dependency 179, 182, 184, 186, 190
dominion 170–1, 174–5, 177, 179–81,
183, 187, 189
intertextuality and literary
convention 171–2, 174, 177, 179,
181, 189
power relationships 169–70, 173–4,
177–8, 183–4, 189
sensory encounters 169, 175, 179–83,
188
moral (ethical) agency 2, 7, 13, 21, 27, 33,
49–50, 57, 60, 62, 66, 70–1, 76, 82, 91,
119, 121–2, 124, 133, 137–8, 144, 148,
151–7, 160, 165, 172, 175–6, 178–81,
183, 188–90, 193–4
moral awakening 1–2, 19, 27, 41, 68, 160,
170, 183, 196n. 3
moral education 1–2, 6–11, 72–3, 81, 136,
138–9, 145, 187–8, 191–2, 195n. 4
Mulligan, Andy,
Trash 129–30, 198n. 25, 200n. 2
Murdoch, Iris,
art and literature 72, 182, 195n. 11
childhood 2–4, 195n. 8
goodness and love 2–3, 30–1, 42
goodness and simplicity 30
metaphor 4
moral choice 33
moral discipline 56
secularizing goodness 37–8
seeing good 5, 56–7
unexamined life and virtue 2–3, 193–4,
195n. 7
unseen (inner) good 3
mutuality *see* Plumwood

Naess, Arne,
ecoeducation 145
narration (diegetic modes) *see* Genette
naturalism (literary) 102–3, 112–13, 122,
126, 171, 201n. 15
naughtiness 15–28, 53, 197n. 8, 198n. 17
Needle, Jan,
Game of Soldiers, A 75
Nietzsche, Friedrich,
'herd animal morality' 7
immorality (beyond good and evil) 19,
26, 44, 47

Norton, Mary,
  Borrowers, The 170, 180, 189–90

Oxford Book of Children's Verse, The
  13–14, 18

Passmore, John,
  nature (definition) 116
  Romanticism and ethics 104
Plato,
  childhood 196n. 3
  dialectics of size 169
Plumwood, Val,
  Aristotelian virtue 149, 158–9
  ethical dualism 143
  eudaimonia 159 *see also* Aristotle
  instrumentalism 153, 156
  mutuality 149, 153–60, 180
Potter, Beatrix,
  Tom Kitten 18
  Peter Rabbit 20, 112, 127, 141–2
Pratchett, Terry,
  Nation 193
Price, Susan,
  Twopence a Tub 83, 85–90, 96–8
puritanism 26, 44, 53

Ransome, Arthur,
  Swallows and Amazons 102, 140, 174,
    204n. 4
Rawlinson, Mary C.,
  fraternity 137, 141 *see also* fraternity
Rawls, John,
  animals and species 115, 129
  liberty 172–3
Rousseau, Jean-Jacques,
  Émile 101, 195n. 4
Russell, Bertrand,
  independent thinking 26
  moral education 7–10, 24, 33, 192

Sayers, Dorothy Leigh,
  Even the Parrot 191
schadenfreude 32, 66–7
  see also Schopenhauer
Schlee, Anne,
  Ask Me No Questions 137, 145–52, 165,
    167
Schopenhauer, Arthur,
  authorship 192

childhood 196n. 3
  schadenfreude 32
  small libraries 8
  will 36, 43
Shelley, Mary,
  Frankenstein 152–3
Sherwood, Mrs Mary Martha,
  Brotherly Love 25–6
  History of the Fairchild Family, The 20,
    25
Singer, Peter,
  animal rights 105–7, 111–12
  refugees 186
  speciesism 105–6, 108, 127, 201n. 8
  status quo 189
Socrates,
  unexamined life *see* Murdoch
Soper, Kate,
  feminism and nature 157–8
  nature (concept and terminology) 115–16
Spinoza, Benedict de,
  moral education 191–2
Stephens, John,
  masculinity 165
  narrative and eco-consciousness 131,
    203n. 37
Stevenson, Robert Louis,
  Treasure Island 5, 42–5, 47–8, 70
stigmatization (labelling) 14–15, 18, 20,
    28, 31, 54
  see also Goffman
Svendsen, Lars,
  aestheticism and evil 51–2
  banal evil 68
  cause of evil 60
  evil (definition) 12, 52
  evil as human/normal 9, 65, 117–18, 127
  remorse 69
Swift, Jonathan,
  Gulliver's Travels 170, 172, 177

terrorism 71, 83, 85, 90–4

utilitarianism (consequentialism) 91, 112,
    120, 160, 163–5
  see also Bentham; Mills

Valentine, Jenny,
  Broken Soup 97
violence 43, 60–1, 93–4, 166, 194

Vipont, Elfrida,
  Elephant and the Bad Baby,
  The see Briggs
virtue 2–3, 7, 15, 18, 40, 135, 149–50,
    165, 169, 179, 182, 191, 193, 197n. 7,
    204n. 5
Voltaire,
  animal consciousness 119

war (ethical conditions of) 12, 71, 75–83,
    162–4
Westall, Robert,
  Gulf 75
White, Terence Hanbury,
  Mistress Masham's Repose 170–9, 181,
    183, 189–90

Wiesel, Elie,
  indifference 11–13, 40–1, 68, 72, 96
Williamson, Henry,
  Tarka the Otter 102–3, 112, 121–2
Wilson, Jacqueline,
  Bad Girls 31–7
Winnicott, Donald,
  child-mother relationship 78
  transitional objects 77

Ziolkowski, Eric,
  Bethel boys 45–6
  concepts of childhood (good and
    bad) 18, 197n. 9
  dualistic theological concepts of
    childhood 45–8

Lightning Source UK Ltd.
Milton Keynes UK
UKOW07f1132200215

246602UK00002B/85/P